Women and Bisexuality

About the author
Sue George has been involved in the feminist movement since 1978 and the bisexual community since 1984. She works as a freelance writer and journalist and her articles have appeared in publications ranging from *The Guardian* to *The Pink Paper*, and *Spare Rib* to *Marie Claire*. Her first novel, *Death of the Family*, was published by Hutchinson in 1989; she is currently working on her second. She lives in London and has a son, Alexis.

WOMEN
AND
BISEXUALITY

SUE GEORGE

SCARLET
PRESS

Acknowledgments

I would like to thank Gail Chester for encouraging me to write this book in the first place, and for her editorial work, particularly in the early stages; and Vicky Wilson for her thorough and persistent editing on the final drafts.

Thanks to all those women who completed the questionnaires, some of whom also wrote letters and helped with their encouragement; and to the women I interviewed for their openness and generosity.

For lending me books, passing on contacts and information, thanks to Alison Butler, Stephen Philip, Brian Robinson, Hilary, I.C. from Los Angeles and, most notably, Zaidie Parr. I would also like to thank Fritz Klein for permission to use the Klein Sexual Orientation Grid. Clare Thompson and Jo Stanley made useful comments on sections of earlier drafts.

Special thanks for her support in so many ways go to my sister, Julia George.

Published by Scarlet Press
5 Montague Road, London E8 2HN

British Library Cataloguing-in-Publication Data
A catalogue record for this book is available
from the British Library
ISBN 1 85727 071 1 pb
      1 85727 066 5 hb

05 04 03 02 01   9 8 7 6 5 4 3

Produced for Scarlet Press by Chase Publishing Services
Printed in the European Union by Athenaeum Press, Gateshead, England

Contents

Introduction

It is nearly twenty years since I began to identify as bisexual, an identity I have maintained ever since (except for a year of thinking of myself as lesbian). For most of that time, I have looked around for other people, for books, or for anything else which would tell me that being bisexual was an option, let alone a great way to be. I looked in vain – and that is why I wrote this book.

Even as a teenager in the 1970s, it was apparent that 'being bisexual' was difficult, especially for a woman. The myths said that women did not really have a sexuality of their own in the first place, and then in any case, everyone was either straight or gay, and anything else was just playing around. My experiences as an active feminist made a bisexual identity no easier, as commitment to women often seemed to require outright rejection of men. I had met few other openly bisexual women until I joined a bisexual women's group in 1984.

It is hard to believe that even in the 1990s, with a rapidly growing bisexual community, queer politics, gender fuck, and constant discussion of sexual issues in many women's magazines, bisexuality remains largely invisible. In the British Library, which holds copies of everything published in the UK, bisexuality would be placed in the subject index between 'Biscuits' and 'Bishops'. The fact that there has never been a shortage of books on either of these subjects, yet between 1977 and 1990 there were no acquisitions of books on bisexuality, must give pause for thought. Moreover, there has never been a serious book published in the UK on women and bisexuality, and most people's perception of bisexuality is focused on men.

Many people (both lesbian/gay and straight) have told me that I am the only bisexual they have met. Of course, this is not the case, but even today, popular misconceptions mean that few people feel able to be open about their bisexuality. This book uses self-identity to define whether or not a person is bisexual, as I believe that anyone who consciously feels sexual and emotional desire for people of both sexes, whether or not they prefer one over the other, and whether or not they act on their feelings, is bisexual if they consider themselves to be so.

There are many stereotypes of bisexuals – as hypersexual, uncommitted, immoral, confused and so on. This book refutes such images, and describes instead a wide range of women who perceive their sexuality in very different ways. It shows the impossibility of generalising about bisexual women, when our experiences and lifestyles are so diverse.

But why is bisexuality so threatening, and individual bisexuals so invisible? As I argue throughout this book, mainstream western society is organised around the heterosexual couple relationship, and by extension the nuclear family. For society to function as it does, this organisation must appear both stable and natural. People who have same-sex relationships are labelled 'homosexual', and by extension unstable and unnatural. To maintain the status quo, it is important that people can be classed categorically as either hetero- or homosexual. Hence bisexuality is invisibilised.

But as can be seen from the women who speak in this book, bisexuality exists, and however much anyone might try to ignore or pathologise it, it is not going to go away. What the experiences in this book affirm and society does not want to acknowledge is that all sexual identities can be seen as fluid; that a woman who identifies as, say, heterosexual this year, will not necessarily identify in the same way forever. However, that does not mean that we should abandon the use of sexual labels altogether: it would, of course, be great if we could all just be sexual, attracted to whoever we liked, but the prevailing heterosexism makes this an unlikely scenario, at least in the short term.

The practical research for this book was conducted through the analysis of 142 ten-page questionnaires. These questionnaires were deliberately designed to allow women to write at length, rather than to give one-word, easy-to-categorise answers. Their responses are quoted throughout, and the numbers in parentheses that follow the quotes refer to the questionnaire serial numbers – allocated in order of receipt. The entire questionnaire is given in Appendix 1.

The first three chapters of the book are historically based. Chapter 1, 'The construction of bisexuality: excluded and absent', looks at how and why sexuality has been constructed to make bisexuality seem an impossible option. Chapter 2, 'Theories of bisexuality', examines the ways bisexuality has been explained or misrepresented from the late nineteenth century to the present. Chapter 3, 'Bisexuality and feminism', discusses the often uneasy relationship between the two.

The remainder of the book looks more closely at how bisexual women live, based largely on an analysis of questionnaire responses. Chapter 4, 'Living as bisexual', describes how bisexual women negotiate different areas of their lives, from sexual desire to bringing up children, and coming out to conducting established relationships. Chapter 5 tells seven women's stories, chosen to represent the wide range of questionnaire respondents, and to show in more detail how individual women live out their bisexuality. Chapter 6, 'Towards a definition of bisexuality', studies some of the different ways questionnaire respondents express their bisexuality, and tries, tentatively and subjectively, to define it. Chapter 7, 'The politics of bisexuality', looks at the various political issues involved in taking on a bisexual identity, and puts forward strategies for the building of a strong, feminist bisexual community. A list of resources and bibliography follow.

This book is written for bisexual women, in the hope that we may continue to develop a positive sexuality based on respect, and for anyone of any sexuality who supports us in this. It is my hope that women wondering about their own potential bisexuality will take courage from the example of so many who have explored that potential. And I hope that this book will contribute to debates on sexuality, and help to ensure that future theories of sexuality include bisexuality. This is a fast-moving and exciting time for the bisexual community and for all sexually progressive people: bisexual women are an integral part of the changes to come.

1 The construction of bisexuality: excluded and absent

Because our society sees everything as so cut and dried, it feels as though bisexuality is the ultimate crime. It's loving people as *people* – shock horror! Heterosexual conditioning is so ridiculous and yet so powerful – it has a lot to answer for. (13)

I tried to tell myself that now I had discovered I could love women, obviously I wouldn't want men because they were so awful. But I was kidding myself because I didn't *want* to be bisexual. It was too awkward, I didn't know anyone else who was – I felt stranded in the middle of nowhere. (120)

Why is bisexuality understood and accepted by so few people? Even individuals who find themselves attracted to people of both sexes often disbelieve their own feelings and try to push themselves uneasily into the categories of lesbian/gay or heterosexual. To many, bisexuality simply does not exist in its own right: it is seen variously as a transitional phase, a desire to hold on to heterosexual privilege, a function of being oversexed, and so on.

For society to function as it does, it is necessary for most adults to be organised into apparently stable, heterosexual couples. Homosexuality (for both sexes) is perceived as something which 'happens': whether inborn, caused by faulty parenting or a stubborn perversity on the part of the individual, society must be protected from it. The Section 28 law (banning the 'promotion' of homosexuality in state schools and by local authorities) introduced in 1988 by the Tory government showed this fear in action.

Bisexuality too presents a challenge to societal norms, and as I shall be demonstrating in this chapter, despite the widespread existence of bisexual desires and behaviour, there is simply no place

4

for bisexuality as a conscious practice within mainstream British, and western, society as it is presently organised. The privileging of the white heterosexual couple and the marginalisation of individuals or units who do not conform to that description is a basic tenet of western cultures, influencing our actions by clearly demonstrating how we should live – whether we agree or not. And as long as individuals who have sexual and emotional desires for people of both genders remain isolated and are told and believe their needs to be abnormal, bisexual behaviour will be minimised.

The following chapters specifically consider the position of bisexual women in the UK. However, much of what is said also applies to western societies in general, and in particular to the US. There is much cross-over in the development of both theory and practice within the bisexual and feminist communities; similarly, psychological theories have international influence. But the UK and US are as different as they are alike – for instance Christianity plays a very different role in each country – and some parts of this book will only apply to the UK.

This chapter will look briefly at how sexuality, particularly female sexuality, has been and is constructed, and some of the implications this has for bisexual women. As bisexuality has to a large extent been constructed as non-existent, much of this chapter describes the ideologies which have led to its absence.

Female sexuality: from constraint to liberation?

In pre-AIDS days I had a long relationship with a bisexual man. He had a lot of sex with other men, and I was very envious. I would have *loved* to be like him, but there was no possibility for bisexual women to behave in such a way. That really hasn't changed. (99)

I felt that as a woman/girl, certain options were closed to me. These were more concrete than the options which were closed to me as a lesbian. (92)

Across ages and cultures, women and men have been presumed to feel and act differently in all areas of their lives. In this first section, I shall be looking at the historical influences on western women's views of themselves and their sexuality, and the ways in which these influences still affect women today.

In ancient times, and until the industrial revolution, women's autonomous sexuality was something of which men were afraid, and which had to be strictly controlled. Many of the fears were focused on ideas about women who lived independently of men, as in convents, and in the sixteenth and seventeenth centuries were manifested in accusations of witchcraft. From the nineteenth century, in British middle-class society, 'good' or 'respectable' women were presented by the law, popular fiction and the Church as sexless, submitting to sexual intercourse only in order to conceive or for the sake of their husbands' satisfaction (men were assumed to have 'natural', uncontrollable sexual desires which it was hoped would be contained within marriage). There was little chance for a woman to express her sexual feelings, whether towards men or women, although sexual feelings did of course exist, as writers from Elizabeth Barrett Browning to Mary Wollstonecraft Shelley attest. This enforced and artificial idea of female purity helped to create a false division, whereby women were perceived as either mothers/virgins or whores (of whom there were between 50,000 and 368,000 operating in the UK in the mid-nineteenth century).[1]

Women who did not work as prostitutes, but were not white, gentile and middle class, were often assumed to be 'loose'. Hence servants would find it hard to escape sexual harassment and colonisers tended to see sexual relationships with women (and men) of the countries they colonised as a perk of the job.[2] The perception of black women as sexually available and exotic was absorbed into western mainstream ideology and persists today. As Gail Wyatt and others have argued, this has constricted black women's sexual expression.[3]

As the twentieth century progressed, perceptions of women's sexuality began slowly to change. Female sexuality was now seen as a delicate flower to be gently awakened by a masterful and active husband whose task was to guide his blushing bride through her passage to true womanhood. As Dr Van de Velde wrote in *Ideal Marriage*, a marriage guide which was a best-seller for forty years until the 1960s, despite (or perhaps because of) being banned by the Catholic Church:

> What both men and women, driven by obscure primitive urges, wish to feel in the sexual act is the essential force of maleness which expresses itself in a sort of violent and absolute possession of the woman.[4]

Women had no autonomous sexuality: sex was something they had to be taught to enjoy. Their sexual feelings were solely a response to the man's, and could only be awakened by him. The heterosexist and sexist assumptions behind these theories were for many years unchallenged. Marriage manuals from the 1920s onwards were usually addressed to medical professionals and husbands, not to women.

The assumption and reality of sex as something to be endured rather than enjoyed was widespread among women, too. Doctors giving contraceptive advice to working-class women in mothers' clinics during the 1920s and 1930s received blank looks when they asked whether their clients enjoyed sex; most of them were unaware there was anything to enjoy. Reliable contraception was for many women a precondition for the enjoyment of penis-vagina sex, and the fight for contraception begun by Marie Stopes and others in the 1920s had succeeded to the degree that by the 1950s contraceptive advice was readily available through family-planning clinics. However, these clinics were allowed to operate on condition that they would only supply married women.[5]

In 1930, Helena Wright, a doctor who had worked in contraceptive clinics for working-class women, wrote the first sex manual by and for women.[6] In common with writers like Van de Velde and Stopes, she believed it to be a wife's duty to enjoy sex. Wright proposed that ideally, sexual stimulation should come through the vagina alone, but that women starting their sex lives usually needed clitoral stimulation – to be given by their husbands, of course.[7] Twenty years later, after receiving countless letters from women who were still failing to reach orgasm through vaginal stimulation alone, Wright was forced to recognise the non-existence of vaginal orgasms.[8]

The importance placed on the vaginal orgasm (and therefore on penile penetration) was vital to ensure women's dependence on men. Its existence was effectively challenged in the 1960s by, among others, Masters and Johnson, who examined people having sex under laboratory conditions for their study, *Human Sexual Response*.[9] Their findings put paid to the notion of two separate types of orgasm, clitoral and vaginal, and recognised that although the vagina was the primary site of heterosexual sexual expression, clitoral stimulation was what led to female climax. Their findings reached a wider audience through sex manuals and books of the period, such as *The Joy of Sex*, *Everything You Ever Wanted to Know about Sex*, *The Sensuous Woman*, and many, many more. While some of these probably did help people to more enjoyable sex lives, many of them promoted traditional attitudes, saying women needed to tease and arouse their men, and men's task was to deal with the 'problem' of female orgasm. It took feminist writer Anne Koedt, with 'The Myth of the Vaginal Orgasm' (1970), to point out the radical implications of the fact that women climaxed through the clitoris: that a penis is not essential for a woman to reach orgasm.[10]

Until the 1960s, marriage was held to be a pre-condition for 'respectable' girls to have penis-vagina sex (though much sexual activity undoubtedly occurred outside marriage, this was not *supposed* to happen, and was therefore kept quiet). Heterosexual behaviour in the 1950s and 1960s became less tied to procreation, however. With the development of the contraceptive pill in particular, women were able to pursue their own desires without fear of pregnancy (though they also lost a valuable excuse for saying no to unwanted sexual advances). The Family Planning Association began to advise unmarried women in 1966 and the abortion laws were relaxed in 1967. Pre-marital sex, 'trial marriages' and 'sleeping around' were becoming common: only 35 per cent of couples marrying in the late 1950s had pre-marital sex compared to 74 per cent in the 1970s.[11]

The so-called 'sexual revolution' undoubtedly changed women's expectations and behaviour. Until the 1960s, women were expected to go from virginity to monogamous marriage; now possibilities previously open only to men existed for them, too. Women also began to expect to enjoy sex, and if they did not, would be more likely to blame their male partners. These changes in sexual behaviour were legitimised, publicised and exploited by the media: the commoditisation of sex, which had always existed in a subtle way, was now openly seized on in advertising, the media, and the arts, and was evident in the increase in readily available pornography.

One theorist who was influential on those women and men who considered that women needed to be liberated sexually was Wilhelm Reich, a pupil of Freud. Reich's ideas on sexual freedom remain radical today, even though they deal only with hetero-sexuality and take concepts such as 'desire' and 'orgasm' as natural and unproblematic. With the aid of a Marxist social analysis, Reich linked the suppression and cultural organisation of sexuality to the authoritarianism of society and proposed that any significant shift in attitudes would occur only as a result of profound social change. In *The Sexual Revolution*, for instance (1951, some parts written in 1930),[12] Reich argues that reactionary forces have maintained the status quo by exploiting women's sexual fears, in the belief that compulsory sexual morality is the only alter-native to sexual and social anarchy:

> Sexually awakened women, affirmed and recognised as such,
> would mean the complete collapse of the authoritarian
> ideology.[13]

Reich also believed that marriage has more to do with economic
and ideological considerations than with love and sex, and is a
construct which makes real love and satisfactory sex difficult.
According to Reich, people are monogamous only because they
are sexually repressed, and though people who are truly orgasti-
cally satisfied within a relationship are more capable of monogamy,
they are few and far between.

Even among sexual liberationists, views like Reich's existed
alongside different expectations – the so-called 'double standard'
– for men and women. Take this example, from 'J', in her book
The Sensuous Woman. Written in 1970, it is a guide to pleasing
your man sexually:

> To a man, love and life are things apart. To a woman, love
> is life itself... It is not unnatural for him to forget all about
> you for hours at a time, even though he loves you dearly. But
> it is natural for you to be unable to erase him from your mind
> and body, no matter how hard you try... You would be insane
> to go against your nature and cheat yourself of many tender,
> sweet, entirely female moments... we women were born to
> love, and only when we love to capacity are we happy.[14]

Such myths, designed to keep women sexually and emotionally
dependent on men, persist twenty years later, and appear in less
blatant form in many women's magazines today. Men and women
are still considered sexual opposites, and the sexual revolution is
widely seen as having failed women by encouraging them to
have sex *on men's terms*. In fact, while the 1960s did encourage
women to behave more like men had in actively seeking out sex
(if usually within some kind of relationship), it did little to change
men's behaviour or level of understanding[15]: as Ehrenreich, Hess
and Jacobs argue in *Re-Making Love* (1987), it was a sexual revolution
for women, but not for men.[16] And as summings-up and verdicts
in many rape trials even today show, sex for men is still regarded
as a physical release to which they are entitled: men need sex,
and once they have an erection they must be 'satisfied'. Women
are supposed to need sex too, but when they act on this need outside
a permanent sexual relationship, they are designated 'sluts'. As
Shere Hite, among others, has pointed out, women are punished

by both men and women for sexual behaviour which is traditionally male. This is true, too, of attitudes to male and female behaviour in many other areas of life.

When I was younger I tried to behave like a man sexually. By that I mean I wanted a lot of lovers, and couldn't see why I had to wait around to be asked. Men couldn't handle it at all: they were often nasty, and treated me like a 'slag'. (99)

For many people, the period of the sexual revolution was as repressive as any other. The much-vaunted hedonism and sexual 'permissiveness' probably reached only a small part of the population, while others actively campaigned to counter it. Though the effects of the sexual revolution are still being felt, and a complete return to the past is not likely, the freedoms of the 1960s and 1970s were profoundly questioned and reassessed in the 1980s.

Sexual liberation, and women's liberation too, seemed to some women to be undermining women's traditional place without giving them a positive alternative. Spokeswomen for the moral right, such as anti-'obscenity' campaigner Mary Whitehouse from the 1960s onwards and more recently Victoria Gillick, seem to want to return to a mythical golden age of innocence, when women were women, men were men, everyone believed in God, there was no sex before or outside marriage, no abortions, and everyone knew their place. Though the backlash from the right was well under way before the advent of AIDS, the epidemic has been exploited to promote the idea that sex – both heterosexual and homosexual – is wrong and dangerous, and that monogamous marriage between heterosexual partners is the only option.

However, many women of all sexualities contend that such moralists are not acting in their interests, and the current obsession in women's magazines with sex (within the context of relation-ships) shows that women are conscious of their own sexual desires. What seems to be happening in the 1990s is that women are trying to work out what is in our interests, and how we can act on our desires – whether to have sex or to be celibate.

Promoting heterosexuality, marriage and the family

My parents' marriage is not a happy one, in fact none of the marriages in my family has been happy and this has put me off marriage completely. (77)

I always felt the need to be a good daughter and never behaved in a way that would upset my parents ... I became pregnant and automatically married at nineteen. (26)

There is such social pressure to be heterosexual, and for so many years, I just didn't know that you could be anything else. (59)

The normalisation of heterosexuality is the area in which 'the tyranny of the natural', as Jonathan Dollimore has aptly described it in his book *Sexual Dissidence*,[17] is most forcefully applied. It cannot be overemphasised that heterosexual relationships are promoted above all others, and that even the variety of heterosexual relationships condoned is very narrow (basically monogamous marriage between two people of the same race and similar ages – unless the man is older – and all points leading to it). That men and women fall in love and get married is presented as the most natural thing in the world. Marriage, which takes days to enter and years to leave, is backed by the wedding industry and is promoted subtly and overtly by all areas of ideology. Heterosexuality is organised and controlled in this way, while other types of relationship are marginalised. The importance given to the couple relationship above all others makes bisexuality very difficult.

From a traditionalist biological perspective, male and female were brought together for procreation. The condoned sexual practice is penile penetration of the vagina, followed by male ejaculation. Penetration *is sex*, and this is still largely true of how 'having sex' is defined today. It necessarily excludes other than male-female penetrative sex, despite the fact that the common use of contraception has loosened the connection between sex and procreation.

That the purpose of sex is procreation has been strongly supported by religions worldwide, and in the west through the Judeo/Christian traditions in particular – although whether or not sexual pleasure is also permissible varies. The Bible has been interpreted in various ways through the centuries, from a commandment for heterosexual activity within marriage, to a condemnation of all sexuality in the early Middle Ages, to a recommendation of loving sex within marriage in the 1960s. The profoundly anti-sexual line dates from the early Christian period: St Augustine, for instance, linked sex with original sin and guilt. This interpretation of religious laws condemns all sexual behaviour which is non-procreative – women as well as men were burned at the stake for homosexuality in the Middle Ages. It is exemplified today in the Catholic Church's continued forbidding of contraception, and debates within the Church of England about allowing 'sexually active' homosexual clergy. The Church of England also condemned bisexual activity in its 1991 policy statement *Issues in Human Sexuality*, which claimed that bisexual activity must always be wrong for the reason, 'if no other', that it inevitably involves being unfaithful.

The heterosexual couple and nuclear family are also essential to the maintenance of patriarchy/capitalism. Far from having arisen 'naturally', the widespread desire for one's 'own', supposedly freely-chosen spouse, own children, own home, has been relentlessly orchestrated and marketed for the benefit of capitalist society: families bond together and consume. The pressure to live in a traditional family unit is also enforced at a practical level: the organisation of housing and economics makes it much easier in our society to live as part of a nuclear family. And because this is the case, other forms of social existence and the structures to support them – for example, different types of housing – are presumed to be neither desirable nor desired.

This perpetual emphasis on the nuclear family denies the legitimacy of other forms of social organisation,[18] so that the rich variety of other family groupings are marginalised. Not wanting to have children is seen as selfish, and wanting them to be brought up by more or fewer than two people of opposite genders as unnatural, wicked and irresponsible, despite the fact that different arrangements work successfully over much of the rest of the world. Limited discussions in progressive quarters about multiculturalism aside, British society, at least, is projected as fundamentally monocultural, the dominant culture being white, middle-class and heterosexual, with anything else perceived as other and different. The standard image of a 'family' is mother, father and children; even the extended families that form part of many people's living arrangements and provide positive enjoyment and support are written out as aberrations. It is hardly surprising, therefore, that there is little possibility for lesbian couples, or people who live alone, or in groups over long periods, to be other than 'outside' society.

Definitions of the family have differed greatly across cultures and periods of history and there have been many debates about its origins and structure. According to Engels' *The Origins of the Family, Private Property and the State* (1884)[19] – a central text for both feminists and socialists – the family as we know it today was established to provide patrilinear descent; the child has to be known to be the child of its legal father in order to inherit his property. Patriarchy, therefore, is based upon the ownership of women and children, and Engels believed that children should be the responsibility of the whole community, rather than of individuals, in order to release women from this subjection.

Dutch sociologist Iteke Weeda[20] has mapped the emotional values invested in marriage and the family over the past 300 years. According to Weeda, the idea of the family in western European culture in the eighteenth and nineteenth centuries was of an unequal male-female duo, in which the partners were entirely separate but mutually dependent. There was no emphasis on love, and sex was for the enjoyment of men and for the production of children. With growing urbanisation in the nineteenth century and the consequent dispersion of traditional kinship groups, the pursuit of individual happiness through relationships became more important.[21] In this scenario, women's closest companions were often other women, particularly when the two sexes spent their days (whether in factories or at home) in single-sex environments. As Lillian Faderman points out in *Surpassing the Love of Men*, unchallenged, intimate, relationships between women were part of many women's lives until around the First World War.[22]

In the twentieth century, the popular model of the heterosexual couple presumed men and women to be different but equal, still mutually dependent, with a lifelong relationship based on 'love'. Sexual satisfaction for both became important, though even in the 1950s, good temper, good financial circumstances and a home of one's own were rated above romantic involvement. This 'separate but equal' view of husband and wife was enshrined in the Beveridge Report of 1942, which laid the foundations for Britain's welfare state. The report encouraged and idealised what it saw as the vital role of the housewife, so supporting the idea of a woman's place as under the control of her husband within the home. It set out as one of its aims:

> to reinforce and encourage marriage, apparent in the proposed material inducement of the marriage grant... and in its ideological construction of marriage as a crucially VITAL occupation and career.[23]

Though British society has moved towards different structures, this family model remains as a pervasive folk memory. Even the more 'egalitarian' marriages of the 1980s and 1990s still see women, not men, as caring for the home, whatever their work commitments.

The Second World War offered many women opportunities for increased economic independence and for new types of sexual relationships, and some seized them. These opportunities were not necessarily heterosexual: women in the forces who had never heard of lesbianism before joining up had sexual experiences with other women. After the war, despite many divorces, a move back to pre-war conditions was encouraged. And though a real return to the past was not possible – women's experiences in wartime had been too wide-ranging for their expectations once again to focus exclusively on house and home – during the 1950s and 1960s, as Elizabeth Wilson argues,[24] marriage became more and more important.

> It is impossible to overestimate the importance of marriage as a central and organising idea in both the 1950s and 1960s. It appealed as much to progressives as to Conservatives... and equally to feminists and those hostile to the equality of women. It was part of a hedonistic lifestyle as much as of a puritanical one.

By the 1960s, the ideal of marriage was companionate – husband and wife doing everything together, sharing.[25] A lifelong, monogamous marriage was to satisfy all women's sexual and social needs, and the previous centuries' norms of romantic/sensual relationships between women, married or not, had gone for good. Marriage statistics from the period indicate that more and more women were or had been married, and celibacy and spinsterhood were no longer a widespread reality in women's lives.[26] Bisexuality is no more possible within this framework than it was when women were straightforwardly owned by men.

> I got married because I found someone I wanted to share my life with, but because I find that sex is high on my list of priorities, other lovers are important. (82)

> My other lovers are important emotionally; my partner and I need a lot of space from each other – he is a pragmatist not a romantic in our relationship. (80)

> My main sexual relationship is with another woman, but I am still married and still love my husband. My female lover doesn't want to end my marriage. (79)

As the above replies from questionnaire respondents show, marriages, and the individuals within them, vary greatly. Married couples do not always live together, are not always in love, may have primary partners who are not their spouses, and may not be heterosexual. However, this is never apparent in the popular conception of marriage, which is always perceived as a primary, loving, monogamous, profound relationship.

Since 1979, Britain has been governed by an increasingly repressive Conservative party, which has tried, subtly and overtly, to lessen the opportunities for alternative lifestyles. The downfall of Margaret Thatcher in 1990 was meant to herald a new, 'caring' face of Conservatism, but the values which Thatcherism inculcated are still very much in place.

In the early 1980s, the Tories seemed most concerned with cutting union rights, restricting social-security benefits, and so on. But from the 1987 election on (Thatcher's third term), moral and social repression became a consistent part of government policy. The social consequences of the economic policies already introduced – increased crime, increased homelessness – had to be explained away, and legislation aimed at strengthening traditional family units and attacking 'alternative' lifestyles began to appear.

For instance, the decline in the traditional nuclear family (the number of single-parent families in the UK nearly doubled between 1971 and 1986 to over 1 million, or nearly 14 per cent), combined with rising crime rates, led the government to assume it was the lack of strong father figures that pushed young boys into crime, rather than increased materialism, cuts in benefits and the growing gap between rich and poor. Yet the motive behind the Child Support Bill of 1990/91, which aimed to make absent fathers contribute to their children's upkeep if the mother was on income support – whatever her wishes – was clearly not the welfare of the mother or child, but the cutting down of money spent on income-support grants to compensate for revenue lost through the introduction of tax cuts.

> It is in the interests of the children that they should be maintained by their parents. Maintenance provides them with a reliable source of income, and they learn about the responsibilities which family members owe to each other.[27]

Mothers should depend on fathers, children should depend on parents. For the moral right, the traditional nuclear family is the cornerstone of society, which must be upheld at all costs. Non-heterosexual and overtly non-monogamous heterosexual behaviour threatens the idea of the family at its core. As we shall see later, when discussing Section 28, alternatives to the traditional nuclear family simply cannot be allowed.

Yet despite social pressures, the percentage of couples who marry is dropping and the divorce rate goes on rising (in 1987, for England and Wales, it was six times what it was in 1961).[28] In 1961, only 6 per cent of live births were outside marriage; in 1981, the figure was 12 per cent; and in 1990, 28 per cent – a significant increase. Sex is less and less connected to marriage, and though the hype around AIDS means that promiscuity is frowned on, sex within a long-term heterosexual relationship, whether or not it leads to marriage, is almost respectable. A 1983 study suggested that 42 per cent of people in general and only 6 per cent of eighteen to twenty-four year olds think that premarital sex is wrong.

After years of Conservative government, Britain is a much tougher place than in the 1960s and 1970s. There is much less trust in the idea that communes, collective living or long-term non-monogamy can work, while the tight economic climate and reduced government spending have made living arrangements other than a couple sharing a bedroom more difficult on a practical level. It is not only heterosexuals who are living in couples: lesbians and gay men are also 'settling down'. However, that does not mean that people are simply accepting traditional ideas of the family – indeed rebelling against increasing conformity was one of the impulses behind the queer politics discussed in Chapter 7.

Homosexuality: questions of definition

I think the worst thing about labels is that once people have pigeonholed you, they won't let you change your mind/label. (142)

It's a shame we have to divide people up, divide love and friendship strictly (and artificially) into sexual/non-sexual. I've nothing against people saying they're gay and being proud, but I think the need is all part of society's prejudice and lies. (14)

How have homosexual desires been taken out of the realm of the 'ordinary', to be perceived as existing only in people who are classed as 'other' and 'different' from the rest of the population? The first use of the word 'homosexual' was by the Hungarian physician, Dr Karoly Maria Benkert, in 1869. Over the next forty years, homosexuality, primarily male, was brought under the jurisdiction of the legal and medical professions, and pathologised. Its causes were believed to be a general moral degeneracy, which could be caused by hereditary weakness, coupled with illness, accident of fate, or too much masturbation.

The first sexologists sought to explore homosexuality from what they believed to be a humanitarian perspective, seeking the 'truth' about what makes a homosexual, or for that matter a handkerchief fetishist or a sex murderer. Although very shocking to Victorian sensibility, sexologists enjoyed a degree of respectability through their links with the medical profession and were able to translate into medical terms what had been thought of increasingly as social problems.[29] In the ten years from 1898 to 1909, over 1,000 publications on the subject of homosexuality appeared.[30]

The late eighteenth to early nineteenth centuries was a period of frequent executions in Britain for sodomy – fifty between 1800 and 1830.[31] The death penalty for buggery was abolished in 1861, although it was still punishable by penal servitude for life. The introduction in 1885 of the Labouchère amendment to the Criminal Law Act, which criminalised 'gross indecency' between men, switched the legal focus from a sexual practice forbidden to both same-sex and opposite-sex partners, to male homosexual acts. This development also meant that for legal purposes, men who were in fact bisexual were categorised as homosexual, the most famous case being Oscar Wilde, who was married as well as a lover of men.

Liberal and socialist sexologists and reformers from the 1890s onwards tried actively to reform both laws and public opinion. Havelock Ellis' *Studies in the Psychology of Sex*, for instance, which detailed variation upon variation of sexual practice both cross-culturally and historically, was a plea for tolerance on the grounds that homosexuality was innate. In *Sexual Inversion* (1924)[32], Ellis discusses 'inverts' in terms both of case histories and of broad, extraordinary generalisations (many male homosexuals cannot whistle, many are physically immature, many are highly intellectual, and so on). Sexologists dealt mainly with male homosexuality (because of lack of data, they said) and the public profile of lesbianism remained low, in part because of the widespread assumption that female sexuality is always a response to male sexuality and that women have no active desires of their own. The concept of sex was also closely linked to penile penetration: the strength of this connection is detailed by Lillian Faderman, who cites women from various European countries, and across the centuries, who were executed for using dildoes, as well as women caught having sex together in eighteenth-century France, whose clitorises were measured to see if they could have been used for vaginal penetration.[33] Even today, sex between men is closely policed (from the high age of consent for male homosexual sex to policemen who try to entrap men having consensual sex in toilets), while sex between women is perceived as unimportant and trivial – not really sex.

British attempts to criminalise lesbianism in 1921 failed because the Director of Public Prosecutions did not want the matter to be brought to the attention of women who had never heard of such a thing. The publication and prosecution of Radclyffe Hall's novel *The Well of Loneliness* (1928) did bring lesbian sexuality to public attention, however, with the result that many women who had previously enjoyed romantic friendships with other women, whatever their sexual content, were now no longer able to do so without comment. This comparatively late creation of a stereo-typed image of *the lesbian* destroyed what was probably a way of life for many women, and although lesbianism was treated less severely than male homosexuality, the legal prescription of sex between men and pathologising of all homosexuality by the medical profession were undoubtedly forces in curbing female sexual expression.

In my youth homosexuality was a crime and lesbianism wasn't talked about much except as something shocking and abnormal. I don't think the options open to me were many or varied – chaste spinster or respectable wife. (79; aged fifty-two)

As a young person I had the usual disdain and lack of knowledge about lesbianism. I felt it was wrong and wasn't interested in a sexual rela-tionship with a woman until I was forty. (74; aged forty-seven)

The sexual revolution is usually discussed in terms of its effects on heterosexual relationships. However, the 1950s and 1960s also saw changes in attitudes to homosexuality. For homosexual men, the 1957 government-sponsored Wolfenden Report (rec-ommending the decriminalisation of homosexual sex, which eventually took place in 1967) led to the formation of lobbying and law-reform groups. For lesbians, the Minorities Research Group, formed in 1963, provided counselling, social gatherings and a magazine, *Arena 3*, which, together with a couple of London clubs, gave lesbians increased visibility. The formation of the

Gay Liberation Front in 1970 saw the beginnings of a public, unapologetic (and fun) face of homosexuality.[34] Within a mood, for men at least, of great optimism, those involved in gay liberation began for the first time to define themselves, rather than being defined by others.[35]

The sexual revolution and experimentation of the late 1960s and early 1970s also created a climate in which bisexuality, or at least the idea of 'swinging both ways', had a certain cachet, at least among the trendy, younger population, and it is arguably around the mid- to late-1970s that tolerance and awareness of bisexuality were at their height until the strengthening of the bisexual movement in the 1990s. The concept of bisexuality that seems to have caught the popular imagination was both glamorous and decadent, with core heterosexual relationships and peripheral, experimental, same-sex experiences. Glamorous, androgynous male rock stars such as David Bowie were important in creating and promoting this image.

From the late 1970s, the question of bisexuality seemed to move back into oblivion, and despite a nascent bisexual community, the subject was barely discussed or written about in the mainstream. The sexual revolution was drawing to a close, and no positive, non-defensive expression of bisexuality was yet in evidence.

In the 1990s, the AIDS epidemic has again put bisexual men in the spotlight by (unfairly) targetting them as the 'conduit' by which HIV is spread from gay men to the heterosexual population. Massive projects by the World Health Organisation, among others, have been conducted to look at men who behave bisexually (as with most research into HIV, women are ignored in such surveys), and the acknowledgment that many people, whatever their self-definition, are bisexual in behaviour is probably the most visibilising thing to happen to bisexuals as a group. Unfortunately, however, the image presented of the secretly bisexual man who has sex with other men in toilets and then infects his wife or girlfriend compounds stereotypes of bisexuals as irresponsible, untrustworthy and promiscuous and discourages honesty.

Although lesbian sex tends to encompass relatively low-risk activities, in many cases public prejudice has thrown lesbians and bisexual women in with gay and bisexual men as 'high-risk groups'. This was particularly true in the mid- to late-1980s: in 1988, according to a government-funded survey, 43 per cent of people thought lesbians were greatly at risk from HIV infection, and 17 per cent that they were quite a lot at risk.[36] This same study

shows a marked increase in anti-gay attitudes, which also applied
to lesbians and bisexual women: in 1983, 62 per cent of people
thought homosexual relationships were mostly or always wrong;
in 1987 it was 74 per cent. 64 per cent thought government
warnings about HIV transmission should mention that some
sexual practices are morally wrong.

The apotheosis of the backlash was Section 28, in law since May
1988, and the most infamous Tory legislation in support of the
traditional nuclear family. Under the misapprehension, along
with the tabloid press and much of the general public, that certain
left-wing councils were 'promoting' homosexuality in schools, MP
Jill Knight tabled an amendment to the Local Government Act.
Councils would no longer be allowed to spend money 'promoting'
homosexuality because:

> ...millions outside Parliament object to little children being
> perverted, diverted or converted from normal family life to
> a lifestyle which is desperately dangerous for society and
> extremely dangerous for them.[37]

According to Section 28:

> A local authority shall not a) intentionally promote homo-
> sexuality or publish material with the intention of promoting
> homosexuality; b) promote the teaching in any maintained
> school of the acceptability of homosexuality as a pretended
> family relationship.

The Tory paranoia is summarised by this quote from the parlia-
mentary debate:

> [homosexuality] will lead to the ultimate breakdown of
> family life, upon which the whole tenor of this country and
> its ways have been formed for generations and upon which
> the whole civilised world has been formed and based.[38]

Perhaps it is not extraordinary that the Tories and others fear that
'pretended' families of homosexuals and children – imposters
claiming the rights of 'real' families – will destroy society as we
know it. Their mere existence shows that there is more than one
way of conducting family life.

Although it is sex between men that is more frequently discussed
and condemned, lesbian sex too is actively forbidden, rather
than simply made invisible, as has been highlighted by the
Jennifer Saunders case. In 1991 eighteen-year-old Saunders was

sentenced to six years' imprisonment for indecent assault against two young women. No violence was involved, but Saunders had dressed as a boy in order to have relationships with them, and the case revolved around whether or not they had known her true gender. The two women said they would not have consented to have sex had they known Saunders was also a woman; she claimed she had been asked to dress as a man by her girlfriends in order to 'keep them in the clear'. On sentencing her, the judge summed up: 'I assume you must have some sort of bisexual feelings', by which he presumably was thinking of androgyny, as there was no indication that Saunders had ever had a relationship with a man.[39] He also made it clear that he felt it necessary to imprison her to deter other women from doing likewise.

So in Britain in the 1990s we are still far from being able to love anyone, regardless of gender. However, all is not gloom and doom: twenty years of 'out' lesbians and gays means that these communities are no longer going to take homophobia quietly. The massive political actions against Clause 28 saw bisexuals, as well as lesbians, gay men and heterosexuals, fight together more concertedly than for many years. The Clause also had a politicising effect on many who had not previously seen their sexuality as political, most famously actor Ian McKellen, who came out publicly at that time.

But where does this leave bisexuality? Society controls people's sexuality by boxing them into categories of acceptable or unacceptable, the same or other. There is no place for bisexuals in mainstream society (that only exists for heterosexuals in traditional relationships), yet as we are not defined as 'other' in the same way as people who exclusively seek same-sex relationships, lesbians and gay men can see us as 'not oppressed'. Lesbians in particular have said that bisexual women will always retreat into a heterosexual identity when the going gets tough, wanting conventional homes for our children and a man's wage. Both straight and gay people have accused bisexuals of having the best of both worlds, presumably with the idea that bisexuals take only what is positive and pleasurable from different relationships and sexual identities, abandoning what is personally or politically difficult.

In some senses, I have the best of both worlds, belonging in the lesbian community, but also fitting into the heterosexual world. In another sense I belong to neither, and am always something of an outsider. (133)

Mainstream society often views homosexuals as sad victims who cannot help their sexual orientation, and therefore deserve compassion and understanding. Bisexuals, on the other hand, are presumed to have a choice and are therefore seen as wilfully refusing to conform. Heterosexual objections to bisexuality often centre on the idea of bisexuals as sex-obsessed: bisexual behaviour implies non-monogamy, which is a threat to marriage, religion and the state. Desire for sex outside marriage is projected on to a sub-group so sexually voracious it will even go to bed with members of its own sex. In this way, the challenge of bisexuality as a genuine alternative is diminished.

Notes

1. Jeffrey Weeks, *Sex, Politics and Society*, Longmans, 1981
2. See Ronald Hyam, *Empire and Sexuality*, Manchester University Press, 1990 and Rana Kabbani, *Europe's Myths of Orient*, Pandora, 1988
3. Gail Wyatt, *Sexual Experiences of Afro-American Women* in Martha Kirkpatrick (ed), *Women's Sexual Experience*, Plenum Press, 1982
4. Theodoor Van de Velde, *Ideal Marriage*, Heinemann, 1965, p111
5. Beatrix Campbell, 'Sex – A Family Affair', in Lynne Segal (ed), *What is to be Done about the Family?*, Penguin, 1983, p159
6. Helena Wright, *The Sex Factor in Marriage*, Noel Douglas, 1930
7. Ibid, p73
8. Helena Wright, *More about the Sex Factor in Marriage*, Williams & Norgate, 1947
9. William Masters & Virginia Johnson, *Human Sexual Response*, Bantam, 1980
10. Anne Koedt, 'The Myth of the Vaginal Orgasm' (1970), in J.P. Wiseman (ed), *The Social Psychology of Sex*, Harper Row, 1976
11. Social and Community Planning Research (eds Roger Jowell & Colin Airey), *British Social Attitudes*, 1984
12. Wilhelm Reich, *The Sexual Revolution*, Vision Press, 1951
13. Wilhelm Reich, *The Mass Psychology of Fascism*, Penguin, 1975, p139
14. 'J', *The Sensuous Woman*, Mayflower, 1970, pp122–4
15. See Shere Hite, *Women in Love*, Penguin, 1989

16. Ehrenreich, Hess & Jacobs, *Re-Making Love: The Feminization of Sex*, Fontana, 1987

17. Jonathan Dollimore, *Sexual Dissidence*, OUP, 1991, p24

18. Michèle Barrett & Mary McIntosh, quoted in Jeffrey Weeks, *Sexuality and its Discontents*, Routledge & Kegan Paul, 1985

19. Fredrich Engels, *The Origins of Private Property, Family and the State*, Lawrence & Wishart, 1940 (first 1884)

20. Iteke Weeda, Family Sociologist and Professor of Emancipation at the Rijks University, Gröningen, Holland, included these theories in a lecture given at the First International Bisexual Conference, held in Amsterdam, 4 October 1991

21. Some of the books touched upon in this chapter deal more fully with the questions of marriage, family and 'the couple'. See, for instance, *What is to be Done about the Family* (op cit); Geoffrey Gorer, *Sex and Marriage in Britain Today*, Panther, 1973; Ehrenreich, Hess & Jacobs, op cit

22. Lillian Faderman, *Surpassing the Love of Men*, Morrow & Co, 1982

23. Quoted in Bland, McCabe & Mort, 'Sexuality and Reproduction' (p89) in Michèle Barrett et al, *Ideology and Cultural Production*, Croom Helm, 1979

24. Elizabeth Wilson, *Only Halfway to Paradise*, Tavistock, 1980, p88

25. Geoffrey Gorer, op cit

26. According to Beatrix Campbell, op cit, p165

27. Quoted in *Children Come First*, HMSO, 1989. This document was the White Paper for the 1990/91 Child Support Bill

28. These figures and those following are taken from *British Social Attitudes*, op cit

29. Jeffrey Weeks, *Sexuality and its Discontents*, op cit, p95

30. Norah Carlin, 'The Roots of Gay Oppression', in *International Socialism*, 2:42, p97

31. *Sex, Politics and Society*, op cit, p100

32. Havelock Ellis, *Sexual Inversion*, F.A.S. Davis, 1924

33. *Surpassing the Love of Men*, op cit, p53

34. Jeffrey Weeks, *Coming Out*, Quartet, 1977, p189

35. Kenneth Plummer, *The Making of the Modern Homosexual*, Hutchinson, 1980, p56

36. Social and Community Planning Research (eds Jowell, Witherspoon & Brook), *British Social Attitudes 1988/89*

37. Jill Knight MP, 8 May 1987. The debates in the Commons and Lords around Clause 28 show how little perceptions of

homosexuality have changed since the early twentieth century. Stereotypes of homosexuality which they present as incontrovertible fact include: you can catch it; it's genetic; homosexuals lead such unhappy lives. Lesbian sexuality is trivialised; gay male sexuality demonised. Parents are *ipso facto* conservative. Most prominent Labour MPs were notable by their absence from this debate: few were strongly against it, a few more thought it 'went too far'

38. Lord Swinfen, debate in House of Lords, 18 December 1986
39. Quoted by Cherry Smyth in *Lesbians Talk Queer Notions*, Scarlet Press, 1992

2 Theories of bisexuality

Until now, I assumed one was either heterosexual or homosexual – I couldn't understand or believe in bisexuality. (75)

Calling myself bisexual, I'm simply using a convenient existing social label. (25)

I read the word 'bisexual' in a book and realised that they were describing me. (37)

Chapter 1 looked at how sexuality has been constructed so that bisexuality is largely invisible, and how it must remain so in order to maintain the status quo. But theories about bisexuality have been developed by some writers, if usually as an offshoot of writings on homosexuality, and this chapter looks at what has been said. In this book I use what I consider to be the correct definition of bisexuality: that is, sexual and emotional desire for and activity with people of both sexes. The term 'bisexuality' has often been given other meanings, however, and it is useful to look at what these are, how they have been created and how they have shifted over time. The confusion between bisexuality and androgyny, and the theories of bisexuality as a stage in sexual development, a defence against one's 'true' sexuality, or as behaviour favoured by the 'over-sexed', still have currency today. Other sexual theorists, writing over the past twenty years, have written about bisexuality from a positive standpoint, or have considered sexuality as socially constructed – which means bisexuality can have a place within it.

Androgyny: bisexuality of the self

As a child I mostly had male playmates and preferred 'boys' games. I felt strongly that males had a better life, and I prayed to wake up a boy. I felt more male than female and sublimated all sexual feelings in sport. When I was a teenager I began to accept that I was a female and was going to stay female. (75)

I love to see boys in pretty clothes and I love to wear jeans all the time. (90)

My friends know that I like feminine men; therefore it's logical that I'd like boyish women. (23)

Sexually I can take the lead and be aggressive with men, whereas with women I act much more passively. (34)

One of the most common mis-definitions of bisexuality is to confuse it with androgyny, and indeed the conflation of bisexuality and androgyny – whether physical or psychic – was common well into the present century and still manifests itself today. Most writers before the 1950s used the word 'bisexual' to mean dual-sexed, to describe the co-existence of masculine and feminine components of the self, or to designate behaviour traditionally classed as masculine in a woman, or as feminine in a man. Often they would slip confusingly from one meaning to another within the same text. Douglas Bryan's paper 'Bisexuality', for instance, (published in the *International Journal of Psychoanalysis*, 1930)[1] begins by asking why the fact that in some circumstances people can use either men or women as sex objects has been ignored. Then, without trying to clear up this issue, he moves to how *types* of sexual response are either male or female. This multiplicity of meaning is still present in Charlotte Wolff's *Bisexuality* (1977).

Nineteenth-century scientists researching the development of human cells saw that they contained within them both male and female components, and considered that the genitals and urological system were also dual-sexed, with people of each gender having the organs of the other in atrophied form.[2] Many sexologists and psychiatrists until at least the 1950s looked for a correlation between homosexual behaviour and genital development, measuring, for instance, the clitorises of lesbians to see if they were larger (more 'masculine') than those of 'normal' women. Sexologists were looking for 'inter-sexed' people, or hermaphrodites – extremely rare, but not unknown, in real life, and a common and powerful mythical element in many different religions and cultures.[3]

At the same time, the idea of the co-existence of male and female characteristics within the psyche was being explored by psychologists, most notably Carl Gustav Jung, who believed that the female unconscious contains a male element or animus, while men have a female element or anima. For Jung, 'bisexuality' was a balance between the masculine and feminine elements of the psyche, rather than a sexual drive.[4] His concept of androgyny was very fashionable in some circles in the early twentieth century, with writers like D. H. Lawrence, James Joyce and members of the Bloomsbury group believing that people were man-womanly or woman-manly.[5]

Today, it is appearance rather than psychological make-up that is the most frequently explored aspect of androgyny. Androgyny is still connected to sexuality within the popular imagination, and is perceived by traditionalists as threatening in its potential to break down gender roles, as witnessed by the hostile reactions that greeted the introduction of unisex clothing in the 1960s and 1970s. Some gays choose an androgynous image as part of the expression of their sexuality; other people, like Carolyn Heilbrun, writing in the early 1970s, see androgyny as a reconciliation between the sexes, allowing male and female attitudes to come together within one person.[6]

The confusion between androgyny and bisexuality seems to have arisen from the idea that one can only respond to a person of the same sex if one has or takes on aspects of the other. And in the case of bisexuals (rather than homosexuals), the capacity to respond to people of both sexes is seen as implying that the bisexual must be both 'masculine' and 'feminine' simultaneously. Some male bisexuals do feel restricted by masculine stereotypes and look to bisexuality to help them express their 'feminine' side,[7] while women have been more likely to want to transform the meaning of 'femaleness' to include things which are/were traditionally male.

The words 'masculine' and 'feminine' have strict and inflexible meanings, connected exclusively to either men or women, and are not terms that can be applied equally and non-judgementally to people of both genders. In addition, power differences between men and women mean that it is not such a simple project for women to express their 'masculine side' by dressing and/or acting as men – power is not so easily grasped. A powerful group can voluntarily 'give up' power; a less powerful one cannot get it simply by taking on the characteristics of a more powerful one.

The queer politics of the 1990s has offered an eagerly-grasped opportunity for women to attempt to 'try on' male qualities in a strictly sexual context. Identifying as butch/femme, dressing up, playing with notions of masculinity and femininity and passive/active within lesbian relationships are subjects of excitement and debate within parts of the lesbian community.

A dangerous stage: from Freud to Kinsey

I often don't like calling myself bisexual because it gives people the wrong impression. They don't take you seriously, think you're mixed up. (127)

I was attracted to girls when I was around twelve or thirteen, but I comforted myself with the fact that everyone knew you grew out of it when boys came along. But I didn't, and because I didn't I was convinced I must be a lesbian. (11)

Sexology, from its inception in the mid-nineteenth century, has almost always classified subjects as heterosexual or homosexual, with the result that bisexuality -- whether as identity, emotions or behaviour -- has received scant attention. Individuals have been pathologised for same-sex behaviour, whether or not they also have heterosexual relationships, so bisexuals are usually subsumed in the group of individuals who at any time behave homosexually. Sexual theorists have, however, occasionally recognised that people do not always exhibit exclusively hetero-sexual or homosexual behaviour and have tried to account for this in various ways.

Richard von Krafft-Ebing, for instance, whose *Psychopathia Sexualis* (1886) was still in print in the 1960s, lists degrees of homosexuality, with categories that include 'psychic hermaph-rodites' (bisexuals) and 'physical hermaphrodites'. According to Krafft-Ebing, psychic hermaphrodites are probably numerous, but because they attract little social attention, they are less likely to consult doctors with their 'problem'. Krafft-Ebing believed that psychic hermaphrodites were predominantly homosexual, but with a heterosexual element which could be encouraged by will and control, hypnotism and treatment, but especially by abstinence from masturbation.[8]

I grew up perceiving sex as secret, and something about which I was ignorant. This was not helped by reading Krafft-Ebing. (52)

The theories of Sigmund Freud, developed between the 1890s and 1930s, have direct relevance to bisexuality in general and to bisexual women in particular. Although there have been widespread debates about how to interpret Freud's views on women and on homosexuality, and whether or not these are positive, his ideas were certainly a great improvement on his predecessors' theories of homosexuality as congenital abnormality.

According to Freud, everyone is born with sexual desires, or a libido, which in an infant is 'polymorphously perverse' (i.e. its desires are directed wherever they gain gratification). During the pre-Oedipal stage, the primary focus for both girls and boys is the mother. Girls, however, have to change their love object from female to male and their centre of sexuality from clitoris to vagina in order to develop into 'healthy' sexual adults. At around the age of five or six, children enter the Oedipus complex. Desiring the mother, for the boy, means fearing castration by the father. But girls discover they are already castrated, and hold their mothers responsible for their lack of penis, which represents power: the infamous 'penis envy'. To resolve the Oedipus complex successfully, the girl has to transmute her desire for a penis to desire for a baby with her father.

For Freud, then, the path of sexual development, for girls in particular, is riddled with pitfalls, and it is clear that for him, women's sexuality does not develop without a struggle. Because of the way girls have to switch object choice from female to male (mother to father), Freud believed that bisexuality was more likely to occur in women.[9]

In 'Three Essays on the Theory of Sexuality' (1905),[10] Freud discusses whether homosexuality is innate, concluding that usually it is not. He believed that homosexuals varied greatly, and that 'inverts' might be totally invert, 'amphigenic inverts' (bisexual), or 'contingent inverts' (exhibiting homosexual behaviour only when a person of the opposite sex was not available). While he saw male/female attraction as the strongest factor in preventing inversion, he also recognised the importance of societal prohibitions. In 'The Psychogenesis of a Case of Homosexuality in a Woman' (1920), Freud discusses the case of a young woman whose father turned to psychoanalysis to 'cure' her of her lesbianism, though she herself was not unhappy about it. Freud said that as she was not ill, nor suffering from a neurotic conflict, there was little chance of her changing. In this paper, Freud stresses the universal bisexuality of human beings, and argues that all 'normal' people have strong unconscious homosexual feelings. While he believed that access to the opposite sex could contribute to 'restoring [a homosexual's] full bisexual functions', he acknowledged that:

> After that it lay with him to choose whether he wished to
> abandon the path that is banned by society and in some cases
> he has done so. One must remember that normal sexuality
> too depends upon a restriction in the choice of object.[11]

Unlike his contemporaries, Freud believed that female sexuality
and femininity did not just 'happen' to women, but were complex
constructs that could easily 'go wrong'. He believed that sexuality
had no natural object and that any choice required some narrowing
of options from the 'polymorphous perversity' of childhood.
Homosexual elements existed in everyone, however apparently
heterosexual.

Many of Freud's disciples -- from Jung to Lacan -- formed their
own schools of psychology that gave weight to and developed
different aspects of his theories. Freud's notion of the universality of bisexuality was developed by Wilhelm Stekel, who proposed
in *Bisexual Love* (1934) that both homosexuals and heterosexuals are necessarily neurotic, as both struggle to overcome and repress
areas of longing within themselves.

> Psychoanalysis has proven that all homosexuals, without
> exception, show heterosexual tendencies in early life. There
> is no exception to this rule. *There are no monosexual persons!*
> The heterosexual period stretches far into puberty. *All persons
> are bisexual.* But persons repress either the homosexual or the
> heterosexual components on account of certain motives or
> because they are compelled by particular circumstances and
> consequently act as if they were monosexual.[12]

Stekel's insights were not followed up by other theorists. But
the idea of bisexuality as a stage, usually found in adolescence,
was expressed by, for instance, sexual reformer Magnus Hirschfeld,
who, according to his pupils (1946), believed that everyone is bisexual
'at a certain stage of development', but normally (sic) people
grow out of it.[13]

From the 1930s onwards, psychoanalysis moved towards a
disregard of Freud's more radical concepts, and abandoned his challenging of the natural. For Freud, male and female were made in
culture, but to many later theorists, biology was of foremost
importance, and much psychoanalytic practice became aimed at
'normalising' its patients. From the 1940s, psychoanalysis and

psychiatry became even more strongly committed to upholding the status quo. Despite, or perhaps because of, a growing homosexual culture (principally among gay men, but also to some extent among lesbians), theories of homosexuality became ever more pernicious. For the psychologists mentioned below, homosexuality *per se* was a mixture of neurosis and congenital disorder, something to be cured. Homosexuals were necessarily full of guilt about their 'condition'; there was no such thing as a healthy homosexual; homosexuals were deluding themselves if they believed society was at fault in condemning them.

The few theories of bisexuality that were developed, mostly in the US, focused mainly on the supposed impossibility of being sexually attracted to both men and women. For instance, many psychiatrists believed that if any homosexual behaviour or attraction existed, then the individual concerned must be homosexual. This was most forcefully expressed by Edmund Bergler in 'The Law of the Excluded Middle' (1956), which claimed that once homosexual behaviour had started, any further heterosexual behaviour must be counterfeit. According to Bergler, bisexuality was an 'out and out fraud', and bisexuals were men (sic) who were capable only of 'lustless mechanical sex' with women.[14]

Other, related, theories considered men and women to be opposed sexual objects, and therefore posited that it was not possible to eroticise both. According to Charles Berg, for instance, writing in 1958, if one sex was associated with gratification, then the other must be associated with castration.[15] Many psychoanalysts in the 1950s and early 1960s considered those calling themselves bisexual to be highly disturbed, full of guilt feelings, chronically unable to choose, and so on.[16]

The Kinsey Reports on male, then female, sexuality published in the late 1940s and early 1950s were mammoth studies of human sexual behaviour that represented a radical challenge to contemporary notions of 'normality'. In his report on female sexuality, (using a sample of 5,940 white American women),[17] Alfred Kinsey and his researchers shocked the establishment by showing, for instance, how few white American women were virgins on marriage, and how few felt guilty about it. As a result of his research, Kinsey developed the 'Kinsey Scale' that graded sexual preference from 0 (heterosexual only) to 6 (homosexual only) and so challenged the myth that people were necessarily totally one or the other. Using the term 'homosexual' to refer to behaviour rather than to individuals, he noted that by the age of thirty, 28 per cent of his female sample had recognised erotic responses to other women, and by the age of forty, 19 per cent had had a sexual experience with another woman.

Challenges such as the Kinsey Report were rapidly dismissed, however. One response, *Kinsey's Myth of Female Sexuality*[18] by Bergler and William Kroger, contends that his 5,940 respondents must be neurotic and vaginally frigid. Bergler and Kroger extrapolate Kinsey's figures to show that if his sample were representative, between 30 and 35 million people in the US would be on the homosexual side of the scale, and homosexuality would therefore be the 'national disease'. Along with Berg, they consider bisexuality impossible, believing that the way a homosexual's unconscious views sexuality and sexual objects is entirely different from the way a heterosexual's does. Indeed, they blame Kinsey for allowing people who behave bisexually to think they are normal when they are not. Though it was often admitted by theorists, including those mentioned above, that bisexuality – either as desire for both women and men, or as male and female components of the personality – existed in the unconscious, individuals who acted on these feelings were dismissed, and either their homosexual or heterosexual behaviour classified as being without desire: a psychological defence against 'true' homo- or heterosexuality known as pseudo-homosexuality, or pseudo-heterosexuality.

The growing homophile movements in the US also tried to dismiss bisexuality. For instance in *The Homosexual and His Society* (1963) – a book predominantly, but not exclusively, about men – Donald Cory and John LeRoy write that one has to admit that bisexuality exists, but that they find it hard to accept the idea.[19] Bisexuals are 'overgrown adolescents'. Individuals on the Kinsey Scale always have stronger tendencies in one direction or the other, and should decide. Although this may be second best for the happiness of the individual, a decision one way or the other is regarded as better than none, as a definite sexual orientation is seen as necessary for psychological stability:

> It is ironic that while bisexuality seems to be innate, and hence natural, the few ambisexuals who do exist would be compelled, by our society, to be far from rational, happy human beings. In fact, they are likely to be psychopathic.[20]

It is a shame that while such writers recognised that homosexuality is problematised by 'society', they were unable to extend this insight to bisexuality.

Anything that moves: the spirit of the 1960s

A friend of mine, in most ways a progressive person, was very shocked when I told her I was bisexual. She said she could understand that men were bisexual because many of them had such rampant sex drives, but women weren't like that. It took a lot of explaining for her to realise that bisexuality was about more than just having sex. (38)

I hate the word bisexual as it has, to me, associations of someone who will sleep with anyone. (2)

'Bisexual' puts too much emphasis on sex, and sounds either very clinical, or projects a nymphomaniac image. (119)

The more liberal attitudes towards sex and sexuality of the 1960s produced sensationalist publications on bisexuality. *The Bisexual Woman*, for instance, by David Lynne (1967), subtitled 'A timely examination of lesbians trapped in conventional marriages' was an American book which appeared in a series of volumes on all forms of societally-taboo sex: drag, promiscuity, lesbianism, and so on. The book is written in a titillating fashion, with lots of heavy breathing and stroking of breasts: an excuse for mildly erotic writing dressed up as investigation.[21]

The first book to be written from a British perspective was *Bisexuality* (1970) by Jason Douglas. This rather strange book, probably written under a pseudonym, purports to be about 'Society's most unhappy but busiest groups of men and women'. It doesn't really show how or why bisexuals are either unhappy or busy, but does deal in broad generalisations, some of which are intriguing:

> The female bisexual is generally tough-minded, clear-headed and passionate. She will be outspoken and will seek sexual satisfaction without embarrassment or hesitation. She will, in all probability, consider herself the equal of men, will not be particularly maternal, and will enjoy the company of other like-minded women as much as men.[22]

Douglas makes no significant distinction between bisexual women and their male counterparts: true (sic) bisexuals always want 'feminine' women and 'masculine' men; other bisexuals see the two sides of themselves as fulfilling opposite needs. The 'permissive society', Douglas believes, allows bisexuality to flourish, and the bisexuals he is discussing have, by his standards, unusually strong sex drives which they are not inhibited about expressing. While Douglas acknowledges that society creates a lot of problems for bisexuals, he believes that this will change given time.

Bisexuality was also taken into account by writers dealing with homosexuality, and the general perception seems to have been that bisexuals were promiscuous and sad.[23] Bryan Magee, for instance, who made several television programmes on lesbians and gay men in the mid-1960s, thought that bisexuals, who according to his definition never accepted one person for a lifetime, must be sad, and ultimately lonely.

Interest in bisexuality was growing in both the UK and US, and in 1974 nine articles on the subject were published in mainstream American newspapers and magazines such as *Time* and *Newsweek*. Most of the articles were highly sensational, focusing on a more-is-better sexuality, which 'experts' would then critique. However, Charlotte Wolff's *Bisexuality* (1977), the most recent UK-published theoretical book on the subject, also appeared. The author was a well-known psychiatrist and someone who believed herself to be bisexual, so clearly the parameters of the book were less framed by sensationalism. She discusses what others -- from Ancient Greek philosophers to twentieth-century sexologists – have said about bisexuality, and looks at 150 bisexual people in some depth, focusing on their childhoods. A number of her subjects also contributed autobiographical articles.

This book was immensely important to me, and to other bisexuals, many of whom were isolated at that time. However, it now seems very dated; many of its subjects naively hedonistic. Parts of it, particularly those looking at possible biological causes for bisexuality and homosexuality, are anachronistic – as they would also have been in 1977.

A positive choice

I would like to believe that to be a bisexual would offer a bridge between two disparate views and lifestyles. But I realise that sounds outrageously idealistic – I think we are a long way from that bridging. (134)

Bisexuality has unfortunate 'swinging' connotations. It's thought of as having the best of both worlds, in a nasty way. (45)

Despite the negative stereotypes of bisexuality which underpin so much sexual theory, some psychologists have posited the possibility of a psychologically healthy bisexuality, and allowed that it may be both a genuine sexuality and a positive choice. According to American Fred Klein in *The Bisexual Option* (1978),[24] bisexuality – which he sees as an openness to sexual and emotional feelings towards both men and women – offers the greatest potential for intimacy. People who are not open in this way, Klein believes, put many boundaries on their behaviour which cut down the possibilities for getting close to others – a fundamental human need. For Klein, the successful resolution of the Oedipus complex relies on the repression of desires for father and mother substitutes, rather than for men or women generally.

Klein distinguishes between what he considers 'healthy' bisexuality, which involves a great capacity for different types of intimacy, and 'neurotic' bisexuality, where relationships with one or the other gender are based on power or over-dependency. Bisexuality as sexual behaviour is intrinsically neither healthy nor neurotic; however, Klein raises the question of whether heterosexuality is intrinsically 'neurotic', pointing to the large numbers of heterosexuals who behave in sexually destructive ways. Klein also developed the Klein Sexual Orientation Grid, which expands on the Kinsey Scale; this is used in discussions of sexual identity in Chapter 6.

Other recent discussions of the psychology of bisexuality (from the *Journal of Homosexuality*) present it as flexibility, rather than conflict[25] and see the bisexual as recognising a co-existence and integration of homosexual and heterosexual feelings and behaviours. This does not mean there is no ambivalence, though it is posited that much of the difficulty is created by society.

Sexual theorists such as Michel Foucault and Jeffrey Weeks have challenged essentialist views of sexuality, asking us to abandon the concept of categorisation, and to question how sexual identity is created and how what is portrayed as natural is constructed.[26] Such writers have helped to provide a background against which theories of bisexuality can exist, but have rarely dealt with the issue themselves. Like past theorists (whether liberal or hostile), they fail to differentiate between bisexual and homosexual subjects, treating both as people who have homosexual

experience or homosexual elements within their character. Most
books of progressive sexual theory still omit bisexuality completely,
and the fact that many people have feelings for and relationships
with people of both sexes is obscured.[27] Once a person is known
to have same-sex relationships, he or she is labelled homosexual,
which becomes an exclusive identity, irrespective of whether he
or she has mixed-gender relationships as well. We need to establish
that bisexuality exists before we can abandon the tradition of
labelling and categorising people. As one respondent put it:

Bisexuality is deeply threatening to the heterosexual order because
it blurs the boundaries between the 'deviant gay' and the 'normal'
straight. It potentially makes the notion of sexuality a much more fluid
issue. Everybody would then be seen as a mixture of male and female
sexuality, the different combinations making up a whole range of sexual
personalities. (34)

It should be clear by now that despite the prevalence of bisexual
behaviours, bisexuality is relentlessly and deliberately left out of
the discussion of the possible range of sexual options. That there
are now more visible bisexuals, and a small but organised and
enduring bisexual community, means that, in Britain and the US
at least, some small beginning is being made to break down these
perceived polarities.

Notes

1. Douglas Bryan, 'Bisexuality', from the *International Journal of
   Psychoanalysis* vol 11, 1930
2. Sandor Rado, *The Psychoanalysis of Behaviour*, Grove & Stratton,
   1956 (a critical examination of the concept of bisexuality).
   He disagrees that mammals are dual-sexed
3. Marie Delcourt, *Hermaphrodite*, Studio, 1961
4. June Singer, *Androgyny*, Routledge & Kegan Paul, 1977 (introduction by Sheldon Hendler, p43)
5. Stephen Heath, *The Sexual Fix*, Macmillan, 1982, p141
6. Carolyn Heilbrun, *Towards Androgyny*, Gollancz, 1973
7. See *Bimonthly*, Spring 1989
8. Richard von Krafft-Ebing, *Psychopathia Sexualis*, Mayflower Dell,
   1967, pp231–3
9. Sigmund Freud, 'Hysterical Phantasies and their Relation to
   Bisexuality' in *On Psychopathology*, Pelican,1973

10. Sigmund Freud, 'Three Essays on the Theory of Sexuality' in *On Sexuality*, Pelican, 1977

11. Sigmund Freud, 'The Psychogenesis of a Case of Homosexuality in a Woman' from the *Standard Edition Of Freud*, vol 18, Hogarth Press, 1955

12. Wilhelm Stekel, *Bisexual Love*, Physicians and Surgeons Book Co, 1934

13. Magnus Hirschfeld, *Sexual Anomalies and Perversions*, Torch, 1946

14. Edmund Bergler, *Homosexuality: Disease or Way of Life?*, Collier, 1956

15. Charles Berg & H.M. Krich (eds), *Homosexuality*, Allen & Unwin, 1958

16. Further information in Gary Zinik, 'Identity Conflict or Adaptive Flexibility?' in Fritz Klein & Timothy Wolf (eds), *Two Lives to Lead*, Harrington Park Press, 1985

17. Alfred Kinsey et al, *Sexual Behaviour in the Human Female*, Sanders, 1953

18. Edmund Bergler & William Kroger, *Kinsey's Myth of Female Sexuality*, Grove & Stratton, 1954

19. Donald Cory & John LeRoy, *The Homosexual and His Society*, Citadel, 1963, pp50–64

20. Ibid, p62

21. David Lynne, *The Bisexual Woman*, Midweek, 1967

22. Jason Douglas, *Bisexuality*, Canova, 1970, p14

23. For instance, Bryan Magee, *One in Twenty*, Corgi, 1968, and Masters & Johnson, *Homosexuality in Perspective*, Bantam, 1982

24. Fred Klein, *The Bisexual Option*, Priam Books, 1975. (In Klein's later work, his first name is given as 'Fritz')

25. Gary Zinik's 'Identity Conflict or Adaptive Flexibility?', op cit

26. Michel Foucault, *The History of Sexuality Vol 1: An Introduction*, Allen Lane, 1979; Jeffrey Weeks, *Coming Out*, Quartet, 1977; *Sex, Politics and Society*, Longmans, 1981; and *Sexuality and its Discontents*, Routledge & Kegan Paul, 1985

27. Jonathon Dollimore's *Sexual Dissidence* (OUP, 1991); for instance, only mentions bisexuality as androgyny. Yet in other ways this book is both thought-provoking and wide-ranging

3 Bisexuality and feminism

When I went to a women's studies summer school, I met 'Greenham-type' women, and discussed issues like sexuality. It was fantastic. Through the women I met there I joined the local women's group, which gave me the confidence and support I needed. (67)

My first sexual relationships with women began through our shared politics. (91)

In a climate as right wing as this, it has to be subversive to go to bed with members of one's own sex and to defend that act. Making any commitment to other women is political. But having done this, to enjoy sex with women, and then to go and have sex with men is regrettably also seen as political. (28)

As the previous chapter showed, women are still unable freely to express their sexuality within our society – whatever that sexuality might be. And in order to create a society where this is possible, women still need to get together and fight. In these supposedly post-feminist days, when we are told we can 'have it all', it is vital that women recognise the continued importance of feminism. 'Having it all' depends both on what we want and on who we are: only a small number of white, upper-middle-class, heterosexual women have ever had anything approaching 'all'.

To judge from the answers of questionnaire respondents, feminism is part of the political credo of self-defined bisexual women: all but three respondents identified as feminists, at least to some extent. And though the relationship between bisexual women and sections of the feminist movement has not always been easy, bisexual women, whether acknowledged as such or not, have been involved in all kinds of feminist struggles. Yet feminist theories of sexuality, which have been a powerful force in liberating women from traditional roles and expectations, have largely excluded bisexual women: bisexuality has been ignored by or absent from feminist theory as much as from non-progressive theories of sexuality in

38

general. In the tough times of the 1990s, sexual theory and politics can no longer afford to ignore bisexual women's experiences and needs.

Feminist theories of sexuality: first-wave feminism

The organisation of sexuality within society has always been of central importance to feminists, and its analysis one of the key sites of the struggle against patriarchy. In this section I am going to look at how sexuality has been addressed within British, US and selected European feminist activity and debates from the mid-nineteenth century to the present day. My perspective on more recent history has been informed not only by written accounts but by my own experience from the mid-1970s onwards. As much feminist political activity has not been recorded in writing, this account is necessarily partial.

Many of the different feminist attitudes towards sexuality manifest today were already in existence from the 1860s. For example, English women were actively protesting against the automatic granting of male sexual licence[1] through the campaign against the Contagious Diseases Acts. These Acts, introduced in 1864, 1866 and 1869 to stop the spread of venereal diseases, allowed the police in garrison towns to arrest and test women thought to be prostitutes. Those who were infected were imprisoned, while their male clients (also presumably infected) were never apprehended. The Acts were the focus of massive feminist protest, and the campaigns against them were followed by other anti-vice campaigns. Many protesters were angered by the stark double standards, by which it was the women who were blamed and punished, when they believed that it was men who should learn to control themselves. 'Control' at the time was seen as the refusal of all forms of extra-marital sex, which social-purity reformers saw as inevitably coercive.

The Suffragette movement, in the decades to 1914, saw the coming together of many different types of women to fight for the vote and look at the position of women in general. Many of its members, most famously Christabel Pankhurst, made the choice to remain celibate – an early form of separatism – rather than endure disrespectful relationships with men, and instead poured their energy into women.

Other women took a very different view of heterosexual relationships, believing that the answer lay not in rejection of men, but in finding new forms of interaction. Many 'free-thinkers' around the turn of the century established committed, but not legalised, heterosexual relationships in which the female partner strove for equality and autonomy. In the USSR, the new forms of society explored in the early post-revolutionary years led Alexandra Kollontai – the only woman in Lenin's 1917 government – to look at the problems which beset heterosexual relationships. Kollontai believed that the 'sexual crisis' was three-quarters socio-economic, but that emotional possessiveness and egoism also needed to be challenged.[2] Other women, such as anarchist Emma Goldman in New York, sought to separate love and marriage, seeing marriage as a purely economic arrangement to which she was vehemently opposed.

At a time when the study of sexology was popular among the radical intelligentsia, politically active women such as British contraception and abortion campaigner Stella Browne were attracted by what they saw as its liberating ideas. Many such women believed that sexual emotions were not weaker in women, but different. However, they were also well aware that society would have to change before attitudes to sex could fundamentally alter[3] and that without the means of preventing endless pregnancies, it would be difficult to promote one of sexology's main theses: that heterosexual sex (i.e. intercourse) is good for men and women alike.

Other feminists lived in lesbian relationships, though this was played down by all sections of the movement. Stella Browne, for instance, believed that 'congenital lesbianism' was tolerable – if inferior – to heterosexuality, but that it should not be put forward as a possibility for 'ordinary' women. Emma Goldman held similar views – despite being involved in what seems to have been at least one passionately sexual lesbian relationship.[4] Although such women were in practice what people would now call bisexual, as women of their time, they considered heterosexuality paramount.

In the 1920s, once women had gained the vote, organised feminism went into abeyance. The only text published over the next forty years to discuss issues relevant to this book was Simone de Beauvoir's *The Second Sex* (1953). Following the publication of her letters, it is now known that de Beauvoir had many sexual relationships with both women and men. In *The Second Sex*, she put forward the concept that the history of an individual is not fatalistically determined, but is comprised of choices. And within this structure, lesbianism is a choice which, given the organisation of power within society, is understandable:

> The truth is that homosexuality is no more a perversion deliberately indulged in than it is a curse of fate. It is an attitude *chosen in a certain situation* that is at once motivated and freely adopted.[5]

De Beauvoir maintained that it is obvious that women should wish to fight against the restrictions placed upon them, including those imposed by heterosexual society. What she saw as less understandable was why more women did not fight back.

Second-wave feminism: the 1960s to the present

By the 1960s, more women were ready to do just this. The beginnings of the women's liberation movement coincided, and to some extent came out of, the theories of sexual liberation popular in the late 1960s. The problem of unwanted pregnancy had been supposedly banished by the introduction of the contraceptive pill, with the result that women were suddenly perceived as unproblematically sexually available to men and able to enjoy sex on men's terms. Women's liberation demanded women-centred heterosexual sex, among other things.

It was at this time, too, that bisexuality was first considered a possibility in the popular imagination. Yet the prevalent image of bisexuality was tainted with a frivolity it has not yet lost -- it was dismissed as a kink in sexual behaviour, the result of unbridled lust and decadence. Within sexual liberation, the stereotypical image of bisexuality was of a man having sex with two women, a stereotype which remains today.

Many of the early works of this second wave of feminist theory addressed sexuality and relationships, usually within a totally heterosexual framework. Among those that questioned the supposed gains of sexual liberation was Germaine Greer's *The Female Eunuch* (1970), which pointed out that the ability to speak freely about sex had led to the creation of other sexual norms, as dishonest as the ones that existed previously. Greer did not believe that substituting genitality for sexuality was at all positive: the women's movement should hold out for ecstasy, not just orgasm.[6]

Mainstream magazines like *Cosmopolitan* played an ambivalent role. Although they promoted an ideology that stressed women's sexual dependence on men, they also told women how to get pleasure, and to ask for it assertively. But the persisting double standard whereby a woman who said 'yes' to sex was often still condemned as 'easy' by both men and women made it hard to win: women who were refusing to remain in traditional roles were often criticised, as were women who espoused more conventional views.

The sexual theory and research that grew out of the women's liberation movement was potentially very positive for the development of a bisexual feminism. Although in retrospect much of it appears naive, it did hold out the possibility that women would be able to choose their lovers regardless of gender. Anne Koedt, for instance, in 'The Myth of the Vaginal Orgasm' (1970),[7] reiterated that women come to orgasm through the clitoris, and proposed that the denial of this fact was politically motivated:

> The establishment of clitoral orgasm as fact would threaten the heterosexual institution. For it would indicate that sexual pleasure was obtainable from either men or women, thus making heterosexuality not an absolute, but an option. It would thus open up the whole question of human sexual relations beyond the confines of the present male-female role system.

In *My Secret Garden* (1976), Nancy Friday's collection of women's sexual fantasies, fantasies involving other women were mentioned more often than any other. Her subjects, who all identified as heterosexual, included other women in a wide range of sexual scenarios, with or without men involved. They mentioned these fantasies easily, which Friday considered men would not have been able to do with their same-sex fantasies.[8]

Certain feminist psychologists in the 1970s were developing pro-bisexual theories. Like Freud (see Chapter 2), Dorothy Dinnerstein and Nancy Chodorow believed that women have a greater potential than men for bisexuality because of their strong early relationship with their mother. Chodorow and Dinnerstein argue that rather than changing the gender of their love object during the Oedipal phase, girls simply add their father on to the original mother-child couple. So girls always remain primarily emotionally attached to their mother (and to other women), even if they become erotically attached to men. Men, whose initial attachment to their mother remains unchallenged, are more likely to direct both their emotions and sexual desires towards women.[9]

The mammoth survey conducted by Shere Hite in the mid-1970s put paid to many of the myths which surrounded women's sexuality. *The Hite Report* (1977), which was based on women's responses to questionnaires, included their views on a range of sexual issues and showed widespread disillusion with men and sex. The report also included a chapter on lesbianism. Although the questionnaire asked no specific questions on changing sexuality, many women who had not yet had a sexual relationship with a woman were considering doing so.[10]

The 1970s was a period in which women got together to talk about liberation, relationships, men and sex. Women within consciousness-raising groups talked of their dissatisfaction with their relationships with men and their feelings of personal failure. For some there was hope that by determining and then demanding what they wanted, women would be able to form more equal and satisfying relationships with men and so effect change; for others, the answer lay in rejecting men altogether. Some women 'experimented' with sexual relationships with women without changing their heterosexual identity; for others, feminism provided the necessary catalyst for a recognition of lesbian sexuality. In Britain, the national women's liberation conferences held between 1970 and 1978 discussed sexuality and different ways of expressing it. The 1974 conference formulated the sixth demand of the women's liberation movement: 'A right to a self-defined sexuality and an end to discrimination against lesbians'.

The UK feminist magazine *Spare Rib* reflected these aspirations and desires. During the early- to mid-1970s, *Spare Rib* contained many personal reflections, discussion articles and general information of interest to heterosexual feminists. Women discussed their lack of orgasms, masturbation and their relationships with men, and the magazine published numerous consumer-type guides to contraception. (The battles for safe, free abortion and contraception were tremendously important at this time, both as a means of asserting women's right to control their own bodies and as enabling them to broaden their sexual experience.) But this discussion of heterosexuality took place without taking power relations into account. It did not consider that the construction of masculinity and femininity, and the inequality between men and women, would necessarily undermine positive heterosexual relationships. The magazine did discuss women's oppression in other areas, but the articles on sexual relations were written as if in a vacuum. It was presumed that if women knew what they wanted and were assertive in asking for it, then men would change to accommodate them. Before too long, however, this hope seemed to die as many women discovered that egalitarian heterosexual relationships were a lot harder to bring about than they had imagined.

So the beginnings of the women's liberation movement were dominated by heterosexual considerations and lesbians were ignored. In Britain, the discrimination was subtle: unlike in the US, there were no public fracas about the place of lesbianism within the movement. There, 'founding mother' Betty Friedan spoke out against the so-called 'Lavender Menace' of lesbians who were, in her opinion, discrediting the good name of feminism. Writer Rita Mae Brown resigned from the New York chapter of the National Organization of Women, and the Lavender Menace group disrupted the 1970 Congress to Unite Women.

The US press was indeed anxious to discredit feminism and saw linking it with lesbianism as a means to achieve this. Kate Millett, author of *Sexual Politics*, was harassed by *Time* magazine reporters asking her publicly whether she was bisexual; her confirmation that she was led to a press scandal during which other feminists were not particularly supportive.[11] Her autobiography *Flying* describes her political struggles in this area.

Of course, the beginnings of women's liberation pre-dated the positive messages about homosexuality put forward by gay liberation, which did not begin in the UK until 1970. The traditional image of the 'sad and sorry' lesbian, forever afflicted by her sexuality, was a strongly entrenched one which any woman coming out in the 1960s or 1970s would have to break through. Even relatively positive discussions of lesbianism, including those written by lesbians themselves, tended to dwell on their supposed psychological immaturity and unhappy lives.[12]

Lesbian groups like London's Kenric, formed in 1963, had tried to promote the image of lesbians as respectable members of society, and aimed to decrease the isolation of individual women. Gay liberation had different concerns. The earliest gay liberation groups, which had a ratio of 5:1 male to female, were concerned with challenging current conceptions of homosexuality. They 'zapped' Harley Street doctors, disrupted Mary Whitehouse's Festival of Light, and held lots of fun-type demonstrations. However, many women felt excluded and uneasy at the misogynist behaviour of some of the men,[13] and in 1972 most women left. Some put their energy into political lesbianism; others joined groups such as Sappho, which operated largely outside women's liberation.

There was some recognition and acceptance of bisexual behaviour at this time. Many groups advertising in *Spare Rib* until about 1975 called themselves groups for 'lesbians and bisexual women'. Some of the women mentioned in Charlotte Wolff's *Bisexuality* belonged to Sappho or Kenric, feeling that even if they were married, their homoerotic feelings entitled them to be there. On the other hand, many lesbians, whatever their politics, saw bisexuality as a cop-out, and believed that bisexual women would always in the end opt for heterosexual respectability and go back to men.[14] The unease female bisexuality engendered and its centrality to any understanding of sexuality as a whole was acknowledged by lesbians Sidney Abbott and Barbara Love, writing in 1972:

> The most important group yet to speak up in the women's movement on the whole topic of sexuality may well prove to be the bisexual woman... It is amazing that there is no bisexual caucus in the women's movement. One reason for the omission may be that bisexual women bring out fears of homosexuality in straight women and also fears of heterosexuality in women who live as lesbians.[15]

In April 1973, *Spare Rib* published an article on bisexuality that pre-dated anything published in the magazine on lesbianism, and was only the second piece on sex of any kind. Unfortunately, the article didn't help to advance understanding of bisexuality; similar in tone to a *Forum* piece (sexually titillating, with details of who did what to whom), it was a personal account of one woman's sexual experiences with both men and women and was totally lacking in sexual politics. The piece attracted a couple of condemnatory letters, one from a woman who said she would not make herself available for this woman and her followers to practise on. The article did bisexual women a tremendous disservice, promoting every sort of stereotype.

As the 1970s went on, it became less and less acceptable to be bisexual within the feminist movement. The publication of Charlotte Wolff's *Bisexuality* (1977) led to discussion in the press, including an interview in *Spare Rib*,[16] in which Wolff said she believed that one could not consciously choose one's sexuality; one fell in love, and although one might try to choose for political reasons, this would always fail – a theory that went against the trend of feminist thinking at the time. The publication of Wolff's book was followed by a conference on women and bisexuality in London in June 1978. Discussion topics included political alignment with lesbians, sex with women and men, and monogamy; however, in practice, the conference focused on support rather than on political discussion.[17]

From this point on, bisexuality seemed to disappear as a positive issue. A one-day workshop at Haringey women's centre in London in 1980, and an article in the socialist-feminist magazine *Scarlet Women* in the same year, are all I can remember. Within the context of a strong political lesbianism, bisexuality became seen as the apotheosis of cowardice, decadence and fence-sitting.

No place for us: political lesbianism and revolutionary feminism

Many lesbians seem to think that bisexual women aren't genuine about their commitment to and feeling for women. They believe soft-porn nonsense about multiple sex. (36)

For a long time I felt two-faced, like I was letting folk down. Now I'm starting to accept that it might be other people's problem and not mine if I don't fit into the categories. (7)

For some years in the 1970s and 1980s it was very difficult for an active feminist to be open about her bisexuality. For many feminists, bisexuality was seen simply as the cowardly holding on to heterosexual privilege. This view was frequently expressed verbally in no uncertain terms (at least, this is my own experience and that of questionnaire respondents), and was written down more rarely.

Sexual separatism had first appeared in the late 1960s. Of course, women's liberation was in itself a separatist movement, in that its meetings, groups, conferences and demonstrations usually excluded men. But now, the idea of removing oneself entirely from the world of men began increasingly to be promoted, not just as a possibility, but as a requisite for true feminist practice. Lesbian separatism began to emerge from about 1970. This had little or nothing to do with sex, and everything to do with political tactics. 'A lesbian is the rage of all women condensed to the point of explosion', said the Radicalesbians group in *The Woman-Identified Woman*.[18]

As the 1970s progressed, lesbians who had discovered their lesbianism before feminism and women who considered themselves political lesbians joined forces to condemn feminism's heterosexual bias and to develop a positive and liberating political theory which explained and challenged their oppression and posited lesbianism as intrinsically disruptive of male power. Lesbianism was, however, in many cases over-romanticised: lesbianism was good; lesbians were wonderful; and heterosexual women were deluded:

> The lesbian is a woman who refuses to be tamed. She is the emblem of eroticism that resists death-by-socialisation.[19]

But especially, lesbians did not have to be sexual. Indeed, to talk about sex *per se* was almost taboo. Women's sexuality has often been posited as intrinsically more gentle or less aggressive than men's (by lesbian feminists as much as others), so it was easy in some way to ignore the importance of sexual desire and activity. To discuss it in real terms would have disrupted the homogeneous image that lesbianism promoted at the time (as indeed happened in the mid-1980s, as we shall see later). The catchphrase was that 'Any woman can be a lesbian' (the title of a play produced by the London-based group Gay Sweatshop in 1976 being *Any Woman Can*). And many women believed it.

The idea of political lesbianism was promoted through several influential books that connected lesbians to women throughout history who had not had the option of identifying in this way. Adrienne Rich's theory of the lesbian continuum, whereby there is and always has been a range of women-identified experience of which genital sex is only a part, was very popular. According to this theory, all women are part of this continuum of experience, being capable of deep emotional relationships with other women, starting with their mothers. Rich also questions whether under male supremacy, with its strong promotion of heterosexuality, female heterosexuality can ever be considered a free choice.

> to acknowledge that for women heterosexuality may not be a 'preference' at all but something that has had to be imposed, managed, organised, propagandised, and maintained by force, is an immense step to take if you consider yourself freely and 'innately' heterosexual.[20]

Heterosexuality as an institution is, of course, promoted as Rich says, but that doesn't mean that individual women do not desire individual men. Her thesis also presents an over-romanticised view of women's relationships with each other – particularly those between mothers and daughters.

Another popular and influential book on lesbianism as an emotional continuum was *Surpassing the Love of Men* by Lillian Faderman (1981), which chronicled the history of women's romantic friendships. To Faderman, lesbian feminism was a follow-on from romantic friendship (in which genital sex was probably non-existent). She agreed with modern feminists, that:

> Women are lesbians when they are women-identified... Never having had the slightest erotic exchange with another woman, one might still be a political lesbian. A lesbian is a woman who makes women prime in her life, who gives her energies and her commitment to other women rather than men.[21]

Rich and Faderman have both been very influential in the development of lesbian theory and have done a great deal to recover a neglected history of women's relationships with each other. But their insistence on the idea that the women they are discussing were 'lesbian' is wrong: it would be more correct (but still incorrect) to call them bisexual, since they were often married or seeking husbands. And although their same-sex relationships were often more emotionally central to their lives than their opposite-sex ones, this was not always the case. It is simply inappropriate to apply current, western-specific sexual identities to other times and places. Besides, other nineteenth-century western women *did* have full sexual relationships with each other: these are the women who should be reclaimed as lesbians.[22]

During the late 1970s, the early theories of political lesbianism were overtaken by the principles of revolutionary feminism, epitomised by a paper written in 1979 by the Leeds Revolutionary Feminist group, later published together with responses from the women's liberation national newsletter *Wires* as *Love Your Enemy?*.[23] The paper expressed the idea that *all* feminists should be political lesbians; that is, not necessarily have sex with women, but definitely abandon men. It marked a change from previous political lesbianism, in that it was primarily anti-men, rather than pro-women, seeing men as the enemy and heterosexual feminists as collaborators. This paper, and the resulting letters published in *Wires*, created a furore, the ramifications of which are still evident years later. The revolutionary feminists reduced the whole patriarchal power structure to fucking, and the complexities of male-female relationships to a for-them or against-them stand. Women-bonding and sexual desire between women, as opposed to political principle, had become irrelevant.

So revolutionary feminism created its own restrictive norms: the necessary abandonment of men; the impossibility of hetero-sexual feminism; the marginalisation of genital sex; and lesbianism as a political credo and way of life, rather than an expression of sexual desire. There was no place to discuss lesbianism except as the apotheosis of correct feminist sexual practice: old-style lesbians, for instance, with traditions such as butch-femme or other, different sexual experiences were presumed to have disappeared or to have false consciousnesses if they had not. As Joan Nestle wrote in 1985:

> ...if I write about butch-femme relationships in the past, I am OK, but if I am writing about them now in any positive way, I am on the 'enemy list'.[24]

Revolutionary feminism saw female sexuality as directly opposed to men's:

> It is surely not in our interests as women struggling to end male supremacy, to assert that our 'sex drive' is as strong as men's, or that our sexuality is not 'passive' but 'active', if, in doing so, we accept as given a model of sexuality which appears ideally suited to the maintenance and reproduction of male sexuality.[25]

Clearly this construction of lesbianism allows no possibility for bisexuality: women either make the correct political choice and become lesbian or continue as heterosexual collaborators. It was not sexual desire for or emotional commitment to women which gained women access to the lesbian fold; it was rejection of men. Bisexuality was ignored in print and abruptly dismissed when encountered in person. In more or less subtle ways, bisexual women were told they were even less acceptable than heterosexuals:

> Bisexuality is not so much a cop-out as a fearful compromise.[26]

> Bisexuality for women in the revolution in any case is col-laboration with the enemy.[27]

> ...until all women are lesbians there will be no true political revolution.[28]

I got away with 'having a relationship with a woman' part-
time. Titillation for her, me shoring up the danger of falling
in love by keeping it up with men too. So wasn't I a lesbian
then? (Come on, you can't have it both ways.)[29]

Heterosexual women, too, increasingly took a background role:
their presence in public discourses on sexuality was minimised
and little theory exploring the possibilities and conflicts of heterosexual feminism was developed. It was as if heterosexuality
became a guilty secret that women felt unable to admit to – some
feminists even wondered whether it wasn't a relief for heterosexual
women to see themselves as deviant collaborators in their own
oppression.[30] Some heterosexual women simply withdrew from
an organised feminist movement, feeling there was no place for
them there; others adopted the 'angry victim' stance, blaming
lesbians for silencing them. *Spare Rib*, for instance, frequently
published letters complaining about the supposedly high profile
given to lesbian issues, and wondering whether there was a place
for heterosexual women in the women's liberation movement.
However, an examination of the magazine during the late 1970s
to early 1980s disproves such assertions: articles about heterosexuality
easily outnumber those about lesbianism, which in any case tend
to be 'issue' articles, for example on lesbian mothers, rather than
on lesbianism *per se*. Yet even this limited coverage posed a threat
to many women, and indicated that heterosexism remained alive
and well.

'Cultural feminism', which saw women as 'naturally' different
from men, also became popular. This essentialist view of sexual
difference, on which many patriarchal justifications for sexual
inequality are based, had been roundly criticised at the start of
the feminist movement. Now, however, women became equated
with a romanticised view of nature and were posited as biologi-
cally opposed to male values of aggression and competition. Male
sexuality, to many women, was perceived as intrinsically aggressive,
organised around penetration which women did not (could not,
never would) desire. Writers like Andrea Dworkin, Susan Griffin
and Mary Daly highlighted the profound differences between men
and women, but saw no possibility of reconciling them. Speaking
passionately about the harm so many men do to women, they
sweepingly and powerfully condemned the whole structure of heterosexual sexual behaviour and the tyranny of behaviour which
wasn't necessarily sexual, although sexual oppression was its aim.

Many women simplistically equated patriarchal institutions with men in general. They saw all men as the same, despite the power inequalities between them. Some black women spoke out against this wholesale condemnation, and reminded white women of other power struggles in society. They pointed out that by holding Reclaim the Night marches in largely black areas, for example, the organisers were supporting the criminalisation of black men and giving credence to the myths that held them to be oversexed and violent. These black women were (publicly) vocal heterosexuals; a strong black lesbian movement developed about five years later.[31]

The issue of why some women remained intransigently attracted to men, although they were politicised and should have known better, received scant attention in the feminist community. How did the institution of heterosexuality connect with women's experience of it? Women who did seek relationships with men spoke almost invariably of the difficulties involved, yet many kept on searching.

> To give up the search for connection, no matter how thankless it may prove to be, is to deny my passion, to betray my power, to abandon my sons.[32]

Other women felt that, through struggle, relationships with men were changing and that this in itself was the creation of a feminist heterosexuality.[33]

New attitudes to sexuality: sex in the 1980s

By the early 1980s, those active feminists who believed themselves to be bisexual often identified publicly as lesbian – and kept quiet about other aspects of their sexuality. But the orthodoxy surrounding feminist sexuality was soon to be challenged.

The main forum for feminist debate on heterosexuality was psychoanalysis: an intellectual debate that often seemed to have little connection with an organised movement. The publication in the mid-1970s of Juliet Mitchell's *Psychoanalysis and Feminism* signalled a new current, which used theories of the unconscious to examine how femininity came into being. Through her reading of Freud, Mitchell presented explanations for the long-term nature of women's oppression, the hold of romantic love over humanity, and the complexity of heterosexual relationships.

Some of the insights developed from psychoanalytic theory came to the fore in the new-style sexuality of the 1980s. Starting with the (in)famous 'Sex' issue of the US feminist magazine *Heresies* in 1981, sex, desire and pleasure began to appear on the feminist agenda. For some women, the opening up of debates on previously taboo topics such as butch-femme, androgyny, the construction of desire and feminist erotica was a welcome breakthrough; for others, such debates were a diversion from the real problems and their admission damaging to feminist unity. These debates signalled the beginnings of a split between two types of feminism – put simplisticly, anti-pornography and anti-censorship – which crossed the lesbianism/heterosexuality divide, and which still remains.

The controversial book *Pleasure and Danger* (1984) was a compilation of papers from the US Barnard conference of 1982 – where feminists speaking for the first time from what might broadly be called a 'libertarian' sexual perspective were picketed by other feminists vehemently opposed to them. The book's basic thesis was that the tension between pleasure and danger in women's lives is a profound issue that must be addressed. To hide women's pleasure is to deny a vital part of ourselves, and will in any case not make the world any safer for us. Many other readers on sexuality were published at this time, and though the issues were discussed among friends, to make statements in any wider, more public context, such as debates or conferences, felt dangerous. It is not clear why bisexuality was not part of these debates, but the fact that it was not indicates how invisible the subject had become. Perhaps there was at least some safety in a solid lesbian or heterosexual identity at a time when every other aspect of sexuality seemed to be unstable.

There were other challenges to revolutionary feminism. Black women became extremely active in feminism in the late 1970s and early 1980s, challenging white women's cosy notions of universal sisterhood, and the white middle-class bias of the movement and the issues it addressed. Both autonomous black women's groups and individual black women disputed the idea that all women (and by extension all lesbians) share the same oppression, pointing out that while all women have some things in common, some women have power over others outside the power men have over women. Many black women worked alongside men to organise politically around issues of race; black lesbians sometimes chose to work politically with black (gay) men rather than with white lesbians.

The most controversial debate to emerge within sexual politics in the 1980s and the issue around which lesbians became polarised was that of lesbian sado-masochism, which still provokes powerful reactions and disagreements. The question became of crucial importance in London with the opening of the Lesbian and Gay Centre in 1985. SM groups wanted to meet in the centre; many other people, particularly, but not exclusively, women who defined themselves as political lesbians, saw SM as an oppressive copying of heterosexual power games and its manifestations as offensive, particularly to black and Jewish women and women with disabilities (though members of these groups did not necessarily all agree).[34] At an extremely vitriolic meeting, it was decided that SM groups could meet at the Lesbian and Gay Centre, but that certain restrictions would apply, namely the banning of some SM clothes and of swastikas. Until this point, the discussion about correct feminist sexual practice had largely been polarised along heterosexual/lesbian lines; now, it became a lesbian/lesbian debate.

Bisexual people were part of this debate: the idea of bisexuals as 'sexual outlaws' put bisexuality on to the agenda and bisexuals found themselves straightforwardly linked with sado-masochists as people whose sexuality was inherently deviant and dangerous. The group Sexual Fringe, which operated in 1985, had bisexuals among its membership, together with transsexuals, transvestites, S-Mers and butch-femme lesbians. It was a mixed group, with an anything-goes attitude to sexual liberation that lacked a clear political viewpoint. The group faded away after it was agreed that SM groups and bisexual individuals (as people possibly in transition to a 'true' lesbian or gay identity) could meet at the centre. Bisexual groups were still banned, as many lesbians were suspicious of bisexual men.[35]

Vitriolic discussions on the nature of correct lesbian sexual practice continued in 1988, and were focused in particular on Sheila McLaughlin's *She Must Be Seeing Things*. This film, about a lesbian couple, one of whom is convinced her lover is having an affair with a man, touched on issues of butch-femme, violent fantasy and lesbian SM. The film was picketed by women who accused it of promoting violence towards lesbians, though many failed to see what the fuss was about. The vehemence of the arguments at this time – about this film, about the UK publication of Joan Nestle's *A Restricted Country* by Sheba Feminist Publishers and about the Sheba Collective's *Serious Pleasure – lesbian erotic stories and poetry* – seems to have put paid to public discussions of lesbian sexual practice for some time to come.[36]

While lesbian attitudes to men and sexual practice now seem to be undergoing further shifts with the arrival of queer politics, and an impatience with what are perceived as restrictive feminist norms is being expressed, open discussion of heterosexuality tends to take place outside the feminist community and to be focused still on the difficulties rather than pleasures of male-female relationships. Shere Hite's *Women in Love* (1989), for instance, an account of 4,500 women's love lives, details widespread dissatisfaction. Of her sample, 98 per cent of those in long-term heterosexual relationships wanted to make basic changes or improvements, while 71 per cent in long-term marriages had tried and had given up.[37] Hite concludes that men just don't take women seriously, and the book is a depressing catalogue of how dreadful so many men are. By contrast, most of my own questionnaire respondents seemed to have reasonable relationships with men, as will be discussed in Chapter 4.

Back on the agenda: new texts and contexts

My lesbianism has been written off by everyone as being less important than relationships with men – even by lesbians. Yet my sexuality too is a political threat to male control and the whole way society is structured. (14)

What has changed in feminist discussions in recent years to put bisexuality back on the agenda? Books from the 1980s merely mention bisexuality, usually as an afterthought to discussions of lesbianism, with an emphasis on its 'dangers': men can get off on it; lesbians have been burned by women who don't want to choose. For instance, from Celia Kitzinger in *A Woman's Experience of Sex* (1985):

> There can be a lot of problems in being bi-sexual. Some women talk about the dangers of using people: using men as meal-tickets, as husbands and fathers to their children, getting all the benefits of being heterosexual in a heterosexual society, and using women for warmth, comfort, and sensual gratification – all the benefits of being lesbian with none of the social discrimination attached.[38]

Here, Kitzinger's depiction of bisexual women as 'users' fails to acknowledge that all women, because of our position in society, may use men, as men, in other ways, use us. The accusation that bisexual women use other women, but in the end return to the supposed comfort of heterosexual society, is also common and is reminiscent of accusations of collaboration with the enemy levelled at heterosexual women in the early 1970s. Kitzinger's piece expresses in a single page almost every stereotype of the bisexual: as cowardly, selfish and promiscuous – an image reinforced by the drawing at the top of the page of a man with his arms around two women. Perhaps because of complaints, and the changed political climate, the latest edition of the book has substantially altered its one page on bisexuality, taking out some of the negativity and admitting that some women are bisexual in good faith. But it still implies that bisexual women put men first, want the privileges of being married, and will necessarily feel isolated because of the disapproval of lesbian feminists. The overall effect remains undermining.

Another anti-bisexual book is *Lesbian Sex* (JoAnn Loulan, 1984).[39] An excellent guide to lesbian sex, with valuable information on, for instance, the effect of homophobia on our sex lives and sex and disability, it remains a painful book for a bisexual woman to read. In the chapter 'Am I really a lesbian?', Loulan discounts completely the possibility that a woman might want to have a relationship with a man without turning her back on past lesbian relationships or on the lesbian community. In this chapter, in which the word 'bisexual' is not mentioned, Loulan distances herself from the reader, avoiding the embracing use of 'we' that is prevalent in the rest of the book. For Loulan, the issue is identity: sex with a man is permissible for a lesbian because lesbianism is about much more than sex. But if a woman is having a relationship with a man, then she should feel duty-bound to identify as heterosexual. Loulan's definition seems somewhat arbitrary and certainly leaves no room for women who do not want to or cannot divide their feelings so neatly.

On the other hand, bisexual women are mentioned twice in Loulan's book as carriers of sexually-transmitted diseases to the lesbian community – again reinforcing one of the most negative stereotypes of bisexuality. Loulan's own personal attitude towards bisexuality is expressed more clearly elsewhere:

Q Do bisexuals bug you?
A Yes, they bug me. But that isn't the point. If you want to
read about how women relate to men, bisexually or hetero-
sexually, there's plenty of books on the subject.
Q Weren't you bisexual once upon a time?
A Yes I was...[40]

There has been some positive writing about bisexuality. In an
essay in the compilation *Sex and Love* (1983), Debby Gregory
wrote from a personal standpoint about being a bisexual feminist.
Gregory was in a long-term marriage at the time of writing,
enjoying an open, apparently distant relationship with her
husband and spending the rest of her life with women. Though
the article is not wholly positive about bisexuality and implies
that the writer would rather have been a lesbian, as this was for
a long time the only available paper that described bisexual
experience, it was very important. Gregory also expressed some
valuable insights into bisexual sexuality, including the idea that
as no one lover can fulfil a bisexual's needs, then bisexual women
have a built-in potential for personal autonomy:

> Bisexuality implies a fundamental separation of ourselves from
> all our relationships. It implies that our sense of sexual
> definition and personal fulfilment can never come through
> any one sexual relationship.[41]

Sex, Power and Pleasure (1985), by Canadian Mariana Valverde,
includes a theoretical discussion of bisexuality. Valverde emphasises
that bisexual means only that someone can and does eroticise both
men and women, and that the term communicates nothing about
a person's morality or politics. For Valverde, bisexuality is a
challenge to the view that everyone is 'really' one or the other,
and she sees a strong bisexual politics as invaluable to the gay and
lesbian movement. This book is very positive, but was available
in the UK only through a few feminist bookshops.[42]

The debate between bisexual and lesbian feminists was taken
up in *Spare Rib*[43] following a letter in the September 1988 issue
about a woman's experiences of trying to come out as bisexual
and the reactions she had received from local lesbians (collab-
orator, it's just a phase, etc). At least one letter per issue appeared
on the subject over the next six months, the vast majority from
bisexual women with similar stories. After a few months, two
articles were commissioned. The first, by Melissa Benn, placed

bisexuality in the context of other feminist debates on sexuality; an answering article, by Sarah Roelofs, accused Benn of ignoring political realities, of ignoring that oppression is directed towards lesbians not bisexuals, and of arguing that the people bisexuals most need liberating from are intolerant lesbian separatists.

Of course, some lesbians are hostile to bisexual women: on a political level, bisexual women have not chosen to reject men, so our commitment to women is felt to be lacking. Despite the fact that bisexual women have always worked within lesbian groups, we are accused of taking advantage of all that lesbians have worked for without giving up any of the privileges of heterosexuality. We are seen as copping out. The difficulties of 'coming out' as a lesbian after a heterosexual past, together with the very real oppressions lesbians suffer, can lead some lesbians to an evangelism whereby in their fervour to embrace a new identity, they abandon their past and believe that other women should abandon theirs, too.

The lesbian-feminist movements of which I have spoken in the course of this chapter have been responsible for powerful changes in the way all women view themselves, and have been in the forefront of women's liberation over the past twenty years. Lesbianism poses an obvious threat to patriarchy, but surely it is sexual activity between women – an autonomous female sexuality – as much as direct or permanent rejection of men which society finds threatening (a woman's sexuality is meant to respond to a man's; we are not supposed to own it for ourselves).[44]

Many bisexual women do in fact live without any 'heterosexual privileges': a woman in an established relationship with another woman, however she identifies, in practice suffers the same oppression as a lesbian. And though a bisexual woman in a similar relationship with a man will not suffer the same practical oppressions, she will suffer emotional oppression if she feels compelled to present herself as heterosexual when she is not. Judgmental moralism has made many women unnecessarily guilty and miserable.

> The straight world treats us much the same as lesbians and gay men and the lesbian and gay world assume that our sexuality, unlike everyone else's, is a matter of choice, so that we can disappear into suburban heterosexuality at a moment's notice when the going gets tough.[45]

The need to know what a person's sexuality *really* is goes very deep, and the prospect that there might not be a *really* is very threatening – even to oneself! Both lesbians and heterosexuals seem highly disconcerted by the blurring of boundaries bisexuality presents, and by the idea that what is chosen can be unchosen. But sexual identity and sexuality are not necessarily fixed throughout a lifetime, and what is right for a person at one stage in his or her life is not necessarily right at another. Some women who change from lesbianism to heterosexuality may do so through inability to withstand heterosexist oppression; for others, who may have identified as lesbian for political reasons, the change in political climate may have brought about a reassessment. The women reported by Shere Hite as having had their first lesbian relationship after the age of forty (24 per cent) were presumably not all unhappy about their previous heterosexuality. For me, however, people who change their sexuality from completely heterosexual to completely lesbian (or vice versa, or back and forth) are not necessarily bisexual, as according to my definition, to be bisexual means always consciously to feel some desire for one sex when loving the other.

The 1990s has witnessed a new openness about sexual practice and identity – at least in some circles. While many lesbians still identify as lesbian-feminists with similar views as they would have held ten or fifteen years ago, other women see themselves as part of a mixed gay movement, as queer, or as pro-sex lesbians. Young lesbians and gay men are reported in Queerzines from the US to be having sex with each other; the opening of mixed, sex-oriented clubs in London is indicative of the same trend. This apparently does not disturb gay people's core identity, and is undertaken in a spirit of adventure, role-playing or affection. Other lesbians (known to me personally) are talking about having sex with men, and the place of men in their lives.

The 1990s has also seen the publication of the first-ever book of bisexual feminist theory, *Closer to Home: Bisexuality and Feminism,* which puts into print many issues which bisexual women have discussed at conferences and groups, developing ideas and suggesting strategies for political action.[46] Edited by Elizabeth Reba Weise, this book is a collection of essays by twenty-two bisexual feminists from various parts of the US, who address a range of issues. The writers come from many different perspectives and backgrounds, although they all consider themselves feminists, and have struggled to make sense of the interactions of bisexuality and feminism, and of how class and race issues are also involved. Some of the writers look mainly at their own personal experiences; others deal more directly with feminist theory, or with specific aspects of bisexuality.

A significant proportion of the writers have identified as lesbian for long periods, and reactions of the lesbian community to their bisexuality feature strongly. Many have long histories of activism within the lesbian community, and describe their struggle with its rejection of them, while maintaining a steady analysis of heterosexual privilege. As Amanda Udis-Kessler rightly points out, bisexual women are in the position of having experienced both the positive and negative sides of heterosexual privilege.

Other essays which stand out include those by Rebecca Ripley, who develops a cross-cultural and historical view of bisexuality, looking at same-sex behaviour and marriage; Eridani, who asks whether women have more choice than men in their sexual orientation, and what impact this might have on political lesbianism; and Kathleen Bennett, who asks which feminist theories should be transformed in order for progress to be made – for instance, the idea that personal sexual desire should give way to an arbitrary ideal. Beth Elliott perhaps best sums up what many of the other contributors say:

> ...it is, perhaps, bi feminist women who can best hold heterosexual relationships to feminist standards... Lesbians who have affairs with men are often too much in denial about what that means to talk about it. Bisexual lesbians do talk about it, if only to understand what such involvements mean to our lives, identities and politics... And unlike straight women, we need not ease up on our feminist analysis of relationships with men for lack of alternatives. Silence bisexual women, and you silence a very important feminist voice.[47]

So it seems that feminist discussion of sex has opened up to the point where it is possible (just) to admit one's bisexuality. Many women have abandoned what felt like the restrictive norms of a feminist agenda and now feel able to buy lace underwear, sexually objectify each other, and use dildoes. But as well as celebrating this 'freedom', we still need to look at the politics behind our sexuality. For example, the terms of the debate are still geared towards white, middle-class women and there has been little open discussion about what women from any traditionally marginalised groups feel, think, do or desire sexually.

Feminists have spent too much time attacking each other. But both lesbians and bisexual women are oppressed by a heterosexist society: oppression is imposed on a less powerful group by a more powerful one, and neither lesbians nor bisexual women have power. Although our immediate struggles may not always seem identical, ultimately our enemies are the same. What we need is a strong, feminist bisexuality which has something positive to offer: theory, politics, community, lifestyle. This should not be apologetic, as bisexual women have often felt forced to be, but proud. Then we will be in a position to connect on a political and social level with lesbians. At this time of homophobia and a fragmented feminist movement, it is essential that we fight together.

Some recent writing by lesbians positively includes bisexual experience as an aspect of lesbianism; the word bisexual has been added to the names of many gay and lesbian organisations, especially in the US – for example the activist group LABIA (Lesbians and Bisexuals in Action); my own experience of writing this book involved far more support from lesbians than I had anticipated. A positive step would be the creation of groups which deliberately set out to recruit both bisexual and lesbian women to work on matters we all believe to be important. That would be a position of strength.

Notes

1. For further information on this period, the following books are useful: Judith Walkowitz, *Prostitution and Victorian Society*, Cambridge University Press, 1982; Lal Coveney et al (eds), *The Sexuality Papers*, Hutchinson, 1984
2. Alexandra Kollontai, *Sexual Relations and the Class Struggle*, SWP, 1984 (1st 1919)
3. Stella Browne, *Sex Variety and Variability among Women*, British Society for the Study of Sexual Psychology pamphlet, 1915
4. Quoted in Joan Nestle, *A Restricted Country*, Firebrand, 1987. Goldman's relationship was with anarchist prostitute Almeda Sperry in 1912
5. Simone de Beauvoir, *The Second Sex*, Cape, 1953, p413
6. Germaine Greer, *The Female Eunuch*, MacGibbon & Kee, 1970
7. Anne Koedt, 'The Myth of the Vaginal Orgasm' (1970), in J.P. Wiseman (ed), *The Social Psychology of Sex*, Harper Row, 1976

8. Nancy Friday, *My Secret Garden: women's sexual fantasies*, Quartet, 1976

9. Nancy Chodorow, *The Reproduction of Mothering*, University of California Press, 1978, and Dorothy Dinnerstein, *The Rocking of the Cradle and the Ruling of the World*, The Women's Press, 1987 (1st 1976)

10. Shere Hite, *The Hite Report*, Summit Books, 1977

11. Sidney Abbott & Barbara Love, *Sappho Was a Right-On Woman*, Stein & Day, 1972

12. For instance, Charlotte Wolff, *Love Between Women*, Duckworth, 1971

13. Jeffrey Weeks, *Coming Out*, Quartet, 1977

14. *Sappho Was a Right-On Woman*, op cit, p157

15. Ibid

16. *Spare Rib*, issue 63, October 1977

17. Personal communication

18. Quoted in Jane Rule, *Lesbian Images*, Peter Davies, 1976, p205

19. Emily Sisley & Bertha Harris, *The Joy of Lesbian Sex*, Simon & Schuster, 1977, p12

20. Adrienne Rich, 'Compulsory Heterosexuality & Lesbian Existence' (1980) in Ann Snitow, Christine Stansell & Sharon Thompson (eds), *Desire: the Politics of Sexuality*, Virago, 1984. Rebecca Kaplan in 'Compulsory Heterosexuality and Bisexual Existence' in Elizabeth Reba Weise (ed), *Closer to Home: Bisexuality and Feminism* (Seal Press, 1992) discusses how Rich's essay can be interpreted with both positive and negative repercussions for bisexual women

21. Lillian Faderman, *Surpassing the Love of Men*, Morrow & Co, p380

22. In Faderman's recently published *Odd Girls and Twilight Lovers: A History of Lesbian Life in Twentieth-Century America* (Penguin, 1992), she does precisely this. This fascinating book also looks specifically at how bisexuality has been perceived at various times

23. The original paper and replies were published as *Love Your Enemy?*, Onlywomen Press, 1981

24. *A Restricted Country*, op cit, p148

25. Margaret Jackson, 'Sexology and the Universalisation of Male Sexuality' in *The Sexuality Papers*, op cit, p82

26. Quoted in *Lesbian Images*, op cit, p207

27. Ibid

28. Ibid

29. Caroline Halliday, Sheila Shulman & Caroline Griffin, *Hard Words (and why lesbians have to say them)*, Onlywomen Press, 1979

30. Deidre English, Amber Hollibaugh & Gayle Rubin, 'Talking Sex' in Feminist Review (ed), *Sexuality: a Reader*, Virago, 1987

31. Beverley Bryan, Stella Dadzie & Suzanne Scafe, *The Heart of the Race Black Women's lives in Britain*, Virago, 1985 and Carmen, Gail, Neena & Tamara, 'Becoming Visible: Black Lesbian Discussions' in *Sexuality: a Reader*, ibid

32. Jane Lazarre, *On Loving Men*, Virago, 1981

33. Angela Hamblin, 'Is a Feminist Heterosexuality Possible?', in Sue Cartledge & Joanna Ryan (eds), *Sex and Love*, The Women's Press, 1983

34. For a clear exposition of this time see Susan Ardill & Sue O'Sullivan, 'Upsetting an Applecart' in *Sexuality: a Reader*, op cit

35. Bisexual groups have been able to meet there since 1990

36. *A Restricted Country* appeared in the UK in 1988 and *Serious Pleasure* in 1989. Cherry Smyth's *Lesbians Talk Queer Notions* (Scarlet Press, 1992) includes a discussion on this period

37. Shere Hite, *Women in Love*, Penguin, 1989, pp5–17

38. Celia Kitzinger in Sheila Kitzinger, *A Woman's Experience of Sex*, Penguin, 1985

39. JoAnn Loulan, *Lesbian Sex*, Spinsters Ink, 1984

40. Interviewed by Susie Sexpert in *On Our Backs*, Winter 1988

41. Debby Gregory, 'From Where I Stand: A Case for Feminist Bisexuality' in *Sex and Love*, op cit, p153

42. Mariana Valverde, *Sex, Power and Pleasure*, The Women's Press, Toronto, 1985

43. The debate ran from September 1988 to April 1989

44. Rebecca Shuster, 'Sexuality as a Continuum: the Bisexual Identity' in the Boston Lesbian Psychology Collective (eds), *Lesbian Psychologies*, University of Illinois Press, 1987. Shuster quotes the example of a schoolteacher who was dismissed for her sexual activities with women. An appeal that she was bisexual failed: it was the fact that she had sex with women that barred her

45. Kate Fearnley in *Pride '89* (Gay Pride week information and newspaper), p22

46. Elizabeth Reba Weise (ed), *Closer to Home: Bisexuality and Feminism*, Seal Press, 1992. The quoted essays are: Amanda Udis-Kessler 'Closer to Home: Bisexual Feminism and the Trans-

formation of Hetero/sexism'; Rebecca Ripley 'The Language of Desire: Sexuality, Identity and Language'; Eridani 'Is Sexual Orientation a Secondary Sex Characteristic?'; Kathleen Bennett 'Feminist Bisexuality: A Both/And Option in an Either/Or World'
47. Beth Elliott, 'Holly Near and Yet So Far', ibid, p248

4 Living as bisexual

This chapter, drawn largely from information submitted by 142 women who filled in the ten-page questionnaire included in Appendix 1, looks at the different ways bisexual women live and their feelings about their sexuality, relationships and lifestyles. Whereas the terms 'lesbian' and 'heterosexual' commonly define a preference for relationships with people of one gender rather than the other, there is no single type of relationship, or sexual act, that the word 'bisexual' describes. So individuals who identify as bisexual can exhibit very different attitudes and behaviours: from the married woman living an ostensibly heterosexual life, to the lesbian who has desires for relationships with men, to the woman who has open relationships with people of both genders.

Any woman who has desires for or relationships with people of both sexes will have to deal with issues which lesbian and heterosexual women do not. Monogamy, for instance, need not be such a pressing issue for someone who is attracted to one sex only. And though in a different world, bisexuality need not be more difficult than any other sexual identity, the existing expectation that individuals will identify as either homo- or heterosexual creates additional pressures. While the sexual histories, practices and preferences of the questionnaire respondents varied dramatically, and the realities of race and class oppression, age, mobility, disability, responsibility for dependants, personality and so on also shaped their lives, they had much in common, over and above these differences. For instance, they had almost all gone through a period of intense questioning of their sexuality (several periods, if they had ever identified as lesbian) and many of them wished that their experience of relationships with women had been greater.

Many of the issues raised in this chapter are new to public debate, for example the questions facing bisexual women with children. As so little on women and bisexuality has been published, any writing on the subject will inevitably open up new areas and new approaches. Much has been omitted in the study that follows; it is to be hoped that the gaps will be filled by future writers.

Respondents' profile

A broad profile of the questionnaire respondents is as follows.

Age group

Under 20	11
21–30	64
31–40	27
41–50	14
51 and over	5
No reply	21

Ethnic origin

White, northern European	123
(includes 4 Irish and 3 Jewish women)	
Afro-Caribbean	6
Southern European	3
Other European	3
(includes 2 Jewish women)	
Japanese	2
Afro-Caribbean/Irish	1
Asian-southern European	1
Mexican-American	1
Pacific-American	1
Australian	1

Geographical location

Greater London	51
North-east	15
Midlands	14
South-east	14
North-west	10
Scotland	8
South-west	7
East Anglia	5
Wales	4
Ireland	3
US	2
Canada	2
Germany	2
Japan	1
No reply	4

The vast majority (90) lived in cities; 19 lived in towns; 18 in small towns; 8 in rural areas. 7 gave no reply.

Living situation

With male partner	59
With female partner	5
Alone	46
With others (not relatives)	22
Families of origin	10

Class background

Upper-middle class	8
Middle class	60
Lower-middle class	11
Working class	34
Mixed (usually working-to lower-middle)	16
No reply	13

Employment

Employed	77
Students	23
Part-time workers	15
Unemployed	10
At home with children	6
Retired	1
No reply	10

8 described their income as high; 70 as medium; 59 as low.

Educational qualifications

O levels or less	13
A levels or less	15
Post-A level qualifications	21
Degree	40
Postgraduate qualifications	26
No reply	27

Disability

4 women identified themselves as having a disability.

Sources

Respondents first read or heard about the questionnaire in:

Guardian	45
Through bisexual groups or conferences	20
Spare Rib	15
Shocking Pink	10
Personal contacts	10
Time Out	8
Forum	6
Bi-Monthly	5
Lesbian and Gay Socialist	4
City Limits	4
Gay Scotland	4
Bookshops (various)	4
Women's News (Belfast)	1
Women's groups	1
Unidentified	5

The return of 142 from a total mail-out of about 230 is extremely high for this type of questionnaire, presumably because bisexual women have not yet had the opportunity to tell their story; the fact that so many women answered a ten-page questionnaire, often at great length, shows that they felt that an important part of themselves had not yet been allowed a voice. Many of them said as much.

The range of women who replied was determined to some extent by where the call for respondents was advertised. For the most part, I relied on editorial coverage rather than paid advertisements, the only exception being *The Voice* newspaper, directed at the Afro-Caribbean community, which yielded no completed questionnaires. Putting paid advertisements in other publications may have led to a different spread of respondents in terms of age, class, race, education or politics; certainly the fact that most respondents' politics were left-of-centre is a function of those publications which would give the project space.

It is disappointing that so few women of colour responded. There are several reasons for this, some of which are discussed by Kristin and Jane, the two black women who speak in Chapter 5. I had anticipated that women of colour might be reluctant to answer intimate questions about their sexuality from an unknown white woman; this may have discouraged women of colour from requesting questionnaires, and certainly personal contacts yielded more respondents of colour than advertisements. Perhaps, too, the identity of 'bisexual' is not one black women use to define themselves. Talking about sexuality is taboo in many non-western cultures; in the case of bisexuality, the stereotypical images of 'promiscuous' and 'exotic' attached to bisexual identity have also been used, in different contexts, to denigrate black women. I hope that future writing on bisexuality can reflect more accurately our cultural diversity. There are other imbalances, too, in particular that no women with disabilities were found for interview.

Press releases to many women's groups, and in particular to groups for women of colour, yielded just one completed questionnaire. The majority of respondents identified as feminist to a greater or lesser extent, despite the fact that the women's movement has not been very supportive of bisexuals (see Chapter 3). Lesbian and gay groups were also contacted, with no result. However, the responses received through, for instance, the sexual discussion/contact magazine *Forum* were not noticeably different from those received through *Spare Rib* or *Lesbian and Gay Socialist*.

Just under half the sample was aged between twenty-one and thirty. It is possible that more younger women think of themselves as bisexual because they are less likely to be in long-term relationships or to feel obliged to identify as exclusively heterosexual or homosexual. The taboos against speaking out about sexuality are also less strongly felt by people who have grown up since the 1960s, though as Margaret's story in Chapter 5 attests, bisexual feelings and activity are not something that began suddenly thirty years ago.

Relationships and sexual partners

For the purpose of this chapter, a sexual partner may be short- or long-term; a relationship implies a romantic, sexual partnership with some degree of emotional commitment, which may or may not be monogamous.

It's worked out that most relationships (and most falling in love) have been with men. Because I'm monogamous, this has restricted my attempts at relationships with women. (60)

When I was in a relationship with a man, I had a feeling that although my bisexuality was accepted it wasn't considered particularly important because my boyfriend didn't consider women so important. Desire for other men would have been more threatening. (120)

I have no sexual preference between men and women. I enjoy different things with both. I do enjoy penetration with men, but with women I love the merging of sexuality/sensuality and the cosiness and safety of feeling that we know how the other feels. (16)

On average, the bisexual women in this sample had had more male sexual partners/relationships than female: this was the case for 114 women, while only 6 women had had more female partners than male. For 37 women, there was a difference between numbers of male and female partners of less than 3. Of those women who gave precise numbers of sexual partners, the highest figure for number of male partners was 100; for female partners 20. The women who had had the largest numbers of male partners were not the same as those with the largest numbers of female partners. The highest total figure was 102, which comprised mostly male partners. The average number of total partners was 18, of male partners 14, and of female partners 4. Many women had not yet acted on their bisexual feelings: 2 women had had no sexual partners, 2 had had at least one female but no male partners, 15 had had at least one male, but no female partners.

At the time of answering the questionnaire, 68 respondents had a primary relationship with a man; 26 had a primary relationship with a woman; 3 had relationships of equal weight with a woman and a man. 2 of these 3 were included in the 14 women who chose to operate 'open relationships', meaning they were open to committed sexual relationships with more than one person (although in practice, they were not necessarily non-monogamous, or indeed sexually involved, all the time). 7 women in primary relationships with men, but none in primary relationships with women, operated 'open relationships'.

Subtly and overtly, society conspires to turn women towards relationships with men. A young girl may grow up simply not knowing that sexual relationships between women are possible; may not realise that her feelings for her female friends are sexual and, if she is also attracted to boys, may become very confused. Men are conditioned to be sexually assertive/aggressive and women are conditioned to respond. Images of romantic heterosexual couples are everywhere, and a family existence based around such a couple is what people are taught to expect and want.

Relationships between women, by contrast, are largely invisible in the media or popular culture and when they are shown are joked about, thought to be sexually unfulfilling (as neither partner has a penis), and are subject to all sorts of vilification. Unless women are part of a lesbian community, it is difficult to find others who may be interested in a sexual relationship; it can also be more difficult for women to initiate relationships, even if both partners are sure of the other's sexuality, as neither has been taught how to make the first move. It is therefore hardly surprising that respondents had more male than female partners, and that this was true of past and present, committed and casual relationships, whatever their ideal preference.

One popular way of meeting lovers – male and female – was through lonely-hearts columns. 42 women had tried this at least once, 11 with 'good results' (they met someone they liked), though these did not always become sexual relationships. Another 9 had also tried to meet men, women or both through the magazine *Forum*; 2 of these had produced sexual relationships. As a way of meeting potential female lovers, this has its advantages: at least you both know why you're there.

There was also variation between women who found sexual relationships easy to come by, and those who found them hard. This transcended age, how sexually attractive or generally charismatic women felt themselves to be, and any other generalisations. 2 women, when asked how they got lovers, said 'You tell me!'. Another 5 wished they had lovers. For their information, the most popular way women met their sexual partners, whether male or female, was 'just through living' (27 respondents in all). Others listed a variety of ways: 22 women said their relationships were friends first, 10 found lovers at work, another 10 through lonely hearts. 3 women found lovers through the lesbian 'scene'.

Sexual preference

The expressed desires of respondents differed in many cases from their experience. 37 respondents preferred women as sexual partners; 9 preferred men. 21 women had no preference, and 35 said they preferred sex with particular individuals, regardless of gender. On being asked why they had had more sexual partners of the 'group they did not prefer' – in most cases, why they had had more sex with men if they preferred women – 32 respondents gave as their reason that heterosexual society made it easy for men and women to get together. 13 women said they didn't meet other women with whom it would be possible to have a relationship; a further 3 that they found the lesbian scene too intimidating. 8 respondents expressed a fear of being rejected by another woman – either because she may be anti-lesbian, or on a personal level.

Men are an easy pick-up, and I lack self-confidence in approaching women. (129)

My only really amazing orgasms are with women, but more men are available. Most are as easy as anything. (84)

Women who live largely within the lesbian community may, of course, find it difficult to meet men, though the dominance of heterosexual assumptions means it is possible literally to meet a man on the street in a way that would be far less likely with a woman.

So why did most of those who had a definite preference prefer women? It is clear that women, at present, are conditioned to be more nurturing, more giving, and better at communicating. This is true both sexually and emotionally, going hand in hand with a woman 'knowing what another woman wants'.

I prefer sex with women, but I go through phases of really wanting penetrative sex with men (30)

I like looking at women's bodies, and they feel better – softer, rounder. (126)

It's easier to have an orgasm with a woman, but the degree of emotional closeness is much more important to me. So far this has worked best with one of my male lovers. (119)

Over one-third of respondents did not prefer one sex over the other as sexual partners, although how this lack of preference was experienced varied. Some women felt they did not differentiate:

I have no preference between men and women, both are just as exciting. At different times in my life I find I spend whole periods of months finding one sex more exciting, attractive, interesting – but then it might be the other one, or both. (1)

If someone fits my categories of 'fanciableness' it doesn't matter what sex they are. (71)

I tend to explain that I fall in love with people, rather than bodies. (36)

If you love the person, the sex is terrific whether the person is male or female. (79)

My top ten would include both women and men – it's more the individual and my relationship with him or her that makes for great sex, rather than whether they're male or female. (115)

For others, sexual (and for some women, emotional) relationships with men and women were experienced as so different, they could not state a preference:

It's very hard to compare the psychology, and the sexual feelings are also very different. (10)

I have slept with women with whom I was not in love, and not particularly enjoyed the sex. I can enjoy sex with men I'm not in love with, although I don't always reach orgasm. With women I'm in love with, I can have quite earth-shattering orgasms. With men, mostly less so. (92)

For other women, the fact that they had no preference meant that they wanted sexual relationships with both women and men contemporaneously.

What I would ideally like is to live alone and have lovers/friends of both sexes, because the friendship and sex of/with men answers different needs to that of/with women. (86)

Ideally I would like to have a relationship with a man and a woman at the same time. However, in practice I cannot see how this would suit anyone but me. (34)

As the above responses indicate, sexual preference is more complicated than simply desiring one type of body or behaviour. Love and emotion can also be important factors, though feelings do not necessarily correspond with desire. Some respondents preferred one sex emotionally, the other sexually; some women sought a nurturing relationship from women, and excitement from men, or vice versa. For some respondents, sex was profoundly important in and of itself, one of the driving forces of life; for others, it was only important as an expression of love and intimacy.

I see sexual intimacy as a way of communicating with someone I feel close to. This could be an old close friend or a short-term intense friendship. (133)

Sex is high on my list of priorities. (82)

Sex only seems important when the chemistry is right. Otherwise, good friends are much more important. (135)

While most respondents (92 in all) felt that emotional intimacy with women was stronger than with men, the developing of that closeness into a relationship was less usual. I asked no specific questions about 'falling in love', though previous research by Charlotte Wolff indicates that both male and female bisexuals tend to 'fall in love' more easily with women than with men.[1] Of course, the definition of 'falling in love', too, will vary from person to person.

Male partners

I am excellent friends with my husband, and we love each other very much – we just don't have a sexual relationship any more. (79)

There are some men whom I feel relaxed and friendly with, and whom I like very much. But basically I prefer women. (75)

Respondents had different types of relationship with men and different views on them. Most common, however, was a tendency to be critical of men in general, while liking some individuals.

Perhaps because of good relationships with my brothers, I have never felt distanced from men. Some things only other women can understand, but this doesn't make me feel more intimate with women friends than with close male friends. (57)

Some bisexual women feel apologetic about their relationships with men, even when these are positive. Bisexual women have often been accused by lesbians of wanting heterosexual privilege – that is, of wanting the acceptability, lack of oppression, financial rewards and freedom from physical attack that relationships with men can bring. Without doubt this tips the balance in favour of heterosexual relationships, but 'privilege' cannot in and of itself be sufficient reason to have them. And in any case, many aspects of this privilege exist only for people whose relationships fall within the confines of same race, similar age and so on.

Under patriarchy, men have power over women. Society gives men some roles and women others, and although individual experience may give lie to this, the stereotypes influence how we behave. Men are taught from childhood to act tough, deny their feelings and only express superiority. These are not qualities conducive to a successful intimate relationship.

Is it possible to have a truly intimate relationship with a man? (91)

Men are at present non-progressive human beings and I don't wish to waste my time on them. I fancy men who are conventionally physically attractive; then they open their mouths and I don't fancy them any more. (69)

Not all men are like this, however, and at least some are trying to find ways to express both strong and gentle aspects of themselves. Others are genuinely capable of responding to women, and some fortunate questionnaire repondents believed that they had found such a man.

On the whole, respondents seemed to be happy with their relationships with men. There are reasons why bisexual women could have better relationships with male lovers than heterosexual women: unlike heterosexual women, relationships with men are not the only route to sexual/emotional fulfilment, and there is therefore a greater element of choice; also, having experienced relationships with women that are not governed by power differences, bisexual women may be able to bring the insights they gained from these to their opposite-sex relationships.

My closest friend is a man, and has been for many years; we have been lovers on and off. I feel we always will be, although I would define myself (if I had to) as someone who preferred the company of women and sexual relationships with women. (63)

My most intimate relationships are with women, or with men who show a mind set or sympathy to a female point of view. (77)

My emotional relationship with my present male partner is the most intense and intimate I have had since my first relationship with a woman.

I would say that I was more woman-oriented; my partner seems to be an anomaly! (72)

Feminine characteristics in men relax and inspire me. (137)

The men I have been involved with have been very good at sensuality, and we spend/t hours cuddling and being non-specifically erogenous in the way that I would expect to be in a good sexual relationship with a woman. (13)

However, sexual politics and personal experience mean that some women remain wary of a longstanding commitment to a man.

In my experience, living with a man involves too many compromises and 'discussions' and reminders about things like whose turn it is to clean the kitchen floor, etc, etc. (115)

As a feminist, I have become more and more aware of male power, and less and less happy about relating to men on any deep level. (142)

Women are emotionally expressive and generally more open than men, who can be very manipulative and also very guarded over their feelings, or conversely totally over the top and frighteningly possessive. (69)

Some feminists certainly find it hard to see how heterosexual relationships can be other than ridden with power struggles. However, men are *not* all the same, and power dynamics within a relationship are mitigated by other circumstances such as class, age or race. For some women, men seem so different that a similarity of background is necessary if heterosexual relationships are to work. Others only have relationships with men of other races or backgrounds, but would have relationships with women without these strictures.

I made a conscious choice that if I was going to have a relationship with a man then I wanted that man to be Jewish. I have come to value the fact that my lover knows exactly where I'm coming from and loves me because of it, not despite it. As far as women are concerned, the Jewish/non-Jewish dilemma didn't enter the picture, because the relationship itself was so far out of any acceptable frame of reference. (117)

Some respondents saw relationships with men as easier than relationships with women. That men tend to be less capable of profound emotional depth – the sort which claustrophobically absorbs both partners – was perceived by some women as an advantage. Others found it easier to insist on what they wanted with male partners as they did not feel they were oppressing another who was already oppressed. Casual sex with men was seen as easier, though many respondents who indicated high numbers of male sexual partners had had them in the early- to mid-1970s, a period when contraception was readily available and AIDS was not known about. Younger women had had comparatively fewer male sexual partners and a more equal balance between female and male partners.

Given that one-off sexual encounters (taking account of safer sex measures) may be good experiences actively sought by women, why were these felt to be easier with men? Men's desire for sex is constructed as a purely physical response – relentless and urgent – so presumably a woman wanting sexual contact without emotional involvement would choose a man. It was also not unusual for women to desire men sexually without liking them very much or wanting to become deeply involved – a scenario less likely with another woman. To judge by respondents' replies, they had had a lot more, and a lot less satisfying, sex with men than they would have liked – probably in common with women of all sexualities.

My present male partner is the best lover I have ever had. But even when I preferred sex with women I had more men for sex as it was easier to pick them up. I never found what I was looking for, though. (72)

I've only ever had sex with men and let's just say I am very disillusioned. (70)

I had sex with lots of men because I kept hoping one of them would be half decent, and because it is far easier in every way to be straight than gay. (30)

Female partners

More than twice as many respondents were currently involved with men as with women. As mentioned above, this is not surprising: to find a female sexual partner, unless one is particularly brave or lucky, one has to be within a lesbian community – often difficult for a bisexual woman. The fact that many more bisexual women have male than female partners is not lost on lesbians: this completes a vicious circle whereby lesbians are reluctant to become involved with bisexual women because so many are involved with men.

According to some respondents, the numerical imbalance is because relationships with women are more rewarding and therefore more likely to last:

Men were always incapable of giving enough emotionally, and incapable of knowing how to know me. Until my current relationship, I have always been far closer to women. (28)

Several respondents expressed their surprise at the emotional depth possible in a woman-to-woman relationship compared to most heterosexual relationships.

Relationships with women are quite new for me. I've always dreamt about having one, and now that I do, I find that I'm afraid of losing myself. (121)

For far too many respondents, however, desire for or fantasies about women, or a particular individual, had not developed into action.

I have a greater fear of rejection by women as I worry (perhaps unreasonably) that it would jeopardise our relationship. (9)

I live with a man, but I fantasise a lot about women. My dreams are lesbian. Yet it has never happened to me to have a woman lover and now I am fifty. Perhaps it never will, and that's something I regret. (88)

To act on such fantasies requires enormous courage, particularly if they are deep and longstanding. It is particularly difficult for a woman who is already in, say, a fairly happy heterosexual relationship, and who feels she will risk losing a lot. As the lesbian scene caters mainly for young women, this can exclude those who discover their attraction to women later in life.

I think it is very difficult for bisexual women to form relationships with other women. I felt it would be wrong of me to try to have a sexual relationship with a lesbian because I knew I would continue to feel attracted to men. Instead I formed relationships with heterosexually-identified women, and these weren't very successful because of their ambivalent feelings. (37)

To say that you are bisexual means, to many lesbians, that you must be prioritising men. In fact, it means nothing of the sort: some bisexual women prioritise men, some women, some neither. Once in a sexual relationship with a woman, a bisexual may feel a great deal of pressure to identify as a lesbian. This can create tension between the partners and between the individual and the lesbian community.

My girlfriend would prefer to think of me as a lesbian, but she is trying to come to terms with it. (34)

Nevertheless, most respondents described their lesbian partners as supportive of their sexuality:

Her reaction is positive, accepting. We met at the Bisexual group, though she isn't herself bisexual, and as she says, that wouldn't have happened if I hadn't been bisexual! Also, bisexual political campaigning is a major part of what I am and, she says, makes me interesting! (1)

She understands and wants to know more about bisexuality. Once I'd reassured her I'm not likely to go out with anyone else at the same time, things were OK. (112)

Relations between respondents and the lesbian community tended to be uneasy: more than half the sample (79 in all) did not feel part of the lesbian community; most of the others (52 women) were involved to a greater or lesser extent. The (non)existence or gender of a woman's current sexual partner(s) seemed to have little impact on her feelings of belonging: roughly equal numbers of women with female partners, male partners or no partners did or did not feel part of the lesbian community.

I've been on the outskirts of the lesbian community for some ten years, belonging to a Black women's group which was one-quarter lesbian; hanging out at women-only bars and clubs. I like the idea of being part of that community, particularly some of the lesbians I know. I feel comfortable, safe and have great fun. (134)

Where I live there isn't any 'scene', but I'm part of a women's group where I'm out as bisexual and I feel very comfortable. (113)

I get on well with the lesbians I've met, and although I expected some hostility I haven't encountered any. (95)

I am positively aware of a tremendous strength and sisterhood, the fringe of which I only touch upon. I am proud that my life is linked to such a dynamic force. (103)

Some women saw membership of the lesbian community as necessary to enable them to have sexual relationships with women.

I had learned very well how to suppress my desires for women because usually if I fancied a woman she turned out to be het. I found that I got myself so deeply into expecting to be rejected that even if I did fancy a woman, I would never bother to try anything. Sometimes I found out later that she did fancy me too at some point, but our over-het environment kept us apart. (126)

Many (48) of the 79 women who said they did not feel part of the lesbian community did not go on to answer the next section of the questionnaire, but the majority of those who did expressed feelings of exclusion. Several respondents said the most hostile reactions to their 'coming out' had been from lesbians.

At the moment, I have given up on the lesbian community. (55)

Many of my friends are lesbians but I always feel that edge between us. It makes me sad, that old chestnut about having to suppress one's sexuality because it just isn't 'cool' in certain circles. (83)

I'm partly angry at being excluded or made to feel uncomfortable; partly understanding of this exclusion. (97)

I feel that bisexual women share many/most of the concerns of the lesbian community. But I do feel that I'm there on sufferance. I'd prefer complete acceptance, but given the limited resources and space available to lesbians, I don't see it happening. Not until the pressure lesbians (and us!) live under is relaxed. (1)

The lesbians locally have been very hostile. I'm sad that separatist feminists are too narrow-minded to accept that their beliefs don't suit everyone. (24)

Other women, especially those in long-term committed relationships, felt their position to be fraudulent. They appeared to be lesbian, but they knew (and sometimes only they knew) that this was not the whole truth.

Lesbian is an important word in a political sense and I'm involved in that political struggle. But I'm unhappy that I can't disclose that part

of me which is attracted to men. Although I can see how important
it is for a united lesbian front, why should I be excluded from it because
I'm sometimes attracted to men? (45)

I'm not generally known within the lesbian community as a bisexual,
and I feel uncomfortable about it, like a fraud. (34)

When I'm with friends in London or Manchester I am part of the lesbian
community, but sometimes I feel a fraud when I talk to advocates of
separatism. I don't subscribe to the 'castrate all men' school of
thought. (40)

Like mainstream society, lesbians have often devalued bisexual
women's relationships with other women, and over-valued their
relationships with men. And the hostile reactions of some lesbian-
feminists (who may believe bisexual women are letting feminists
down) and non-feminist lesbians (who may feel personally
threatened) has been transmuted into the myth that all lesbians
are against all bisexuals.

As mentioned above, casual sex with women was a less common
experience than with men. However, it seems that many lesbians
are currently exploring the possibilities of more casual sex, so future
figures may change. The emergence of lesbian, 'queer', and mixed
gay clubs which are blatantly about sex and sexual encounters
shows that women are more freely expressing their desires.

Only two respondents lived a predominantly heterosexual life
in which their interest in other women was purely sexual – a more
common pattern, perhaps, for bisexual men. Women seeking
other women for sex only do advertise in listings magazines such
as London's *Loot*, but none of these women answered the call to
complete the questionnaire. It is possible that women who match
this pattern identify as heterosexual; perhaps by refusing any
emotional involvement with the women they have sex with they
can regard their feelings for women as unimportant, manageable
and therefore less threatening.

Bisexual partners

Out of a total of 97 respondents currently involved in a relationship,
17 had bisexual partners, of whom 9 were women and 8 men.
Several respondents expressed the belief that a relationship with
another bisexual contained the basis for a deeper level of under-

standing, in particular about the idea that one might want to maintain a committed relationship but might not want to confine one's desires to a single individual. 14 of the 41 partners considered by respondents to feel positively about their bisexuality were also bisexual themselves:

She and I share similar values about the variety and fluidity of sexuality and sexual desire. (32)

He's supportive, sees it as nothing remarkable, because he has had gay affairs himself. (7)

However, a partner's feelings in theory do not necessarily carry through into practice: bisexuals too can feel jealous and insecure. That one desires people of both sexes oneself does not make it necessarily less threatening when a partner is found to desire other people too.

He's bisexual too, and supportive, but potentially jealous of other lovers. (10)

Bisexual partners may also be uncertain of their own sexuality:

She felt more uncomfortable about being in a long-term relationship with a woman than I did, which is why I have just ended it. She's now sleeping with a man. (54)

Partners' attitudes

85 out of 97 respondents' partners knew of their bisexuality and 12 did not. Of the 12 who did not know, 10 were men and 2 women. One of the respondents whose female partner did not know was unsure as to whether she now identified as lesbian, and so had not told her partner about her past heterosexual experiences. The other knew her partner was strongly anti-bisexual. Of those with male partners who did not know, 2 respondents said they did not want to upset their partners, 4 felt it was not relevant, and 2 that their husbands were too narrow-minded. Of the partners who knew, 41 were positive, 29 had mixed feelings and 9 had negative reactions – often because they felt personally threatened. (6 respondents with partners did not answer this question.)

Among respondents with male partners, 3 reported an initial reaction of excitement, followed by a feeling of threat once their partners realised that they took their sexuality seriously:

At the beginning, my husband was interested in my bisexuality, and wanted to take part in a threesome. When my last lover appeared, he got jealous. It turned into a very traumatic experience for us all, including her husband. (15)

Non-bisexual female partners were more likely to have felt threatened from the outset. Committed lesbians may well feel angry that their sexuality is potentially connected to a man. And the fact that their partner could be involved with a man can be especially painful because of the inequality of the situation: a heterosexual relationship has society on its side, whereas lesbians have to fight for sexual autonomy.

My lover knew I had had relationships with men prior to our living together (this caused many problems in itself) but believed I had been 'converted' and become a true lesbian in our four years together. She was outraged and violently angry when I told her of a recent 'het' encounter. (48)

Reactions from male and female partners were also conditioned by whether or not the respondents had known about and admitted their bisexual feelings at the start of the relationship, or whether they had discovered them later. In the former case, partners at least knew what they were letting themselves in for; in the latter, they often felt scared or cheated when the issue arose.

However, it seems that many partners, both male and female, are able to accept without too much difficulty that a woman's bisexuality is an integral part of her personality. Or a partner may be quite happy as long as the relationship is monogamous. A woman whose bisexuality expresses itself as serial monogamy poses no threat to her current partner. However, the partner may imagine that a bisexual woman is bound to leave sooner or later for a person of the other gender. She might – as a monosexual person may leave for another partner, too.

My boyfriend's attitude is amused tolerance, so long as my bisexuality remains theoretical. Putting it into practice caused massive rows. (86)

He is totally accepting of my past life and does not object to me talking about my sexuality or saying if I 'fancy' some women. I have had open relationships but it was me who became jealous, even when I had other partners myself. (72)

Monogamy and non-monogamy

Monogamous heterosexual relationships have been viewed traditionally (and still are by the moral right) as the only safe and natural way of life. Sexual licence was seen as the biological predisposition of men, which their female partners were to 'tame' and control. But throughout history, many people of all sexualities have had a primary relationship (usually marriage) from which they would 'stray' occasionally, or outside of which they would establish a more permanent secondary relationship. In the late twentieth century, lifetime monogamy can no longer be presumed as a norm.

People with no personal knowledge of bisexuality are likely to assume that bisexuals want multiple relationships: that one lover, male or female, can never be enough because a bisexual has needs which cannot be met by one sex or the other. This section explores how far this is true, and details what questionnaire respondents said about monogamy and non-monogamy. Some aspects of the issue are common to people of all sexualities: how to maintain excitement in a long-term relationship, for instance, or how to maintain two simultaneous relationships with the least hurt to everyone involved.

Bisexuals have been considered incapable of monogamy, and by extension of commitment and deep feeling. Respondents disprove this stereotype: 51 women were in favour of monogamy (10 because it was easier, and 8 because of fears of HIV infection); 52 had mixed feelings, or considered monogamy unrealistic; 7 women thought it depended on the relationship or individuals concerned; 23 women felt monogamy to be destructive.

Having been rather promiscuous as a young woman, it's almost a relief to be monogamous. But it depends whether all your needs can be satisfied by one person. (38)

I am working on being monogamous at the moment. It has its rewards, like any other emotionally demanding project. It helps me grow. (37)

It seems unrealistic to me to expect only ever to be sexually attracted to one person. I do not feel naturally monogamous, but the difficult part is balancing your life if your partner does feel monogamous. (34)

I feel that if you are in a relationship with someone you have deep feelings for, it is probably better to be monogamous, but if you are in casual relationships with people and are honest with them, then polygamy is OK. (33)

Monogamy seems to work best for most people (security, trust, etc), yet it is rarely maintained (there's a lot of hypocrisy about it). (32)

I think monogamy is tempting but ultimately destructive. (30)

At the time of answering the questionnaires, 72 women had monogamous relationships and 25 women had primary relationships with other sexual partners outside of these. Only 3 of the women who thought monogamy a good thing (and who were in primary relationships) were not monogamous.

The effect of secondary sexual partners on respondents' primary relationships varied: some said the effect was complementary, others perceived it as destructive, though many women seemed able to minimise potentially destructive effects. It has been presumed – by the lesbian writers cited in Chapter 3, for instance – that female bisexuals will have primary male partners and secondary affairs with women. 20 respondents fell into this category, while 5 respondents had primary lesbian relationships and secondary relationships with men.

I have been with my female lover for a number of years and in that time have had several short-term affairs with men and one longer affair. (34)

I have lived with my husband for fifteen years and have had other relationships which provide me with passion, excitement and so on. No one individual can offer everything. My husband accepts me totally, provides emotional and domestic support. We have an 'arrangement': as long as I tell him when I am involved and am discreet and sensitive, there is no problem. (17)

People whose primary relationships are little affected by other sexual partners are likely to have decided in advance that this will be the case, a situation that can be difficult for secondary sexual partners. The fact that it is heterosexual relationships, however inadequate, that receive the support of society means that lesbians involved in relationships with, for instance, married women, are perhaps most justified in feeling at an unfair disadvantage. However, the lesbian partner may also have good reason to be involved with someone not able to commit herself totally – like having another partner herself. Married respondents also reported having married women lovers:

Everything is fine between myself and my girlfriend because I am married and she is also going to be married soon. (100)

The type of relationship developed by many gay men and some heterosexual couples – for example, Jean-Paul Sartre and Simone de Beauvoir – in which the couple is strongly bonded, but within which partners may openly conduct other sexual relationships, seems to work well for some people, though the danger that other sexual partners will be marginal and feel exploited is still there.

Some respondents had no desire for more than one sexual partner: of those involved in relationships, 28 were not interested in other relationships; 9 were involved with partners who wanted monogamy; 8 didn't want the ensuing complications. However, for some bisexuals, men and women meet different needs, and over the long term the unsatisfied part of themselves craves expression. It can feel like sexual repression not to be able to explore that part.

I know that when I had more than one lover at a time I did so because I was in some way dissatisfied, and felt I needed something else all the time. When I was with a man I longed for women's company; when with a woman, I suddenly began to appreciate male qualities. Now I assert that two people can be enough for each other, if they both want and allow it. (31)

Monogamy can be very nice indeed, but it's hard for me as a bisexual on a long-term basis. (10)

The desirability, as a matter of principle, of having more than one serious sexual relationship at a time is nowadays rarely expressed. Twenty years ago, at least among certain sections of society, there was a lot of hope that 'new', 'open', non-possessive, non-exclusive, loving relationships with numbers of people would be possible. Sex and friendship would be less clearly divided, and the claustrophobia of oppressive, traditional couples dispelled forever. This non-monogamy differed from traditional notions of 'unfaithfulness' in being founded on principles of honesty and openness (whether or not this was the case in practice).

Non-monogamy was often espoused by 'idealistic' bisexuals in the 1970s. It was seen as logical that people who were looking for a new type of relationship would be less constrained by considerations of gender. In the 1980s, the climate began to change, and even before the threat of AIDS was used to discourage non-monogamy, people seemed to be moving back to more conventional relationships. Respondents were on the whole unenthusiastic about non-monogamy, but attitudes seem to have changed again recently, at least in bisexual activist communities. This may be the result of the new emphasis on 'sex-positive' strategies – the need to reiterate that sex is good in and of itself, and that safer sex is not lesser sex – as a reaction to the fear of sex and homophobia the AIDS epidemic has generated.

14 respondents operated open relationships (although by circumstance these were not always non-monogamous and the respondent did not necessarily have two partners of different genders at the same time). 72 did not, of whom 8 strongly disapproved; 21 had done so in the past. Of those who operated, or had operated, open relationships, 11 did so for emotional reasons, 7 for sexual reasons, 4 for political/idealistic reasons, 9 for a mixture of all three. For 4 women, open relationships 'just happened' and were not consciously chosen. Many women who had been non-monogamous in the past saw this as belonging to an experimental period of their lives, which had not worked out.

I have had them and would like to again, but in practice, it's difficult. (21)

I thought I could do it with M and my other two lovers, but I realised that M meant a lot more to me. (83)

I once tried to do it, partly out of a belief in the absurdity of monogamy and partly as an emotional safety net. But almost immediately I wanted to spend my time with one rather than the other – the one who had been usurped hated the idea of non-monogamy anyway, which didn't give it a very good ground base. (28)

I look back with some nostalgia, though at the time I know there was pain as well as fun and affection. The main upset was fear of being marginal. The main joy was the feeling of power and freedom. (37)

Respondents who were successfully non-monogamous were usually helped by favourable circumstances: they and their lovers lived far apart; their relationships fulfilled different needs; their relationships were 'sexual friendships'. However, even in these relationships different insecurities come into play: for instance, a partner may be threatened by another same-sex lover, but not by one of the opposite sex; some people feel fine about sexual non-monogamy, but suffer jealousy over friends, work or time.

I have two sexual relationships at present – one fairly longstanding with a man, and a newish one with a woman. I don't really consider them 'open': they have a fairly equal, though very different, importance. My woman lover has a male lover as well, which I can cope with. I would feel differently if she had a female lover. I suffer from time, rather than sexual, jealousy. Non-monogamy may be a great utopian ideal, but I think most of us are too needy and emotionally damaged to cope with it easily. (108)

In the course of a lifetime, a woman may have long-term relationships with men or women, sexual friendships, short-term flings, and periods of celibacy. It is not always appropriate to have deep, intense relationships, and while those who criticise non-monogamy for being the perfect way to avoid deeply committed relationships may be right, so what? Similarly, does it really matter whether being in a monogamous relationship is constricting if it is also enjoyable and rewarding? In practice, the most important thing is to conduct oneself with honesty, respect and love for oneself and one's partners.

Marriage

Girls in most western societies are brought up to want to have a wonderful wedding and to live happily ever after. The state of marriage represents love, contentment, security and acceptance by society – forever. This indoctrination affects most women, regardless of their sexuality: most women want to marry and the majority succeed. This is as true for bisexual women as for heterosexuals, despite the fact that marriage is a public proclamation of heterosexuality – whether or not the spouses are heterosexual in reality. Openly having sexual relationships with other women requires an enormous amount of courage, whereas heterosexual relationships, and particularly marriage, are almost universally approved of.

Yet marriage seems to be decreasing in popularity in much of western Europe and North America at present. Some 87 per cent of women in the UK marry before the age of fifty – though there is no reason to suppose they all have primary sexual relationships with their spouses – but the rate is dropping rapidly: in 1990/91 less than 40 per 1,000 unmarried people over the age of sixteen married, compared to more than twice that number (82.3 per 1,000) in 1971. 28 women in this sample were currently married; 16 were divorced or separated. This is proportionately lower than society as a whole, which I think has more to do with the fact that many respondents identified as feminists, than even that most of them were relatively young.

Respondents were asked why they were or were not married. Some expressed hostility to the idea, presuming that I thought they should be, which is far from the case. The 28 women who were married identified their reasons as follows (some gave multiple reasons): 15 said they were in love; 6 responded to pressure from their parents; 4 married because that was what they expected; 4 were not sure why they had married; 3 married for security.

I'm not quite sure why I got married. Basically, not to hurt my family's feelings, for tax incentives, and to some extent to provide my child with security. (80)

I met someone I wanted to share my life with. (82)

Married for emotional and financial support. Now I can't break away from my husband for fear of losing our child as a result of him finding out about my lover and proof of my lesbian tendencies. (62)

I was getting too much hassle to do the right thing from my aging parents. (52)

The respondents who were most likely to be (or have been) married were those over the age of forty. Of the 19 respondents over forty, 15 had been married at some point – of whom 8 were now divorced. Other than age, there seemed to be no definable difference between the women who had and had not married: they were not more or less likely to have had significant sexual relationships with women, for instance.

Some married respondents expressed vague regret at having married, without regretting their relationships with their husbands. Others were unsure as to why they had married in the first place:

Why am I married? I honestly don't know! (44)

I married because I was pregnant (this was thirty years ago) and it seemed a good idea at the time. If I could choose now I wouldn't have married, but would live with the same man. (51)

Respondents who had rejected the idea of marriage, at least for the time being, gave the following reasons: 20 did not agree with marriage; 18 were not interested; 10 thought they were too young; 6 hadn't yet met Mr Right.

Marriage is bad for people, especially for women. (69)

I don't believe marriage works. (70)

Disapprove on political, emotional, sexual and any other ground you can think of! (86)

I don't feel it would suit me. I'm too independent. (78)

Others had watched their parents going through destructive or empty marriages, and were determined not to make the same mistake. The 20 women who disagreed with marriage from a feminist perspective expressed the strongest feelings about it.

Divorce in the UK is increasingly common: 153,000 divorces in 1990 compared with 74,000 in 1971. While many divorced people remarry at some point, remarriage figures are dropping at a similar rate to those for first marriages. Of the 16 respondents who were divorced or separated, most cited the reason for their marital breakdown as growing apart, or their relationships becoming boring, though 2 women suffered violence. 3 marriages ended because either one, or in one case both partners, were convinced they were with a person of the wrong sex.

My husband discovered his bisexuality, and did the gay male scene at the age of forty-two. But perhaps it would have ended anyway, because our sex life wasn't working. (59)

I found marriage too restrictive, and we were moving in different directions politically. (67)

Women increasingly choose not to marry, and the effect that has on their social acceptability depends on culture, geographical location, and the people they mix with. In some areas of some cities, marriage seems almost rare; in more religious or conventional communities, non-marriage will be heavily disapproved of.

24 questionnaire respondents had experienced overt pressure to marry from their families; another 15 had felt covert pressure. 14 of them complied and married, although others reacted by laughing, getting angry, or simply ignoring it. 11 women had experienced pressure *not* to marry – either one person in particular,

or to resist marriage in general, because their own parents had
had such a miserable time.

My mother was giving me pressure: I wanted to carry on living
together for a while longer. But I cracked! (125)

I never had overt pressure, although I felt pressurised, which is similar.
Once I asked them if they minded that I didn't have children/wasn't
married. My mother reassured me very unconvincingly; my father I
think couldn't care less. (123)

4 married respondents had female lovers who were at least as
emotionally important to them as their husbands. 3 of these
respondents were over fifty, all were over forty, and all had been
married for over twenty years.

I have had one very deep and sexual relationship with the same woman
for eleven years now, and that is just as important as my relationship
with my husband – sometimes more. (35)

My female lover sometimes worries that she might damage my
marriage... I would hate to lose my husband and if she asked me to
leave him I don't know how I'd cope. (79)

For many women of all sexualities, lack of deep feeling for a
husband has not been a strong enough reason to leave him.
Worries about financial security, emotional security, and desire
for stability for the sake of children all play a part. Loving someone
over a long period, whether or not it is intense or entirely fulfilling,
can be an important part of one's life that one is reluctant to give
up – even for a person one thinks one loves 'more'. For many
bisexuals, loving a woman and a man at the same time might be
an (impossible) ideal.

Children

35 respondents had children, and a further 6 were trying to get
pregnant. One woman mentioned grandchildren (as I had not asked
about them, there may have been other, undisclosed grand-
mothers). As most respondents were in their twenties and thirties,
children tended to be young, though women with teenagers and
adult children were also included. 15 of the women with children
were currently married, 11 were divorced or separated, and 9 had
never been married. One of the 9 had her child when involved

with another woman, but the relationship had ended. 7 women had told their children something about their bisexuality and 7 had told their children nothing because they were 'too young to understand'. 9 believed their children had some idea, but they had not explicitly discussed the subject.

They know I had affairs before my husband and I separated, they know about affairs with men subsequently; my son knows I sleep with my woman lover but I do not discuss this. My children like and accept her. (116)

I think my daughter may have guessed, but we haven't talked about it yet. All my children had left home before I became conscious of my internal struggle. (64)

My children, who are eight and ten, are not aware as far as I know of me being anything other than heterosexual. (38)

Of the 7 women whose children knew something about their sexuality, only 3 knew definitely that their mothers were bisexual: the others only knew that their mothers had female lovers.

My daughter asked me if I was bisexual because I support gay rights, go on marches, etc, but still live with her dad. I replied, 'yes', and she hasn't mentioned it since. (17)

My husband told them when they were about eleven and fourteen in a general discussion on women loving women. I was very proud of him, but anxious, because I wasn't there. (35)

My children, who are now in their mid-twenties, have known everything about my sexual identity for the past fourteen years. (139)

As bisexuality is increasingly acknowledged as a valid sexual identity, more bisexual parents will feel it incumbent on them to discuss their sexuality with their children, in ways appropriate to their age. At present, it is hard enough for a bisexual woman to forge her own identity, let alone to know what to tell her children; most respondents found it hard to be out as bisexual even to friends. And there is no support network as yet for bisexual mothers, as there is for lesbian mothers. Perhaps, too, bisexual mothers do not want to 'confuse' their children, and so keep their sexual relationships apart from them – unless they are in long-term relationships.

Yet there are ways of talking to children, even those who are quite young, about loving both men and women. True intimacy with one's children, and the capacity to provide a positive role model for them, requires appropriate honesty – and preferably before the children themselves realise that society believes same-sex relationships to be wrong. Children need to receive a positive image of bisexuality from their parents to counter the arguments of peers and adults who think differently. Women who identify as bisexual before having children are now considering this.

Any child that I had, I would tell I was bisexual. How would they know me otherwise? (125)

Many areas of British society (particularly white British society) work in such a way as to segregate people with children, not just through insufficient provision of childcare and crèches – important though these are – but through an assumption that children should be invisible. Children are very demanding; more collective ways of bringing them up would lessen the burdens of individual isolated mothers.

However, the responsibility of having another, vulnerable, person to consider does change parents' priorities for good: all women (and some men) make compromises, sexual and otherwise, when they have children. 15 respondents said they had compromised their own desires for the sake of their children; 15 that they had not; 2 were not sure.

I feel I owe it to my baby to preserve a fairly stable home environment, even if it means a sacrifice. (37)

I keep quiet about my sexuality. Kids can be very cruel at school. (73)

I suppose I have compromised, but it's hard to say how. (79)

Of course I've compromised, I live with their father! (17)

2 other women said that society currently made life so difficult for mothers that they had chosen not to have children.

I have made a huge compromise by not having children because of my sexuality and being an artist. If society was different about these two things I would have had children. (123)

Bisexual women who have children with heterosexual men and then become involved with a woman can find themselves in the same sort of custody struggles as many lesbians. The threat of losing their children in a custody battle can operate as an additional pressure in keeping women tied to heterosexual relationships, whether or not this is what they want.

My ex-husband knows about my attraction to women. He is about to remarry and has mentioned he wants care and control. He believes my lifestyle to be inferior to his. I nearly joined a lesbian housing co-op but decided not to because of this. (67)

I am unable to break away from my husband for fear of losing our child as a result of him finding out about my lover and having proof of my lesbian tendencies. He has always been suspicious of my female friendships since I told him I was bisexual. (62)

The knowledge that their male partners could try to claim custody of their children at some point in the future mitigates against bisexual women being honest about their sexuality at the outset or in the course of a relationship. A man who appears to be sympathetic and even encourages his partner to have sexual relationships with other women can still, if he wants custody, play the 'unfit lesbian mother' card.

Custody courts are not interested in how someone defines herself; they are hostile to non-conformist lifestyles, and in particular to same-sex relationships. Any woman who has a primary relationship with another woman, and whose fitness to care for her child is questioned by her male ex-partner (not necessarily ex-husband) needs expert legal advice. It is a moot point as to how much a woman who does not have a same-sex relationship at present but has done in the past would be disadvantaged, though any extra-relationship affairs can be used as proof of a woman's instability.

There has been a lot of debate between black and white feminists about whether or not the family is oppressive to women. Part of the division arises from different concepts of what the family is: white feminists have tended to see the oppressive family as a nuclear one; black feminists, although less hostile to the nuclear family because of the supportive role it has played to its members in racist societies, are also talking about extended families, which may include people who are not blood relatives.[2] Many people who have been rejected by their families of origin, or who live far away from them, have created their own families of friends. And networks of people in committed, non-monogamous relationships can also provide 'family'-type support. Increasingly some men and many women

are choosing to have children outside a primary heterosexual relationship, either as 'single parents', within same-sex couples, or
with a network of friends, within or outside collective households.

Sexual relationships rarely last forever, and putting more energy
into creating friendships and closer relationships with other
family members and our own children (if we have them) can be
very valuable. Alternatives to the nuclear family are perceived as
deeply threatening to the basis of society in the 1990s – and not
just by the moral right. The family – in its most narrow sense –
is paramount, and any attempt to bring children up in an alternative scenario is subject to attack. In particular, two people of
the same sex fulfilling parental roles poses a threat to many
people. Significantly, the major target of Section 28 was 'pretended
families' – those who claimed the rights of families without being
families in the traditional sense. Gender roles are always posited
as 'natural', and parenthood the most natural part of that. Certain
sections of society are scared that children who are shown other
possibilities may take them up, and the world of the future will
spin out of control.

My own ideal is that children should be brought up in a stable
environment by a number of people, whether or not they live with
them, or are blood-related. This would lessen much of the suffering
imposed by claustrophobic nuclear families and the heartache of
those children whose parents separate (as very many do), as well
as encouraging children to relate in different ways to a number
of different people. 'Idealistic' bisexuals probably also want their
children to be brought up feeling that however their sexuality turns
out, that is a cause for happiness and celebration.

Families and communities

It is difficult to discuss the influence of families of origin on
sexuality without implying that that is what 'makes people
bisexual'. Conventional psychoanalytic theory certainly posits that
this is the case, implying a norm of heterosexuality from which
people are forced to deviate because of parental neuroticism.
Lesbians and gay men have fought against this notion for many
years, trying to convince the straight world that there is nothing
particularly natural about heterosexuality, and that people are most
definitely 'made' heterosexual too.

It is true, as one respondent put it on refusing to answer the relevant section of the questionnaire, that 'no one knows what makes a person gay', while clearly one of the factors that contributes to making a person heterosexual is the phenomenal pressure from society. The nuclear family is the earliest and deepest way in which society's values are transmitted to us; it is also the filter through which a child learns about the rest of society.

What I want to look at here, rather than what might 'make' a woman bisexual, is how respondents' families of origin, and the communities in which they were located, affected the *expression* of their bisexuality. Early influences can work in complex and con-tradictory ways: for instance, a woman may have a religious background which connects sexual desire with guilt, yet has been taught, through education, to challenge given truths.

28 women felt that the restrictiveness of their backgrounds had negatively affected their possibilities for sexual expression, and a further 9 that they had been restricted by the heterosexist expectations of their parents:

My parents had a completely Victorian morality – it was all right to fiddle the income tax, but not to sleep with someone you love. They have been dead for five years and I have been married for twenty-four, but I think they gave me hang-ups which I shall never overcome. (79)

I feel that because I had a normal/conventional happy family background, I naturally fell into the 'normal' sexual category, i.e. het-erosexual. (19)

20 women felt strengthened by positive female role models, 15 by a liberal upbringing, and 10 by a happy and loving childhood.

My father died before I was born, so my mother gave me twice as much love. I never felt I was lacking as a child; feminine influence was very strong in my life. (58)

They tried to raise me as believing gender was not a barrier, that I could do whatever I put my mind to. When I finally looked at myself I realised how positive their efforts had been. They in turn accept my sexuality totally, though they do not fully understand it. (50)

My parents' attitudes were fairly liberal, in as much as they assumed I'd be sleeping with my boyfriends. I don't think a girlfriend ever crossed their (or my) minds. But it was always stressed that really you should only sleep with people if you loved them. Not a bad philosophy. (86)

10 women mentioned sexual abuse, all of whom considered it had had serious effects on them:

Last year I retrieved a vital early memory: sexual abuse by my grandfather when I was around three. This must have had a great effect on the direction my sexuality took. (64)

18 women thought their families had not affected them, 10 were not sure what the effects were, and 20 mentioned a variety of other perceived effects.

No one had a gay parent as a child. One woman's mother is now a lesbian, and another's has told her that she had a relationship with another woman when she was a student. A further 7 parents (both mothers and fathers) were likely, respondents thought, to have had same-sex experiences, though they had not discussed this with their children.

The influence of respondents' communities of origin was also perceived as important. 41 mentioned heterosexism and the idea of heterosexuality as 'compulsory' within the wider community as strong influences; a further 21 felt that bisexuality was simply 'not possible'. 7 women said that as teenagers they had had to keep very quiet about their sexual feelings.

Heterosexuality is forced upon us by the mass media, including the music industry, with soppy songs about falling in love and becoming a man's slave. (129)

I feared the wrath and ridicule of the wider society; as a teenager that put lesbianism or bisexuality out of the picture. (22)

I grew up in a Muslim, male-dominated society. There were no options other than heterosexuality. (134)

8 women each mentioned sexual libertarianism, education, feminism and contact with lesbians as helping them to recognise and express their adolescent sexuality and 3 the influence of other girls. 11 women felt there had been few influences on them.

Religion was cited by a number of women as having affected or as affecting their capacity for sexual expression. Organised religion is a powerful force in society, and plays a controlling role in maintaining the family unit as a container of sexuality. 58 questionnaire respondents were brought up to be religious, whether by their family, school or community. 27 of them thought this upbringing had had a negative effect on their sexuality, primarily in making them feel guilty. 8 women felt the effect was positive, or mixed, and 23 that religion had not had a lasting impact.

Homosexuality is condemned in the Bible as the ultimate in wickedness. It has taken me years not to feel guilty about how I feel sexually; religious reasons are also the main ones for not telling my parents about my sexuality. (29)

I was brought up a Catholic: it's hard to split its effects from the results of the way I was parented and my parents' own interpretations of religion. Although it can be about passion, energy and humanity, religion can also be about bigotry, narrow-mindedness and a rule book to hide away from life. (34)

I come from an extremely religious Jewish background and I think it has taken me much longer than other people to realise that I am attracted to women, as well as to men. The true importance of a relationship I had with a woman has been obscured from me for a long time. (138)

Adolescence was remembered by many respondents as a time of confusion and unhappiness. 40 respondents had felt they were definitely heterosexual, 22 confused, 18 bisexual and 14 that they were heterosexual but had crushes on other girls. 6 thought they were lesbian. Many fell into a pattern of crushes on/intimate friendships with other girls and tentative approaches to boys, which is a form of bisexuality.

I was very confused about myself and my sexuality. I would not have sex with men, although I had boyfriends. I knew that I was attracted to women as well, but I never acted on it. (17)

I went through agonies trying to make myself pretty so that boys would fancy me. I was boy-mad and did all the things girls did in the early 60s. (90)

I wasn't attracted to men sexually, but to women. Yet I only had relationships with men, and never with women. (26)

My initial orientation was towards other girls, but by around fifteen I was unhappy with the label of lesbian that was rumoured around school. So I made the effort to be 'normal' and found I could be, although I realised I was still attracted to women. (22)

I still am an adolescent and I'm bisexual. (77)

I had a crush on a female youth leader when I was about thirteen and considered myself a lesbian until I was about twenty-two. (92)

17 women said they had not experienced themselves as sexual beings during adolescence, 8 had felt unhappy about sexuality in general, 5 defined their behaviour as 'promiscuous'.

I felt a lot of frustration about it without being sure why. (32)

As an adolescent my sexuality didn't seem to belong to me. Other people got to make decisions about it, but I was too young to be consulted. (11)

I worried that I was asexual because I was sixteen before I fancied anyone, much later than my classmates. (9)

The increased openness in the discussion of all kinds of sexuality may make it easier for young women today to recognise bisexual feelings. Bisexual and gay role models can help teenagers to think through their sexuality and to recognise the existence and validity of their same-sex attractions. None of the respondents reported knowing any bisexuals in their youth and meeting homosexual people in childhood or adolescence did not seem to have had much effect: 36 women had had some contact with gay people; half had felt interested, or liked them; half had not. 6 women had seen gay or bisexual people on television, or known about them from books. No one reported relating to them, in fact most felt that such characters had little connection with their own same-sex feelings – if indeed they were able consciously to recognise those feelings at that time.

Once into adulthood, women had more power to choose their own living situations and to escape their families or communities of origin if they wished to do so. Further education, the discovery of feminism and different perspectives on the position of women in society, and meeting lesbians and other bisexual women were all mentioned by respondents as enabling factors.

If I didn't live where I do, didn't have divorced parents, didn't know any gay people, never read a book, never heard a woman sing, never saw one I liked, I suppose I'd be almost heterosexual! (125)

I was 'privileged' to go to Oxford University, where most options were open and accepted. (91)

Respondents' relationship with the communities in which they had lived or lived now was often complex. The amount of pressure they felt to conform and the extent of their dependence on the support of a wider community varied according to culture, geographical location, class and race. For instance, many Afro-Caribbean Britons live within a strong, Christian-based community, which is very supportive in the face of a racist society. However, although women do have sex with each other (see Kristin's story in Chapter 5, for instance), it is not spoken about, and same-sex relationships are presumed by many in the community not to exist. The support of a 'community' can be very important – particularly for people outside mainstream white society; most people need to feel acceptance by some group or other, and may tailor their behaviour to gain this acceptance.

28 women said their past community had no effect on their behaviour now. For 15 women, the effect of the community at large was restrictive; 11 women thought it made them conform. 10 women were conscious of protecting their familes (their own parents and/or children); a further 10 had little contact with them. 3 women still felt the need for their parents' approval.

Everyone is totally curtailed in their life-choices by the community in which they live. My whole maturation process has consisted of trying to 'tame' my sexual activities to protect myself, and to fit in. (7)

Conditioning creeps out after years of working on egalitarian attitudes; you constantly have to confront 'inbuilt' attitudes to determine their validity. (36)

It has a big effect subconsciously. I still mind very much what my parents think. I got very excited when my father asked me recently how the bisexual stuff was going; similarly I get devastated when my mother ignores it and looks upset about it. (123)

15 women felt the effects of their present community to be positive. They either had supportive relationships with their families, or had an actively-chosen and supportive community of friends.

I live far away from my family, but I'm still quite close to them. I worry about them and feel buoyed by their successes. My friends who have similar sexualities to mine make me feel more secure about my sexuality. (65)

My community is very political and supportive. I have never felt repressed for saying how I feel about my sexuality to people I know here: it's given me confidence and never a sense of shame. (61)

2 women described themselves as living in two different worlds; 2 others felt their small town/rural communities severely limited their options.

The community is important as I appear to live a split/polarised lifestyle, where for the majority of my life I have to live a lie and pretend to be straight, or else risk a brick through the window, risk getting beaten up or getting the sack. (33)

I live in a small town and feel very constricted by the community. I do feel self-conscious, and could not stay here if I was in a lesbian relationship. (38)

Negative reactions to their bisexuality from feminist and lesbian communities were mentioned by 4 women, who felt that their desire for acceptance within these communities had hindered their openness about their bisexuality.

I came out as a lesbian ten years ago, but to do the same as a bisexual seems much harder. I feel it will meet the disapproval of both the straight and gay parts of my world. (34)

Religious and spiritual practices of various sorts were important to 32 women. 5 were Church of England/Scotland, and 5 were matriarchal/pagan. 3 women each were practising Catholics, Jews and Quakers; 2 were Buddhists, one was a Baptist and one practised Transcendental Meditation. 6 women described their religion as, 'my own' – generally a mixture of spirituality, ecology, meditation and ethics. 3 others described a belief in Christianity, but a lack of faith in the organised Church. No women were currently practising Muslims or Hindus.

Most women who had a religious belief said either that it had a positive effect on their feelings about their sexuality, or no effect at all. Only 3 women found its effect negative. Indeed, unorthodox religion may be positively supportive of bisexuality:

The Goddess doesn't care what two consenting adults get up to in private. (6)

However, even within religions which don't explicitly outlaw same-sex activity, it is often perceived as an unimportant diversion, with heterosexuality still posited as the 'natural' option. This applies to Taoism, for instance. In other cases, there is a connection made between fertility and sex, or (as in some New Age treatises) a discourse in which male and female essences are seen as 'naturally' complementary.

It is easy to see, then, that the communities women had been or were part of directly and indirectly shaped their sexuality. Some people, sadly, felt that they had had to cut themselves off from their past cultures, communities and families in order to act as they wished; those women who lived at some distance from their parents often perceived this as liberating. All communities exact a price; equally, all individuals need to balance their desire for acceptance with their desire to be true to themselves.

Is sexuality a choice?

To judge by the responses to the question, 'Is sexuality a matter of choice, or were you born/made bisexual?', choice is a continuum. At one extreme, women felt that they had been swept away by passions over which they had no control; at the other, that they had consciously chosen their bisexuality. The majority of respondents fell at points along this line.

43 respondents saw their sexuality as a choice, though some added provisos. 12 women thought they were bisexual through a combination of choice, birth and external factors. A further 12 thought they had been born bisexual, but had chosen to act on it, and 2 thought external factors had 'made' them bisexual, but again that they had chosen to act on their feelings.

Socialisation is the biggest factor, but obviously how it works is very complex. I've made the choice to recognise that I find both men and women attractive; others choose not to recognise or to suppress the desire for anything outside the norm. In this sense it is a choice. (68)

Once you feel it's OK to fancy women as well as men, there is no impediment. (25)

I suppose I was brought up quite liberally to like all people, but it was my choice to enter a physical relationship with a woman – although after that I felt a lot happier about my sexuality and couldn't understand why I'd repressed it for so long. (27)

Others definitely recognised an element of choice, but were not clear about how this had operated. 24 women thought it was difficult to say, or that they simply did not know why they were bisexual.

It's a choice, in that I 'chose' *not* to repress the sexual attraction I felt for women; but I don't know where that comes from. Why did I get crushes on female movie stars at about the age of thirteen? (56)

To express/explore my sexuality is definitely a choice, but I did not *consciously* choose to be bisexual. (98)

I suppose it's a choice, but it took me a long time to be happy with myself. (26)

It isn't exactly a choice – I never *chose* to be attracted to women or to men. But I think if I hadn't (for reasons not too clear to me) chosen to confound my lesbian and gay friends and start a relationship with a man, I might not have changed from being a lesbian. I think I could perhaps have suppressed that part of me, if I didn't have some little part of me that likes to be a bit of a rebel. Ditto at school, maybe I could have chosen to conform to heterosexuality? I don't know. (1)

Other women felt that choice was not involved: 27 respondents considered themselves to have been born bisexual; 14 that external factors had 'made' them bisexual. 3 women said that though they did not know why they were bisexual, their sexuality was not a choice.

My sexuality is not really a choice. Having 'discovered' women I could not give that up, yet I am still attracted to men. I developed into a bisexual over the first twenty or so years of my life. (2)

I suppose that considering that I've often wanted not to want men, and have not managed so far, I must have been born bisexual. (127)

I think I'd say that I was born/made bisexual because there were times when I wished I was something else but I knew I wasn't. (126)

If I could have chosen, I would have chosen heterosexuality. Life would have been so much easier. (48)

15 women thought that everyone was bisexual:

I believe we are *all* born with the capacity to be bisexual and choose one end of the spectrum, i.e. heterosexuality or homosexuality because in many ways that choice is 'easier'. To allow full rein to bisexuality is very difficult. (17)

I think most people are made heterosexual/homosexual, but born bisexual. (114)

Whatever the degree of choice over our latent sexuality, choice does come into play in the areas of identity and action. Bisexuals are supposed to be able to choose which side of their sexuality to express, although for many bisexuals, to express both sides *is* their sexuality. Bisexual women may feel under pressure to choose; conversely, if they do choose, they may feel guilty about the choice they have made. Heterosexuals believe bisexuals should behave as heterosexual, lesbians that they should behave as lesbian. This amounts to sexual repression: ignore part of your sexuality to fit in (wherever it is). Women in long-term relationships may feel happy to describe themselves as lesbian or heterosexual, despite an underlying knowledge that such a description is not the whole truth. This is quite different from feeling compelled by other people to identify as something you are not.

Several respondents saw loving women *and* men as the way forward to a new kind of society. Others felt very aware of their attraction to people of both sexes, but chose not to act on certain options. This sounds a lot easier in theory than it is in practice, though obviously the decision not to act on sexual feelings is taken in certain situations by people of all sexualities, especially those in monogamous relationships. Yet for bisexuals, it is as likely to be social pressure as loyalty to a partner that leads to a rejection of possibilities.

My own opinion is that we are born with the capacity to love people of both sexes, but that this capacity is modified by personal and social/political circumstances. Factors from our past clearly affect us subconsciously in powerful ways, yet we can often come to terms with these and so achieve some measure of real choice in our lives, in particular around action: choosing, for whatever reason, to act or not on our feelings, despite the limitations imposed by society. I reject the idea that bisexuals ought to try to be heterosexual; nor do I believe that everyone is really – here and now – bisexual. I also reject the idea that women should be lesbian for the sake of the advancement of feminism: feminism exists for women, not the reverse, and in any case I don't believe it works. Sexual repression is one of the more pernicious aspects of organised religion, in which we are taught we must restrict our sexual behaviour to marriage. The 'shoulds' of some kinds of lesbian-feminism often seem uncomfortably connected.

Coming out

'Coming out' – disclosing your sexuality – means different things to different people. For some, being 'out' means not lying when discussing one's sexual past or present. For others, it means prefixing sentences with 'as a bisexual woman...'. It may mean identification with an open bisexual community, or simply being openly yourself in different, sometimes hostile, surroundings. But for everyone, the first step is to admit bisexual feelings to yourself.

Bisexuals have often been accused of being open only about their heterosexual side; bisexuals who run their lives in this way are as much 'in the closet' as lesbians who are not known as such, and suffer to the same degree if only the most acceptable part of their sexuality is acknowledged and validated. Bisexuals may need to declare their sexual orientation more often and more insistently than heterosexuals or lesbians, as all but longstanding friends will assume their sexual preference to be that of their current relationship. A bisexual woman with a male partner will have to insist very loudly that she is bisexual, not heterosexual; a woman with a female partner will be assumed to be lesbian. Women who are currently celibate may have the easiest time convincing people that they are in fact bisexual.

Coming out is risky, but there are important reasons for doing it. First, secrecy about key areas of one's life create a distance from other people, preventing potentially enriching experiences. Second, while some people argue that their sexuality is their own business, society thinks differently, and it is important politically to challenge the attitude that people are heterosexual until proved otherwise. It is not realistic, however, to believe that everyone can be out in all circumstances. The risks are enormous, ranging from mild distaste and ridicule, to violence, loss of children, job and so on. Some people of colour have also argued that the emphasis on coming out which permeates the white western lesbian and gay communities is inappropriate for them, as it is more important to them not to jeopardise their positions within their communities of origin.[3]

Coming out as bisexual (as opposed to lesbian) has additional complications because public knowledge of bisexuality is limited.

The bisexual community is far smaller and less influential than the lesbian and gay communities, making it more difficult to counteract negative myths and stereotypes. A woman who has previously identified as lesbian is likely to be wrongly perceived as on her way back to heterosexuality; a woman in a same-sex relationship as a lesbian who can't yet admit it.

24 respondents considered themselves absolutely out, 22 as somewhat out, and 58 as not out. 20 of the 24 who described themselves as out 'in general' had identified as bisexual for over three years; 5 were students and 3 gave their main occupation as mother of young children. 5 of the 24 said they played an active part in the bisexual community; however, as other respondents were also bisexual activists, activism did not necessarily mean respondents were out in areas outside this community, particularly at work.

Respondents had disclosed their sexuality more freely to friends than to anyone else in their lives: 30 women were out to all their friends, 100 to some, and only 6 to none.

The friends that I am out to are either bisexual or gay or know other bisexuals or gays. My brother found out when he woke me up in the morning and found another woman in my bed – but I was only just finding out myself. We talked about it. (127)

I am out as bisexual to all my bisexual friends, but not to others, as it's not important to me that they know. I don't want people knowing everything about me, so I'm only going to tell people to whom the knowledge is directly relevant. (20)

I think it's very important to be out as much as possible, both politically and to make my own life easier. (99)

Many women had chosen to tell only those people they were sure would be supportive. Several respondents said they found it easier to tell men that they were bisexual than women, as heterosexual women could appear threatened by the idea that the bisexual might want the relationship to become sexual, while lesbians reacted in a patronising or hostile way.

From some gay friends, vaguely patronising – I'm half way on to the true path. From straight women friends, very relaxed. (132)

One female friend, who had also been attracted to women in the past and is now married, was great. I tried to talk to another, which was useless and was met by not much more than 'I don't know what to say'. (136)

Reactions to my hesitant admission of bisexuality vary. Gay men appear keen for me to come out 'properly' and refer to me as a lesbian. My lesbian friends seem to regard me as an imposter if I show more than a passing interest in their politics and lifestyle, while at the same time trying to convince me that I am really a lesbian. But in fairness, lesbians and gay men project the most positive reactions to my sexuality, and it is my heterosexual friends who have the most disturbing attitudes. Heterosexual men regard me as someone with a particularly unusual and exotic sexuality who is all the same available to them. Very few of my straight female friends are aware of my attraction towards women as I've found them extremely narrow-minded in the past. It is instantly assumed that I want them as lovers (sometimes they are right!) and thus the friendship is distorted. (94)

The reaction has been very mixed: some people have said, 'isn't everybody?'; some people have looked horrified (a gay friend told me how politically wrong it is to be bisexual as it is colluding with a heterosexist society!). Others have just accepted it as part of me. (133)

Assumption that I'm promiscuous; change the subject quick; off-hand 'so what?'; 'you must know everything there is to know about sex'; from lesbians: 'do you think you take energy from women and give it to men?'. (123)

Some women were out as lesbian, and then faced another sort of coming out which they considered in some cases even more difficult.

I am not generally known as bisexual, and I have only voiced this new identity to my lover and a close girlfriend. (34)

I had the whole range of reactions, because I came out everywhere as a lesbian and then realised I was really bisexual – so disbelief, anger, acceptance, support, rudeness. (139)

Reactions from lesbian friends have varied from mild disappointment and a philosophical kind of attitude to outright hostility. None of them wants so much to do with me now. Straight friends have been generally supportive, but one or two of them have said they're glad I'm with a man now, and express anti-lesbian sentiments they never admitted to before. If I let them get away with that, it would feel like betraying the relationships that have been most important to me. That's also why I can't tell my family I'm seeing a man now: they'd be so pleased. (7)

Bisexual women going into lesbian social or political situations often feel they have to come out as 'lesbians plus'.

I feel sad and cowardly because I don't dare mention that I'm bisexual to most lesbians: they assume that I'm totally lesbian too. Maybe it will be different when I'm more established in this new identity. (16)

I always felt a fraud when I spent a lot of time with lesbians: perhaps if I'd had a big 'B' stamped on my forehead I would have felt more comfortable, and not as though I was unintentionally deceiving people. (85)

Far fewer respondents were out in work situations or at college, etc, than to friends: 22 women were out to everyone at work, 26 to some colleagues, 65 to none. I did not ask respondents what they did for a living: however, 4 women out at work were self-employed (3 mentioning they had 'artistic' occupations); 6 were students, teachers, or otherwise connected with education; 2 had jobs on the gay 'scene'.

I am out at work but I'm in a very small, right-on office, with only three other women, all feminists. If I worked in a more conventional place, I probably wouldn't be out. (16)

At work I am only out to my boss – an individual I trust 100 per cent. (17)

Reactions to respondents' declarations of their bisexuality varied considerably: 58 reported good reactions to their coming out; 27 mixed-to-good; 37 mixed reactions; 10 mixed-to-bad; 7 bad reactions. Although these replies look encouraging, many of the 58 women who reported good reactions said they had only told people they thought would react in a positive way.

I've had a supportive reaction, but then I've chosen my friends carefully. (140)

Fine so far, but I've done a lot of testing the water and avoided telling people whose reaction I'm not sure of. (119)

Many of the 'bad' reactions were from people who women had told because they were close (for example, families of origin), but whose politics were far from their own. Only 10 women were out

to all members of their family of origin, 65 to some, 40 to none.
Even women who considered themselves out 'in general' had often
not told all their family members.

Part of my family, including my mother, has rejected me. (138)

Indifference, shunned, I've been physically assaulted because of it.
Isolated from both straight and gay communities because neither accepts
my choice and feelings. (129)

I have drastically curtailed the way I used to let everyone know I was
bisexual, because a lot of men think this means I am completely 'available'
and I have been unpleasantly harassed in the past. (37)

Different stages in one's life and different living situations
clearly demand different approaches to coming out. For example,
it may not be appropriate for a woman in a state of tentative explo-
ration to declare her sexuality too loudly or confidently. 3 of the
6 respondents who were not out to any friends were in this state
of self-questioning; another woman was living with her male
partner (who did know) and children in a small town and did not
want other lovers at present. The remaining 2 were both in their
fifties: one was married (and had a female lover who knew of her
sexuality), the other was divorced, but spent most of her time with
lesbians.

Declaring your bisexuality can spark off deep fears and hos-
tilities in people, which you and they may be unaware of until
it happens. Finding out how people are likely to react, and being
prepared for it – knowing when, after all, it may be best to stay
silent – are strategies learned over time by each individual. At
present there are so few out bisexuals that anyone describing herself
as such is liable to be perceived as 'the' bisexual – a tiresome but
understandable reaction if you are the only out bisexual people
have met.

Coming out is a lifelong process; being out when a student, for
instance, may be a lot easier than in many jobs. And the first time
is always the worst: at least once you have told your mother you
never have to do that again! Knowing that you are not alone can
give you strength, and as awareness of a bisexual community grows,
whether or not individuals are personally involved with it, coming
out will surely become easier.

My own strategy is to be out wherever possible, though not necessarily immediately on meeting someone new. While it may be
easy to be out to one's partner, or to some of one's family, or in

a particular job situation, bigoted and ignorant acquaintances also need to have their opinions challenged. Presuming acceptance and support (except where it is totally unlikely) makes other people more positive towards bisexuality. And the more bisexuals they know, the more likely they are to feel this way. It may even make them reconsider their own sexuality!

Celibacy

I prefer to live and be on my own. I like sex, but don't make much effort to initiate sexual relationships because I think there are more important things. I prefer being on my own in my own bed. I don't regret this attitude – neither do I envy or despise friends who have regular sexual relationships. (45)

Because the image of bisexuality has often been connected with excesses of sexual activity, the idea that many bisexuals have long periods of celibacy may be unexpected. 35 women in this study (25 per cent) were celibate by their own definition at the time of writing, a higher average than that of a recent UK government survey, according to which only 14 per cent of women of child-bearing age are not having heterosexual intercourse (this figure obviously includes lesbians, and therefore is not an accurate guide to whether or not women are sexually involved).[4] Respondents' definitions of celibacy varied: for some, it meant the absence of sexual activity, whether within a relationship or not. For others, it simply meant the absence of a primary sexual relationship. Some women mentioned that they were celibate with women, but not with men, or vice versa.

I was celibate for about five years during my mid-twenties because I wasn't sure of my sexuality. I hadn't yet had any relationships with women, but several bad encounters with men. (48)

For the past three years I have been sexually active with my husband and celibate with women. The latter is a pity. (15)

Feminists have been anxious to show that celibacy is a valid choice. Being seen and seeing yourself as a sexual person, regardless of whether or not you have a current partner, is an important step to sexual autonomy. But celibacy is not always a choice for women, and many respondents said that their celibacy was not something they were always happy with. The feelings of the 35 respondents who were currently celibate ranged from desperation to anxiety, satisfaction and happiness, with some women feeling ambivalent.

I have been celibate because of fear of sex with men; lack of self-knowledge as to lesbian feelings; always picking the unobtainable (on purpose?); being a loner. (120)

Celibacy due to choice: I needed all the time to myself. Celibacy not due to choice: I can't/couldn't find the partners I want/ed. (109)

I'm not entirely sure why I'm celibate – but it's got something to do with sexuality and confusion. Also having been very hurt by a woman. (138)

I was aware that I could only be creative in other fields, or give my work my full attention and energy, if I wasn't in love. (115)

A further 62 women had had what they described as 'extensive' periods of celibacy at some point in their pasts (the terms used were deliberately left open to subjective interpretation: the definition of both 'celibacy' and 'extensive' can vary dramatically from person to person).

For me it was part of thinking about/deciding on my sexuality. (91)

I needed a long time on my own to find out who I was and what I wanted. I haven't got there yet, but I feel a lot better about myself. (85)

Respondents gave many reasons, both positive and negative, for past and present celibacy. Most common was lack of opportunity, or of mutual attraction, which were mentioned as factors by 21 women. Feelings of shyness and insecurity were mentioned by 9 women, as was a positive desire not to have sexual contact with anyone. The ending of a relationship, a desire to concentrate on other things, and a feeling that sex was something to be shared only with a special partner were each given as reasons by 8 women. A further 7 felt a lot of unhappiness and confusion, both in general and about their sexuality. Other reasons given included parental repression, illness, fear of pregnancy and sexually-transmitted diseases, ambivalence about men, independence, work, and a desire to avoid intimacy.

I am not promiscuous and do not fall in love very often. (79)

I'm too shy and quiet. (80)

I take no for an answer and don't keep trying! (60)

Sex doesn't seem that important. (78)

I have been celibate for so long due to lack of contacts, lack of opportunity, dislike of the lesbian 'scene'. I want to form a relationship with another woman because I know and like her, not just because we are both women. Women who have fallen into this category have either clearly found relationships between women distasteful, or I haven't been able to find out how they felt and was scared to lose them as friends. I have had relationships with men who seemed to be able to relate to me on an equal basis; I quickly found out they couldn't and ended the relationship. (69)

There are other things I want to do at the moment, which seeking out and having a relationship would hinder. (111)

Some women who had *not* experienced long periods of celibacy also felt the need to explain why this was the case. Reasons given included a need to be touched, a hatred of being alone, and the capacity to fall in love quickly. Some of these women saw a possible period of celibacy in the future as a positive prospect.

I need to feel in love, to have someone to cuddle with. I wish I didn't. (122)

Touching people is desperately important to me, and in the past I've gone to great lengths to find people to touch. Sex usually comes with the package. (14)

While many of the reasons given for being celibate or not could apply to women of all sexualities, there are factors specific to bisexual women. For example, the decision to have a relationship with a man can mean giving up one's place, however tentative, within the lesbian community; the decision to have a lesbian relationship can mean alienating heterosexual friends and family. Weighing up the advantages and disadvantages of being involved with a person of one gender rather than the other can lead to total inaction. Yet ironically, it may well be easiest for other people to believe that a bisexual woman is indeed bisexual when she has no partner by whom her sexual identity can be defined.

Group sex and swinging

Sex between a group of people (usually one man and two women) is for many non-bisexuals, *the* image of bisexuality. Sexual activity without emotional commitment is supposedly what bisexuality is all about, which is perhaps why the subject has been almost taboo among bisexuals in the UK, particularly those with some political consciousness; at the time of writing, this is just starting to change. Things are different in the US, as I will discuss later.

60 questionnaire respondents (about 42 per cent) had had sex with more than one person at a time at least once. Of the 77 who had not, 8 were strongly interested in the possibility. 23 of the 60 women had had only one experience; 24 had had between one and four; 7 more than four, but not regularly; and 5 'many' such experiences, usually with the same group of people. 19 women had had sex in various combinations of people; 18 in a combination of another woman and a man; 2 just with women; 4 just with mixed-gender groups of more than three people.

I have done it three times, with three different lots of people – all a mixture of men and women. I was excited and turned on and it was amusing at times! I was amazed to see how excited men get when they see women fondling each other. (62)

I have not had sex with more than one person, but I would like to do it with two men sometime if I found two I liked who were into it. (25)

I wanted to explore all possibilities, and I feel happy that it happened. I think it is good to have an open mind about sex. (90)

I haven't done it but I'd like to; or better, my boyfriend and I would like to. (105)

Feelings about the experience(s) were predominantly good for 25 women, predominantly bad for 14, OK for 11, and mixed, depending on the experience, for 8 women. For some respondents, having 'both sides' of their sexual personality expressed at once was a thrilling experience; other bisexuals find the idea repellent and emotionally 'unsafe'.

Many times, I have had sex with a woman and a man together. It is as if the two sides of my personality have been brought together. Physically, I find the whole thing very exciting. (40)

It happened twice: the first time, two men and me; the second, two men, one woman and me. The first time it felt deliciously immoral. I could cope with this development in the relationship with my boyfriend, but I worried that he couldn't. I was right. The second time, when I realised the situation I was getting into, I refused to take part. I felt it was a set-up for the other woman and myself to put on a show to thrill the men. (107)

I found it difficult, uneasy. I was worried about leaving someone out or being left out. (123)

These quotations highlight many of the potential difficulties and pleasures of group sex. Although it is assumed to be an experience without love, many deep and often highly confusing emotions may be evoked, making it emotionally (as well as practically) tricky. It is difficult to give sexual attention to more than one person at a time, so in the case of a couple inviting another person to their bed, partners may find it painful to feel neglected, however momentarily, in favour of someone else. This type of threesome is also potentially exploitative for the third person, as the couple maintains its bond, re-forms, and can discuss the experience afterwards, whereas the third person is expendable.

This third person is usually imagined to be a second woman invited by a man to have sex with him and his female partner. The survey disproved the predominance of the stereotype: other men were invited to join heterosexual couples, female couples invited others (both female and male) to have sex with them, and groups of friends found that it 'just happened'. For 17 women, there was no one initiator; in 15 cases, the respondent was the initiator; in 11 cases, it was the man (or one of the men) involved; for 10 women, it was a variety of initiators over a variety of occasions; in 6 cases, it was the other woman (or one of the other women). On the whole, questionnaire respondents had initiated sex more often than men in these situations.

With a man, a woman and me, the man thought he was initiating it, but the woman and I were doing what we wanted/had decided. It was wonderful! (10)

Both times I've done it, I was the main initiator – although my boyfriend was also willing. I really enjoyed it both times, but I'm not sure if I'd have the guts to do it again. (72)

As Susie Bright points out in *Susie Sexpert's Lesbian Sex World*[5] many lesbians (and bisexual women) have their first sexual experience with another woman as part of a male/female/female threesome. They may not have realised that sex with a woman was what they wanted or dared to do it without the protective (in societal terms) presence of a man.

For me, it was only once: myself, my best woman friend and her boyfriend. At the time I found it very exciting; I was very interested in her, and for me the boyfriend was peripheral. That episode confirmed for me the desirability of women lovers, and so has great significance. (115)

In the 1970s I was a teenager, and I desperately wanted to have sex with a woman. I didn't have a clue how to meet anyone I could have a relationship with, so I answered an ad in *Time Out*. I thought it would be just from a woman, but it was actually a couple. I wasn't quite sure what to do about this, but I went round to have dinner with them and we ended up having sex. The experience was a good one really, although I didn't want to repeat it, but it lessened my desperation for a while! (99)

Although none of the respondents said they had taken part in organised sex parties, it is worth mentioning 'swinging' here, as it has been so closely connected with bisexuality in the popular imagination. Indeed, one Californian bisexual activist calls swingers 'the drag queens of bisexuality';[6] certainly they are the most obvious recipients of the flack directed at all bisexuals. Swinging is an organised subculture, in which groups of people (individuals or couples) get together to have sex. There are several ways they can do this: for instance, there is the (possibly apocryphal) story of a group of men who throw their car keys into a heap and the women go home with the owner of the keys they pick up. Alternatively, there are sex parties at which individuals may join sexual scenarios involving one or more people they don't know.

'Wife-swapping' and swinging were much talked about as part of the sexual-liberation movement of the 1960s. As the term 'wife-swapping' implies, it seems to have been men who were instrumental in initiating and organising this. However, it was also thought by both men and women that for women actively to pursue sexual pleasure was liberating, and the label of 'wife-swapping' rather than 'partner exchange' may simply reflect the assumptions of the gutter press. According to the *Records of the San Francisco*

Sexual Freedom League,[7] a swingers group operating in the 1960s, bisexuality was seen as just another diversion in the more-is-better stakes. Same-sex sex took place almost solely between women; men did not admit to bisexuality in public. This replicates the scenarios of mainstream pornography (aimed at men), where touching between men is taboo, yet women are often posed together. According to a later book,[8] women who 'swung' were usually over thirty-five, married, and had been initiated into it by their husbands. But having started, women were usually keener on the idea than men.

From its beginnings in the 1950s, and, predominantly, the 1960s in the US, swinging has travelled to many other countries, though there is less evidence of organised sex parties in the UK than in much of the US, where swingers clubs, which are often advertised in 'adult' papers, are a feature of most major cities. This is true even post-AIDS: swinging has simply absorbed safer-sex practices. (*The Sex Maniac's Bible,* written and published in the UK, tells the reader which sex clubs worldwide insist on safer sex, and how to get your partner to practise it in many different languages.) Contact magazines, some specifically for bisexuals, are also readily available in the US. *Bi-Lifestyles* from New York, for instance, contains nude photographs of many different types of people wanting different kinds of sex in every possible combination, including single women who specifically state they want no money and female couples seeking men for sex only. These magazines also exist in the UK, but are less widely available because of stricter pornography laws, though contacts' sections of publications like London's *Loot* contain advertisements from bisexual women seeking others for sex.

As with group sex, swinging contains the potential for exploitation – Thomas Geller, in *Bisexuality: A Reader and Sourcebook,*[9] refuses to include information on sex and swing clubs, which he believes to be predominantly coercive. Many women may wonder about swinging in fantasy, but would be wary of acting out of fear of not being able to set their own limits. Yet while some women are possibly coerced by their male partners to take part in sexual activities they dislike, others do seek out such experiences for themselves. For single women who do not want a relationship, but do want sex, swinging may be a relatively simple way to get it.

The necessity to counteract the sexual puritanism which has overtaken much of the public agenda since AIDS has led, in the

US, to the development of a celebratory form of swinging that incorporates sexual politics, safer sex and sex education. Loosely connected to queer and bisexual activist culture, the new sex parties aim to teach people that responsible sex is safe, desirable and exciting. For instance, Mother Goose Productions in San Francisco hosts Jack and Jill-Off parties (basically safer-sex orgies) for lesbian, gay, bisexual and heterosexual participants. The rules are strict: safe sex only, nothing without asking, no penetration. No physical contact at all is allowed without explicit verbal permission: no categorically means no, and breaching this leads to permanent ejection. A guest has to be introduced by a member, and may then become a member after a period of sustained good behaviour.

These are the only sex parties of which I have heard personal reports – and they were enthusiastic!

AIDS

No book on sexuality written in the 1990s would be complete without a discussion of the impact of HIV and AIDS. Even after ten years of the epidemic, AIDS is still widely perceived as a problem which affects only 'abnormal', high-risk groups, in particular gay men and IV drug users. Within this scenario, the bisexual male, often referred to simply as 'the bisexual', is portrayed as the shadowy figure who 'spreads' the virus to 'ordinary people'.

This perception has been promoted through the gutter press, as well as through newspapers and magazines which might have been expected to know better. The Sunday tabloid *News of the World*, for instance, infiltrated a conference for bisexual activists, and then reported that students were 'flaunting their bisexuality in a murky and dangerous world', spreading HIV from gay men to the general population.[10] But even so-called 'quality' or liberal newspapers such as the *Guardian* have confused the issue: the news item headlined 'HIV bisexual jailed for sex with girl, 13'[11] confused serious questions about sexual abuse, consent and safer sex with the worst kind of tabloid sensationalism.

Women's magazines have used scare tactics which seem almost designed to foster biphobia. For instance, the cover of the June 1990 issue of *Cosmopolitan* read: 'Bisexuality: One Man's Defence of Dangerous Sex'. Yet the article inside was not a description of random, unsafe sex with many partners, but the story of a love affair between two men in the 1950s.[12] The magazine continued the theme in its December 1990 issue, in which women were told they should beware of their boyfriends having casual sex with other men, as almost all men do this at some point in their lives. The hyping of the subject seems almost set up to reinforce fear of bisexual men.

It is acknowledged even by official bodies that AIDS was in part responsible for the rise in homophobia in the mid- to late 1980s. Increased homophobia and the perceived link between AIDS and homosexuality have affected lesbians too: in the mid-1980s, when gay men were believed by much of the public to be the only group at risk from AIDS, lesbians were seen by many as being at risk to almost the same degree.[13] Even today, popular articles on AIDS do not always specify the gender of the gays or bisexuals quoted. Homophobes do not care who does what with whom, rather they rely on bigotry and scapegoats, for which anyone perceived as 'different' will do. For instance, there is public sympathy for a woman whose (secretly) bisexual male partner gives her HIV; probably this would be considerably mooted if an acknowledged bisexual man gave it to an acknowledged bisexual woman.

In many parts of the world, AIDS is a heterosexual disease, and is very widespread. 18 per cent of women attending an ante-natal clinic in Malawi were found to be HIV positive; at a clinic in Abidjan in the Ivory Coast, the figure was 6 per cent; in Africa generally, 80 per cent of AIDS cases are estimated to have arisen from heterosexual transmission.[14] In the UK, 533 people contracted AIDS from heterosexual sex between 1982 and 1992 and 2,007 women have tested HIV positive.[15] These figures are small compared to the prevalence of HIV among men who have sex with men, but heterosexual transmission rates are increasing. Yet despite the fact that many UK health-education campaigns have been directed at heterosexuals, the small-scale surveys which have been done[16] indicate that unlike gay and bisexual men, heterosexuals have not altered their sexual behaviour and tend not to consider themselves at risk. So though it seems that the scare figures of the 1980s (when a 1985 report estimated that one in five people in the UK would be HIV positive by 1990)[17] have proved to have been wildly exaggerated, the message that unprotected penis/vagina sex is unsafe must still be reinforced. Contracting HIV, as we should all know by now, has more to do with risk *behaviour* than with sexual identity.

Probably because of the perceived risk of HIV transmission from gay men to heterosexuals, bisexual men have been targeted in several officially-funded campaigns. The World Health Organisation has investigated men who behave bisexually in countries around the world, and in the UK the Middlesex Hospital's 'Personal History, Health and Lifestyle' project looked at the sexual behaviour of men who have had sex with men and women in relation to safer-sex practices. But the desire of gay activists to fight the idea that AIDS is a gay disease, together with establishment fears that the virus will be transmitted to and among heterosexuals, has, some gay men now believe, marginalised the issues they face and the funds available to them, when in fact gay men in the UK are more likely to be HIV positive than any other group (68 per cent of all cases up to May 1992; 12 per cent of cases were bisexual men).[18]

Women are now becoming HIV positive at a much faster rate than men,[19] and it seems that women are more likely to become HIV positive from infected men than the other way round. AIDS is the single highest killer of women between the ages of twenty-five and thirty-five in some areas of the US, yet no large-scale research on women and HIV has been carried out. Ensuring safer heterosexual sex (using a condom; no penetration, etc) is not always easy for women: to many people, heterosexual sex is synonymous with vaginal-penis penetration, and to suggest alternatives threatens many men. Advertising campaigns which equate condom use (or non-penetrative sex) with virility may possibly have some effect on men who otherwise falsely consider they have no motive to change. For women to be open with their male partners about desiring sex at all, let alone to discuss the possible risks of HIV transmission, is to challenge traditional assumptions about female sexuality.

There has been much discussion and dissemination of information about safer sex by and for lesbians and there are many debates within the bisexual, lesbian and AIDS-activist communities about the safety, or lack of it, of sex between women.[20] Some women believe that all forms of lesbian sex are safe; others that transmission of HIV is possible through oral sex or sharing sex toys; yet others, that no one knows what the risks may be. No research has been done on woman-to-woman transmission, and the few reported cases remain contentious. But there are lesbians who are HIV positive, whether through sex with men or IV drug use.

Bisexual women have been accused by some lesbians of bringing HIV into the 'lesbian community'. This is clearly biphobia at work: many lesbians have had sex with men at some time in their past, or have been IV drug users; HIV can take a long time to develop into AIDS, and sex with an infected man may have happened years before a woman identified as lesbian. Blaming people – any people – for becoming HIV positive is simply inappropriate. If HIV were not transmitted sexually, blame would be out of the question.

Of course, it is essential for all women to practise safer sex if they have any doubt about their own HIV status or that of their partner, and many women in this survey spontaneously (I had asked no specific AIDS-related questions) said they had modified their sexual behaviour because of AIDS. But just because it is no longer responsible to have unconsidered, unsafe sex does not mean the renouncing of all sexual experimentation. Sexual experimentation, with care and respect for partners, can be a good thing, and may well be a better option now than twenty years ago, when the pressure to appear 'sexually liberated' made it seem almost compulsory rather than a choice for many young women. There is a danger of allowing ourselves to be persuaded by moralists that AIDS should mean the end of pre- or extra-marital sex, and that only heterosexual monogamy (one partner in a lifetime) should be practised: fine if that's what you want; not so good if it's the only alternative. The lifetime-monogamy idea is simply a return to the values of the past, which were *not* beneficial to women, and were positively damaging to all kinds of people whose sexuality did not fit into the prescribed mould. Supporters of such ideas usually espouse the 'AIDS is the Wrath of God' view, demonising gay male sex and ignoring lesbian sex altogether. Of course, unprotected sex carries risks, but that is a reason to change sexual practice, not to abandon it.

Our aim should surely be an increase of choice, not a narrowing of it. More open discussions about sex and sexual activities in the public arena mean that many different practices and identities are now on the agenda, including male gay sex, bisexuality and lesbian sex. That everyone must now talk to their sexual partners about what they have done and what they want greatly increases the potential for intimacy – and for satisfying sex.

Notes

1. Charlotte Wolff, *Bisexuality: A Study*, Quartet, 1977
2. See, for instance, Beverley Bryan, Stella Dadzie, Suzanne Scafe, *The Heart of the Race: Black Women's Lives in Britain*, Virago, 1985

3. Carmen, Gail, Neena, Tamara, *Becoming Visible: Black Lesbian Discussions* in Feminist Review (ed), *Sexuality: a Reader,* Virago, 1987

4. OPCS monitor, *General Household Survey,* 1989 (women who gave 'no partner' as their reason for not needing contraception)

5. Susie Bright, *Susie Sexpert's Lesbian Sex World,* Cleis Press, San Francisco, 1990

6. Lani Kaahumanu, *San Francisco Examiner,* 22 June 1990

7. Jefferson F. Poland & Valerie Alison, *Records of the San Francisco Sexual Freedom League,* The Olympia Press, 1971

8. Lloyd Lewin, 'Women in Swinging' in Martha Kirkpatrick (ed), *Women's Sexual Experience,* Plenum Press, 1982

9. Thomas Geller (ed), *Bisexuality: A Reader and Sourcebook,* Times Change Press, 1990

10. *News of the World,* 29 March 1992. This article was part of a series which looked at the growth of the bisexual community (sic) – swinging and so on – in the UK

11. *Guardian,* 2 May 1992

12. It referred to Colin Spencer's book *Which of Us Two?*

13. According to Social and Community Planning Research, *British Social Attitudes,* published in 1988, 87 per cent of the population surveyed thought gay men were greatly at risk from AIDS; 43 per cent thought lesbians to be greatly at risk too

14. According to the *Health Education Authority Report on HIV and AIDS,* symposium proceedings 1989

15. *Communicable Disease Report* vol 2, no 25, 19 June 1992

16. See, for instance, the survey in *Elle,* April 1992

17. Official reports giving much higher predictions of HIV prevalence than have occurred include the Cox Report, 1988 and the Day Report, 1989

18. Simon Watney, *Gay Times,* May 1992

19. According to the *Communicable Disease Report,* op cit, the number of AIDS cases resulting from sex between men and women increased by 49 per cent from June 1990 to May 1992; female cases were 51 per cent of this increase

20. See Sue O'Sullivan & Pratibha Parmar, *Lesbians Talk (Safer) Sex,* Scarlet Press, 1992

5 Seven women's stories

The average composite bisexual woman, according to the responses discussed in the previous chapter, would be a white woman aged between twenty-one and thirty who lives in Greater London and has a job, a degree and a middle-class background. However, although women who conform precisely to this description filled in the questionnaire, many bisexual women do not. Bisexuality does not presume a particular lifestyle, a common set of attitudes towards sexuality and relationships, or a common politics. And it is precisely to illustrate some of the differences between women who identify as bisexual that this chapter is included.

Previous writing about bisexuality (what little there is) has been criticised for being overly anecdotal, and of course anecdote alone is not enough. But bisexual women do need to know that we are not alone and to share our experiences with one another. Much lesbian publishing of the 1970s fulfilled this function; now bisexuals need to do the same. The sharing of personal histories is an important means to enable us to learn from and grow from each other.

Kristin

Kristin is a thirty-two-year-old black woman living in outer London. She is married and at the time of our interview was expecting her second child.

I'd describe myself as a professional working woman of the twentieth century. An individualist, which is to say I wouldn't work for Marks & Spencer.

I've always been bisexual. I think I've always been attracted to women more than to men, but mainly it's because I've always made a stand of being myself, with my own mind and ideas. I do not class myself as a lesbian because I have a lot of men friends and enjoy men's company. But in general, I don't find that men come up to the standards I would like for a human being. From being a child, I've thought boys always wanted to dominate and bully; they've always put their physical strength first and not their brains. I think that's how I look at men: they're more being macho-man than a person.

My first sexual experience with a woman was when I was four... Or to put it more accurately, my first sexual experience was with another child of four, my sister. I wasn't interested in boys until we did sex education at school – then we said 'Oh! So that's why we're all different', and went out to 'experiment', as they say. When I first had sexual intercourse I didn't like it – I thought: 'It's messy and it's quick and that's what it's all about'. It happened to me in a field and I was lying on an ants' nest, which didn't help.

In the late 1960s, early 1970s, when I was about sixteen, it was the in-thing to sleep with men at parties and so on. I suppose the group of people I went around with were the last of the intellectual hippies, and I think we really did have the last of the freedom. There was no AIDS, and it was the thing for parents to make sure their daughters were on the pill once they were fifteen or sixteen. So I did go through a time when I was playing the total heterosexual, though I think it was because most of my friends were doing the same thing. It was like a competition: three or four of us would like the same guy and would see who would be the first to lay him! Talking among my friends now, I find that women do not get total sexual satisfaction from men. Nowadays, I think most of my friends have leanings towards bisexuality, even if they aren't actually bisexual.

I've been married for nine years; a long time. My husband doesn't like my being bisexual, but just because you're married to someone doesn't mean you have to take up their ideas or their way of life. I married my husband because I loved him, nothing else. Not because I liked him, or wanted to be friends with him. I did love his stupid little ways, and his piggishness and I am prepared to put up with him, as he is prepared to put up with me. A lot of people think that when they get married, their own lives should come to a halt and they should take their partner's friends and so on. You come together in making a home, having a family, and I'm quite prepared to do some of the things which are expected of me, but I'm also going to hold on to me as a person with my own personality. It's not easy, but you've got to be determined to stand your ground, because you can go out with somebody today and two years later they're dead. You're still you and you've given up everything for that person, but you're left as just a hollow tube.

I also have a girlfriend and we have an open relationship. I'm not the sort of bisexual who's into foursomes, wife-swapping or whatever; I think that's a different sort of sexuality altogether. That side of things doesn't appeal to me and it wouldn't to my husband, either. When you look into a lot of these relationships, they're about the man having a licence to sleep with other women.

I am faithful to my husband because he is the only man I would want to sleep with (I think most men look funny with their clothes off, anyway). I would not be happy sleeping with another man because I think it would be committing adultery; sleeping with a woman is a different sort of thing altogether! I don't have the same feelings about women because I think a woman partner I might have is free to sleep with other women if she wants to, and so am I. But I wouldn't be happy with her sleeping around with different men.

Like most black bisexual women, my sexuality is a personal thing. Admitting it can be dangerous, and lead to rejection and harassment. A lot of black women I know are professional women who have girlfriends – they have a small circle of friends who sleep with one another, but nothing's ever said about it. They're just a group of women – with an added bonus!

I think a lot of black women who are gay tend to be very attractive to men, not stereotyped at all. I can go down the road and think: 'Aha! I spot you, darling!' It's also a way of hiding, because who would believe that gorgeous woman was sleeping with another woman? Men have a lot of power over career life, and if you do come out, there's a lot of jobs you can't get into. You're not acceptable. So you'll find a lot of women have disguised their sexuality and it's only by playing the same game yourself that you'll recognise the other women out there doing it too.

Any children I may have will have to work out their own sexuality, and if they get to an age of wondering what they are and they come to me, then I'll tell them about myself. If they decide they're heterosexual, then why should I tell them anything: I don't want to cause a family storm? My children will have their private lives, and as a parent, I have mine. Some of my family know about me – but only because I told them. I think they only find out if you come out as a political lesbian, not otherwise. As they say, the family is usually the last to know. I don't think people should be pressurised into telling if they don't want to – it's not everybody who can cope with coming out to the world.

Most of my friends know I'm bisexual. I do explain that a lot of ordinary women are; it could be the person you're working next to. I tell people when I want them to know; for them, it can be a relief that their friend whom they've known for years, have slept with in the same bed without being pounced on, is bisexual. And once you've explained that most people can be bisexual, whether they practise it or or not, most of them turn round and say: 'Well, I know what you mean'. So I take it that most of my friends are bisexual, whether they've come out or not. I find that once you've been able to sit down and talk to them, they are more free to turn round and talk about their problems, and there is an increased closeness. You do get the odd one who tries it on, and it's something you've got to be aware of.

I think it can be difficult for people to sort themselves out; trying to work out your sexuality is often not an easy thing to go through. I needed to know there were other bisexual people in the world, that I wasn't abnormal – which was how I felt at the time. I felt isolated, and although I'd always accepted myself to a certain extent, after a time you want to meet people who are the same as you.

And that's when the problems start. You've sorted yourself out, now who can you turn to for support, where are the people of like mind? That is one of the problems I find in this country: you always have to make a choice and state what you are. And when you just don't know, there's nowhere to go. I phoned up this, that and the other gay line, and I got the reaction: 'Well, we can't help you unless you're lesbian'. I was put in touch with two bisexual groups for men, but I didn't want to be a part of that. I wanted a group of bisexual women to talk to.

So you could have come together in your head years ago, but it's finding a group of women with like minds. You're not going to agree with everything everybody says and vice versa, but at least you know that there are women around who are bisexual, and they are the people next door, the person who works in the office next to you, the teacher: these women have got on with their lives and some have openly admitted they're bisexual outside the group, some haven't. And you can be strengthened, really.

There are a lot of questions that come to your mind that you'd like answered. I find that, if you're isolated, you have the tendency either to ignore your bisexuality and lock it away in the cupboard, or to turn around and say, 'I'm really a lesbian'. Either way, you're not being true to yourself, and a lot of times you're causing yourself a lot of emotional and psychological problems. I think that to have more women's bisexual groups, discussion groups, up and down the country, would bring a lot of women out and make them happier.

I know it sounds as if my bisexuality has been very easy and idealistic – but it hasn't. It was hard work for me to get to the state I am in now, and I had nights when I stayed awake and thought: 'You must be mad'. Then I had days when I thought: 'Right, I'm totally lesbian'. Another day, I'd say: 'Oh no, I'm not'. Being part of a group with women who are much older than you, you get to know that your bisexuality doesn't stop; you don't get to some magic number and stop being bisexual.

Rachel

Rachel is a thirty-nine-year-old white Jewish woman from an 'upwardly mobile' working-class background. She currently lives alone in London, but will soon be living with her male partner.

When I was eleven I went to a girls' school, and it must have been there that I learned about lesbians. In the kind of upbringing I had, it was never mentioned; it was never a possibility for a nice Jewish girl. People would talk about 'lezzies' and so on, and I remember being intrigued, but also relieved that there was nothing wrong with me! With boys, I was very scared; if I saw a boy I thought was attractive I could no more have acted on it than flown to the moon! The first memory I have of fancying someone is Cliff Richard. I'm not sure I felt sexually aroused by him, but it was very strong – I became a member of his fan club and used to go and scream at his concerts.

When I was about twelve or thirteen, a wonderful teacher came to the school to teach physics. She was a small, dumpy woman with short cropped hair and a very deep voice, and I used to long to see her and got very excited when she paid me attention. I wouldn't have admitted this to anybody, because I knew these were the signs... I remember when I first had the horrible sensation there might be something wrong with me: spending hours in the bath, maybe for the first time consciously feeling sexually turned on and thinking about her and thinking, 'Oh my God', and deciding that I couldn't be the way I was or look the way I was and still think like that. I'm sure things aren't that wonderful for young lesbians and gays now, but it just wasn't possible, coming from my family and living the life I did.

This continued through my teens. I used to get ribbed a lot at school because I never went out with boys. It wasn't that I wasn't attractive, but boys didn't come near me, I think because I was so icy. Also, although I would have loved the fact of having a boyfriend more than anything, I wasn't particularly interested in individuals. It was a time of great confusion.

When I was eighteen I went to university, where it was mainly men because I did a technological degree. I completely panicked at being surrounded by so many men; my thinking went completely and I'm only just getting over it. At the time, I thought I didn't like women and I didn't like men either, and I didn't know what that made me. I knew I wasn't a man, but I didn't feel like a woman, although I looked very feminine and used to wear lots of make-up and wigs.

One weekend I went on an encounter group given by a visiting American professor. I was completely attacked, mainly by people saying what a nice, middle-class Jewish Princess I was, and how privileged I was. That night, three men came back to my room and started to say, 'There's something really funny about you, you don't like men, do you?' I felt completely panicked because they were saying there was something wrong with me sexually and that they were going to bring it up tomorrow in the group. When they left, I thought for the first time that I was cracking up about this thing of men and women and sex. I remember shaking all night so badly that the bed was banging against the wall. They never did bring it up, but after that I knew I had to get help.

The message was that there was something wrong with me. My tutor told me about a psychotherapy place and I went along and had interviews with the psychiatrist. I ended up in three years' group therapy, labelled as the frigid woman. There was the woman whose husband cross-dressed, so she was a problem; there was a man who was impotent; there was a man who was a closet gay; and I was the frigid woman. They thought my problems were inter-personal, so I'd do better in a group. I feel so angry about it, although I know that not everyone's experience of therapy is like this. I was also very heavily dependent on valium.

I always knew that my feelings of going crazy were about sexual identity. Afterwards, when I had relationships with men, I'd start to crack up when they'd start to go wrong. So there's something very closely connected in my stability, feeling like a woman, and so on.

Over the past eight to ten years I've come to remember being sexually abused as a child. At times, when I haven't been able to understand what's been going on with my sexuality, it's been something to hold on to, because I think that a lot of why my sexual feelings are so distressed comes from that abuse. Unravelling what happened and remembering more and more gives me a framework. I was mistreated sexually from a very young age, and that was the beginning of my confusion about sexuality: who you could love and whether they were also the source of pain – a lot of confusion.

After about three years of therapy, I moved away from London and had my first sexual relationship as an adult (I didn't know then about the abuse). I chose the weediest man – the least threatening, should I say. And from then on (I think I always knew this would happen), once I started to be sexual, I couldn't stop. I ended up putting myself in situations where I got abused. Then I fell in love: he was married and when his wife had a baby and he didn't want me around any more, I just cracked. I couldn't cope, and I moved back in with my parents. I don't think I thought about women then; I just felt devastated.

I went back to university for my final year (I'd taken a year off) and went from being frigid to being a nymphomaniac, or whatever label was going. I remember men were pretty shocked – I think I was trying to sort something out, and they felt used. Every time it went wrong I remember thinking I wanted to try to meet women. The lesbian group Sappho must have started to meet (this was about eighteen years ago) and when we got really pissed off with men, a friend and I would say: 'Yes let's go, really just to look at the lesbians you know, nothing to do with us'. But in fact we never went.

Then I started a relationship with a man that lasted for eleven years. For the first nine, I was completely involved and didn't pay much attention to women's issues. I was totally unpoliticised. We lived in the Home Counties and I remember for some reason I decided to go to a women's group. I walked in with high heels and eyelashes, feeling very contemptuous of the women there and how they couldn't get men. Then I got a job doing research with

young women and I became politicised through that and began
to go to women's events. Towards the end of the relationship, when
things were difficult, I saw a woman and I remember thinking,
'If I were a lesbian I would really find her attractive!' I didn't think
about it much, but when things went badly with men, I would
think about women.

I left the relationship and moved to London. I was incredibly
lonely and it felt a ridiculous thing to have done in my thirties,
to have given up that relationship. I went to a women's counselling workshop, and one night we had a party. I think I'd been
counselled very well about sexual abuse and my feelings about
myself. There were loads and loads of women dancing together
and I thought it was all a bit strained, but then a slow dance came
on and a woman said, 'Come and dance'. She put her arms round
me and when I felt her body, there was a complete lack of
antagonism in every bit of her body, and I felt 'Ohhhhhhh!' It
wasn't that I found her sexually attractive – I thought at the time
I did, but I could see afterwards that it was just the relief of being
physically close and how wonderful it felt. I got completely, but
completely panicked; this thing shot through my head: 'You're
a lesbian and you've always been a lesbian'. Everything I'd ever
denied about the teacher, and not knowing whether I was a man
or woman: it just made sense of everything.

One of the things I still have to battle with about bisexuality
as an identity is my own feelings about what lesbians are like. I
remember looking in the mirror and thinking, 'You can't be a lesbian,
you can't be a lesbian! You wear mascara!' Then I met somebody
who is wonderful, wonderful and gorgeous, and I love her a lot.
She identified very strongly as a lesbian, a black lesbian. I went
up to her and told her she was gorgeous, then I got scared and
ran away. Then she came up to me, which had never been my
experience, and we started seeing each other. She lives in mainland
Europe and she would come over every month. It was a year, I
think, before we kissed; I used to take her to the place where she
was staying and we'd sit in my car and touch hands and kiss on
the cheek and sweat and giggle and get so embarrassed. I think
what was wonderful was that she was so obviously accepting of
me as a lesbian and as a white woman. I learned so much from
the way she loved me and let me love her.

Gradually, it became a sexual relationship. She was much
younger than I was and smaller and a lot of the time I'd feel I was
sexually abusing her, even though she told me I wasn't. Also, I

got very confused about whether I could be a woman and feel like that about another woman. It's really deep: 'If you feel like that you can't be a real woman', all those messages.

So I had a relationship with her, and then I went to the States. She was going to fly out to join me and we were going to have an idyllic week and a half in New York. But I met a Jewish woman. I've had a lot of negative feelings in my life about Jews, especially Jewish women, but when I met this woman, it was so romantic. She was older than me – I've never had a woman lover who's older. And J... well, it was the beginning of the end for us as lovers.

At about this time, while I was still identifying as a lesbian, I had a crush on a young man. We had a tortuous relationship: I knew I was a lesbian, but this man was just lovely. We were never sexual together, but the night before he went away for a year we slept together and kissed and touched. It wasn't at all like sex with men had been until then, which was very frenzied. And it didn't knock my sense of lesbian identity, because I loved him like a brother.

Then I fell in love with a woman who worked in London and tried for about a year and a half to have a relationship with her. It was one of my greatest failures! I heard afterwards that she was scared – I used to want to see her all the time and I must have been a bit passionate! I certainly didn't feel like the world's most successful lesbian. I loved the community; at the time I came out there were a lot of Jewish lesbians, a lot to gel together around, and that was my social life. I went to the Jewish lesbian conference and transformed from being a very successful heterosexual to thinking that everything with men had been a complete con and I was totally lesbian.

I used counselling consistently, and was working a lot on my abuse, so I thought I was ready to have a relationship. I thought a lot about who I could have a relationship with, and my first choice was a woman I knew. Again, she was younger and smaller than me, and I realised when I was with her that it wasn't right. I was very attracted to her, but I didn't like that part of lesbian life – going clubbing and getting completely stoned on Saturday nights and sleeping all day Sunday. When I realised that I was fancying a fantasy, I started to look more clearly at who I might want to have a relationship with. And much to my horror, I realised that it might be a man.

A friend of mine was directing a course and I was tutoring on it. I used to sit and watch him, but now I saw him in a quite different way. When I first met him, I thought he was lovely. I was very scared of him and found him physically very attractive, but I knew I was a lesbian, so it was OK. And we got closer and closer and it became very apparent that he really liked me too. He had been married for fourteen years and had two children; now his marriage started to get rocky. One day, he said his wife wanted to meet me, and she came and sat in my car. I was going off to see a woman I was besotted with, and she cried, and said, 'Just leave my husband alone'. I said, 'Look, I'm a lesbian, I don't want your husband! We're really close friends, but I'm taken with this woman. I don't feel sexual towards him'. And she said, 'You're going to be sexual, men and women are sexual. I can see what's happening and it's going that way'. And then, of course, we did become lovers. It has been very hard for her, and I felt as if I betrayed her. What I told her at the time was true, but then in the course of about a year things changed dramatically.

I do think that kind of change is possible and I think it's a matter of choice. I don't know what pushed me to make the decision – I think having worked with P was important and having a lot of counselling workshops with him, and seeing who he really was and what the struggles were for him. And so I set it up, really, that we would become lovers, and we did, and we've been lovers for maybe two years. My belief is that feelings aren't a good guide to action, and that once I've dealt with some of the feelings I have, I'm much more able to think effectively and to make the decisions I want to, including deciding what's going to be in my own long-term interests.

I think I could have carried on trying to make a relationship with a woman, but when I looked around for my best bet in terms of who was going to challenge me and who was really going to love me for me, I realised that it made more sense to think strategically. I don't think it's easy to do and I make a lot of mistakes, but I do think it must be possible to make choices about sex. It may feel as if you have urges you have to act on, but I think the urges are often stimulated by the past. I would much prefer to get beyond fantasy and to work on being more methodical and rational about decisions.

Sexual fantasies scare me, which goes back to the abuse: a lot of things that turn us on are things that have been abusive in the past. When I was being sexual with the man I was with for eleven years, I would sometimes think about women, which was horrible, and then sometimes when I was having relationships with women, I wouldn't actually think about men when we were being sexual, but my sexual fantasies about men increased. Now I keep a check on fantasies; they stop me from being with whoever I'm with.

My relationship with P, my present partner, has brought me up against things that I've hated. When we first used to go out together, I would walk behind him or in front of him. He's black, and for him it was another instance of people not wanting to be close to him. We had to talk for a long time before I realised that for me it was about not being able to stand the manifestations of heterosexism, that heterosexual shuffle with your arms round each other. It's partly because it had hurt me so much as a lesbian: I've got a clear insight into what it's like to have your love denied and not to be able to be spontaneous. Yet now I'm in a relationship with a heterosexual man who doesn't understand that.

My best friend, who's a lesbian, always used to say she never wanted me to forget the privileges I have being in a relationship with a man. She's stopped now, but I still find it hurtful when they assume that I'll forget. How can I forget? I haven't stopped being the person I was when I was lovers with J or other women: the whole thing about labels really gets me.

The other thing that makes a big difference in being in a relationship with a heterosexual man who's black is the way privilege is distributed. At one point it looked as though I was going to have to choose between him and my family; my family couldn't deal with him, and my mother still can't cope. So heterosexual privilege is not clear cut. For me, there's being in a relationship with a man and being in a relationship with a gentile, as well as the fact that he's black and I'm white. We're more or less living together now and I've gained a lot from being shown a different perspective every day of my life. On the other hand, I've been positively challenged in the past by women who've had similar views to me, and I've lost a lot in terms of understanding – that sense of being able to breathe easy, to say something and not have to analyse it a hundred times to make sure it's understood.

I was very scared that I would lose friends over this. I remember telling two of them, a lesbian couple: I thought it was going to be make or break. Their first response was shock: it was as if I had betrayed them, and I felt bad about it. But it was the same as having to decide between my family and P, and ultimately I decided for him. One of the couple (they've split up now) is still one of my closest friends and is very close to P; it's changed her life too, to discover that she can accept him. I felt that if other lesbian friends couldn't take it, then they weren't thinking about me, but about themselves.

There are people I don't see and that makes me sad. When we do meet, usually through work, I feel uncomfortable and judged. I do think I've missed something: it felt like a certainty, for five years I identified as a lesbian and then not to... I don't think I've lost anything from who I am, but other people think I'm a different person. But perhaps they weren't people I was close to anyway; the ones with whom I had a good connection stuck in there, whatever came up.

I've steered clear of bisexual politics until recently. To me, it seemed like a nothing, like neither one thing nor the other. It didn't feel like having a strong identity, and I'm not sure it does now. 'Fragmented' is the word I'd use around labels. I feel I may lose the core of myself, not knowing where I am or who I am, do I stand here or there, and can I not be in both? It's a very fragmenting experience, and I'd prefer to hold on to the unity I have in myself. So perhaps that's a good reason to want to look at bisexuality, to see that I'm not fragmented, it's just the construction of sexuality that makes me feel I can't be who I am. Because you're not supposed to be like that, either from a lesbian and gay stance or a heterosexual stance.

But it's also the labels that get in the way. I much prefer to say, 'I'm having a relationship with P', if people ask me how I define myself, though of course it's more than who I'm having a relationship with. I feel passionate about women. Now that I've allowed myself to have the experience of being sexually and emotionally involved with women, it's opened something that will never close.

I have two friends with whom I discuss it. One is a married man who goes out cruising a lot, and we talk about what bisexual means, although we both scream with laughter when we talk about being bisexual because it seems so ridiculous. Then I have a woman friend, who's a wheelchair user. We've always concentrated on disability issues, but recently we started to talk about sexuality, and she feels like a heterosexual woman who happens to have had lesbian relationships.

In real terms, my options are narrowed for the moment by being monogamous, so in some ways I think everybody would see me as heterosexual. But I want to transcend that and be able just to be Rachel and to know that's OK. I also feel that sex isn't so important any more. I used to be frenzied about it as well as having long periods of being completely disinterested, so now I don't trust the stuff about fancying people. Of course I see women who I think are attractive; it's nice to feel that, but it seems superficial in comparison with the feeling I'm getting in this relationship. On the other hand, I have a hankering to find a Jewish bisexual woman who will make me feel complete!

As long as I'm monogamous with P, it feels as if I can't express myself fully. It's not that I want to have a relationship with a woman, but rekindling my relationship with J has led to some interesting discussions. If you've got a primary relationship, what do other relationships look like? We have said that being lovers with someone else is up for grabs, and I'm sure it's achievable. But now we're buying a house together and I feel more and more as if we're getting into a visible commitment to each other. Yet I'm determined not to shut down my vision of what's possible. It's going to be interesting: I don't know how it will work out.

Margaret

Now aged seventy-eight, Margaret was born into a white middle-class family in the north of England, spent her working life in London, and since retirement has lived in East Anglia. She lives alone.

Now in my seventy-ninth year, I am still attracted to men, and in particular to women. I have a very close woman friend, rather younger than myself. She has no knowledge of how I feel about her, but we are great friends, and it's marvellous for me to have this close relationship.

When I was fifteen I was seduced by the nursemaid to my half-brothers and sisters. We were discovered by my father and stepmother. The nurse was dismissed, and for years afterwards, Father 'warned' me about lesbianism. After that brief experience, I was not interested in a woman again until I was about twenty-three. I had one or two men friends, and was seduced by one of them, but had no lasting affair and was not in love with him.

Then I had a sexual relationship with a young woman who was bisexual, though I think she was mainly heterosexual. We shared a flat in Chelsea where she entertained her men friends, which I found rather disconcerting because of my feelings for her. One of her men friends, whom I liked very much – he was such a gentle, warm person – told me that although he was infatuated by her, she wasn't the sort of person he wished to marry and he wanted to marry me instead. This, of course, I could hardly believe: I said he mustn't mention it again until he had recovered from his infatuation, and I refused to sleep with him, though we both wanted to. Needless to say, he and my friend were married soon afterwards. He was in the Air Force and was killed within a few weeks, but I would have married him had I had the opportunity.

When I was in the WAAF I didn't form any relationships at all, male or female. But in the early 1950s I became deeply attached to a colleague, a true lesbian. After some months I realised that she had other affairs and I was not of any real importance to her, other than to help her out of her financial and other difficulties. She took me to a renowned lesbian club in Chelsea, which I found very frightening. All their relationships seemed so casual; there was an almost hard, cruel atmosphere. I didn't go again.

I was never involved in a lesbian community, though I realise now that that Chelsea club was a sort of community. But lesbians met in other ways, too – at places of work or at parties. Chelsea was full of artists and writers and people who felt free of convention, so of course these things went on in a more open and free way. I was very shy and withdrawn and was never part of this way of life; although I, too, have an artistic nature. My relationships were formed in a more private way – they came about naturally, in places of work and so on.

I had a lasting sexual relationship with a married man, a family friend, which we kept private for four years, apart from my brother knowing. This man had a very warm personality and we were in tune with each other. I broke off this relationship before it came to a more natural end, as there was no solution to it, and we did not wish to hurt his wife. We always remained friends. My last affair was with a woman half my age, who was temporarily attracted to me, though she's really heterosexual. I was deeply attracted to her, and we are great friends now.

My sexual relationships with women have been short-lived, by which I mean that though my relationships with them could have been long-lasting, their feelings for me ended in every case within weeks or months. I think I was perhaps too possessive – over-anxious to have a permanent relationship with someone.

Despite all that's happened, I must say that I've always wanted, not necessarily to get married, but to live with a partner. I would love to have had children; I had half a dozen half-brothers and half-sisters whom I adored, and I was many years their elder. Several friends have asked me why I've never been married, and I've always found it difficult to answer without revealing my sexuality. Perhaps had I married, I would have lost my feelings for women, which society deems taboo. I believe that if I could have had a lasting partnership, it would have solved many problems, because I am a faithful sort of person.

Although I have indeed been 'in love' with women, I've never been 'in love' with a man, never in my life. However, I've been very fond of several. I felt I could have lived with the two I've mentioned and would have married either had the circumstances been different. And I think that these two men have been the only ones who've been sexually attracted to me: I think that because I was so shy and withdrawn, with a sense of inferiority, I didn't know how to make myself attractive; it didn't occur to me that any man would be interested in me before these two came along. In later life, men have been much more anxious to be friendly with me, I think because I've loosened up a bit and I've become much freer now.

I've always felt wretched about my sexuality, not because I felt it was wrong, but because others would think it was wrong. I was really frightened of this, and thought I would lose friendships because of the attitude in those days. The attitude towards lesbians and bisexuals and homosexuals made me nervous of anyone finding out, and it still does. I wish I'd been born what is called 'normal', because life has been rather full of frustrations and unhappiness. I kept all that inside myself: all that unhappiness and misery was due to my sexuality and wishing I'd been born 'normal'. Although how I feel seems normal to me, of course: I was never really conscious of changing from men to women, it just seemed natural. So I've always found it strange that society couldn't consider bisexual relationships possible.

In my Chelsea days, I formed a close relationship with two homosexual men, a couple. With one, I had a lasting friendship until he died, five years ago. I felt so at ease with him, and in fact do with all homosexuals, as I've had friendships with a few since. Only this first couple knew I was bisexual; they were the only people who knew of my sexuality. We were very free in conversation about the subject, and to me it was a sort of freedom to talk about any subject whatsoever with them. It was wonderful.

I think that society should recognise that bisexual feelings have always existed, even if it's only since the word was coined or used that people have appreciated this sexual condition. It's good that attitudes today have changed so radically, and I realise that this 'burden' I seem to have carried all my life is entirely due to the attitudes towards sexuality and condemnation I suffered when I was young. But it must not be thought that I'm still a wretched, miserable creature, because I'm not. I am more content and happy now than I've ever been, with all that life has to offer. I'm only too glad that I'm no longer young!

Stella

Stella is a thirty-one-year-old white woman who lives in London with her female lover. She is from a working-class background, with a 'middle-class education'.

I feel very much that I am the product of my times and of the opportunities I have seized. Had I been born fifty years ago, I'd be in some unbearable marriage to a lower-middle-class man with three or four children, unhappy, repressed and frustrated. I don't know whether or not I would have managed to have any same-sex sex. I am a product of the 1960s and 1970s, of an upwardly-mobile, conservative, petty-bourgeois family which got through the permissive age without doing anything more daring than buying jazzy curtains. I was the first working-class child I knew to have divorced parents; apart from that, I was enabled by the women's movement and the existence of gay bars.

I was always aware that not to get married would be a disaster. But I saw men as an unknown quantity to be admired from afar; I had no idea how I was ever going to get close enough to one to have a relationship. I went to an all-girls' school and felt uncomfortable with boys and didn't understand them. I was aware of their power to reject me or ridicule me, which they did a lot – at junior school it had been horrific; they would make physical comments and I was hounded. It was a great relief to be with girls, even though I knew they could be horrible too.

If you didn't have sex at university, it was seen as a pretty poor state of affairs, so I got it on for the first time in the first term. I screwed around for three or four years and started to develop strong survival mechanisms with men. These centred on being clever and on the way I dressed. I was overweight; I felt embarrassment and hatred for my body. I knew I couldn't survive as a normal woman, being attractive and relaxed, so I had to create some other identity in order to be respected. I took on very bizarre forms of dress – I used to be known as 'the girl in the dressing gown' – and would wear pyjamas, nightdresses and dressing gowns that were loose and didn't seek to define a shape, so I could hide my body within them. And I learned to take on the clever-girl identity, which men also tapped into.

I was sexually hungry, wanting sex all the time. I'd get very drunk and fawn over men who had shown affection to me in the past, believing we'd have sex, but we never did. I would always mess it up, become paranoid or paralytic; it started to make me feel quite sex-starved.

As soon as I started to have sex, I knew I wanted to sleep with women, but I didn't know what they did in bed or anything. When I was twenty, I started to get seriously interested, so I joined the gay society, and people assumed I was a lesbian. By that time I had realised that lesbianism had some relationship to feminism, and my first sexual stuff with a woman was with someone who was part of the women's group. We edged round each other for a while, then one night I said something like, 'It's really strange when you want to say something but you daren't because you don't know what the other person will think'. And she said: 'I find you very attractive'. So we went to bed and had strange, tentative, held-back kind of sex. After that she avoided me and was soon going out with a man.

Then I fell in love with a lesbian. I got drunk and told her, and she said, 'Well, what is your sexuality?' I said: 'I suppose I'm just attracted to the people I'm attracted to'. Her response was: 'Huh! Bisexual! AC DC!'. So I said: 'Well maybe, but what shall I do?', hoping she'd say, 'Come to my room'. But instead she said: 'Well that's your problem', and walked off. Horrible. But I had so little self-confidence, I accepted it as my just reward.

After I left university I got involved with a lesbian and gay group and came out. I had a wild time, then lived with a woman for two years. Then I had a phase of massive amounts of sex: going to clubs all the time, lots of drugs, lots of pick-ups, countless one-night stands. I had several horrendous three- or four-week relationships, many of them masochistic on my part. I was very out; it was as though I'd got religion and it had given meaning to my life. Women found me attractive and liked my body, which was a big step forward. I started to like my body too, and it didn't matter what men thought.

With women, I feel raunchy, confident, sexy, one of the gang, equal, stimulated, unselfconscious. I can tap into who they are, I can like myself, I can project myself. I've related to women in lots of different ways: the two long-term relationships I've had have been very comfortable: we've played child, we've played parent, we've revealed ourselves to each other. The other relationships have been mainly sexual and about role play, with me as the masochistic femme and them as the dominant, sadistic butch or boyish type.

I'd always worked in a lesbian and gay context, rarely within a women-only context, and as time went on I found I was turned on by a lot of men. I'd never tell them or take it any further, but I'd try to get close. All the men I've had crushes on have been gay, and what they've got is a supremely glamorous style and image. They really get off on each other – it's beautiful to see them being affectionate with each other, especially coming from my very straight background, where men only clapped each other on the back and shook hands. I don't know any straight men, and I'm just starting to get to know bisexual men.

Part of my current wish to explore my sexual desire for men is to do with wanting to know the unknown. I've never had an orgasm or a satisfactory relationship with a man and I want to see if this is possible for me. I've never known a man I really trust, not one. I don't know what would happen if I did become close to an individual man – if I would cease to desire men in general or would desire them more – but I know I can't go on having these cycles of obsession with individual men which turn to dust in my hands. Something's got to change.

This pattern has been there since two or three years after I came out as a hard-line dyke, so I've never been free of it, I've never found men unattractive. Yesterday I found an old notebook and inside was a long diatribe about why I wanted a particular man and how I'd never had a proper relationship with one. I wanted to do it and know that it was possible. It was exactly the same as now. The notebook was from 1986.

My current partner, L, has been very good about this. She felt quite threatened when I started to think and read about bisexuality; she wanted to think it was a professional interest. As time has gone by, she has known about my crushes on men and has pointed out to me that it's as though I express my desire for men as a willingness to be abused and to be treated in a way that I wouldn't tolerate from a woman. Recently I've become quite interested in a man, and I've been sitting waiting for the 'phone to ring. With a woman, I'd just ring up and say: 'I feel I'm waiting on you; if you're avoiding me, please tell me'. L and I are moving towards a point where I can have sex with a man and it won't upset our relationship. She knows I wouldn't want to do it on an ongoing basis; I would say to her, 'Look for five years I'll screw around and after that I'll be all yours'.

I want lessons in how to cope with this, but there aren't any. Every time I ask somebody (whatever their sexuality), they say they can't help. I'm getting this over and over again and I'm getting desperate. I asked my sister, who's straight; I asked my friend, who's straight, and her boyfriend; as well as my own girlfriend. All of them say they can't tell me what to do. My sister's terrified I'm going to jeopardise my relationship with L and it'll be divorced parents all over again. My friend K just thinks I should forget it because it only leads to hurt. K's boyfriend is perhaps interested in discussing it further; L just hopes I won't get hurt or go off and leave her. So I've got to start talking to some bisexuals about it.

The lesbian community is very important to me. I have been doing some work on bisexuality, and lesbian and gay friends have started to wonder what I'm up to. I'm aware that they're starting to see me as at worst consorting with the enemy, or at best doing something they don't understand. They're so frightened of it they don't even want to ask.

I'm very out as a lesbian, my name's known, and for me to come out as bisexual would be very difficult. It's important that I have my writing published and my work seen and that I'm part of a culture. Maybe it has allowed me to avoid some of the things I could be thinking about; maybe it has been an easy option. You can write about lesbians for the rest of your life, and I'm frightened of dropping out of that niche because there isn't a bisexual niche to replace it with. There will be in the future, and I think I'm helping to contribute to it, but I'm not at the stage where I can say, 'Look, I'm bisexual, and I'm doing this because it's really important'.

I'm beginning to find it exciting to think of myself as a bisexual in a lesbian relationship. It makes me think of myself as a groovy person. My relationship with my girlfriend is quite public: the neighbours know we're a couple because our flat has only one bedroom. And everyone knows we're a couple when we go out because we're clingy and we dress similarly. To be bisexual in this set-up would be like being a married person in a heterosexual relationship where everyone assumes you're straight and you have a lot of social approval, but one of you is not that at all, and you have an exciting side that nobody knows about. I find I'm starting to take pleasure in foxing people's assumptions. They'll all assume I'm in a lesbian relationship, cosy and married for ever and happy with a mortgage and two cats, when in fact I'm wanting to fuck men and have sex and drugs and rock 'n' roll and still be with L but have a secret life with men, as an amazingly disjointed thing.

We're starting to resist some of the things we do that are a bit like being married. We've managed to identify monogamy and 'hideous married domesticity' as being bound together, and as we reject the latter, we are having to examine what we mean by monogamy. L doesn't understand bisexuality; she's not interested in men, she can't understand them or relate to them and she has no expectations of them. But she knows it's not a threat to her; she knows that I'm not trying to get away from her: I need her and we're having more sex now than we were six months ago. It's as though I'm learning that if you try to make a theory and fit your life into it, it's frightening, but if you take it step by step until you feel sure of each step before moving on to the next, it isn't. Six months ago it would have been unthinkable that we should stand outside the kitchen door with bottles of beer shouting: 'Fuck monogamy and domesticity, we want no part of it'.

I have sexual desires for and emotional dependencies on other people outside our relationship. But since we've been together I haven't had sex or even snogged with anyone but her. I have had deep flirtations and obsessions and there are many subjects I don't discuss with her but do with other people. But the step to non-monogamy is very big. She is completely faithful and interested in me and sits at home waiting for me to come back from my adventures and sink into her arms in tears. At some point she's going to fancy someone else and my world will fall down around my ears. If she does, I hope she'll be as cautious as I've been. But she says that all she's interested in is me. It would be wonderful if that was the way it stayed for the rest of my life: I went off on adventures and came home and my dinner was on the table, but I know that's not going to happen.

I've always had a bravado and self-confidence with women, a sense that I only had to be myself in order to find out whether I was interested in somebody. But with men, I've got to find the script which will enable me to communicate with them so we'll be able to find out whether we want to have sex together. I want a man to say to me, 'You can just be yourself', but I do feel tremendous pressure to be all those physical things: hairless, thin, attractive. I want to have an affair with a man who is not homophobic, who is interested in me as a person with my whole history behind me.

Any relationship I might have with a man would not be a heterosexual one. I think that heterosexuality means a certain set of things in our society: those relationships have taken on a massive social and cultural significance. In terms of men and women relating to each other, we not only have established power relationships in which men have most of the power and expectations are made that women will struggle in the home (if they're lucky enough to have one), we also have the battle of the sexes and post-feminism. I see my heterosexual women friends in relationships with men that are a mixture of regressive and progressive. I can't have any truck with that: what would be the point; I'd rather just be a lesbian. What I want is something completely different, a totally new age.

I don't want any man ever to have any control over my life – of course men in general do, because they control the world, but I don't want one man who feels he owns me. All men feel they own their women, whatever they say. I would never want that. I feel that sex with a man for me would be something that is a development from my lesbian identity; it would be another part of me that has other needs and desires. I want a whole new framework on which to relate to men – and to women as well. I don't want L and I to sink into monogamous domesticity; I want a different framework where we make our own rules. One of the things I would be bringing to a sexual relationship with a man is the knowledge that I've gained through women about my own body and sexual desires. So I suppose I see any sex with men I have in the future not as heterosexual, but as bisexual. I can't think of another way to describe it.

I definitely felt that I was choosing to be a lesbian, but I knew I was giving up something very potent by renouncing a heterosexual identity. I chose to give it up once I knew that a lesbian identity would offer me more, and I think it's fairly clear that I'll do the same with bisexuality.

Many other lesbians are thinking about sex with men. Of course, a lot of them are getting so much out of being lesbians that they don't feel the need to explore it, but I have one friend who feels the same as me, and is tortured by dreams and fantasies.

The others are probably too ashamed to show it, or they feel it's too minor a part of their sexual spectrum to bother with. Part of the reason it's so problematic is that people who prefer sexual relationships with the opposite sex are so alienated from progressive sexual movements. In the US, there are young lesbians and gays who are creating a culture of having sex with each other. So in the future, lesbians and gays won't be so frightened of talking about their desires for each other.

I hate the word 'straight'. I know lots of people who are straight to whom I would apply it, but there are also lots of people who are heterosexual and aren't straight at all. I resent the fact that they've been pushed out of the sexual-liberation movement; they should be there because they're working at surviving heterosexuality like we are.

And I hate it when bisexual people talk about the 'straight side' and 'gay side' of themselves, as though they live in two different worlds. I think the most exciting thing about bisexuality is that it can create a whole new world which can embrace the willing parts of both sides, not hop from one to the other. I think people who talk like that are just reinforcing this thing about living in the middle.

We have to have class and race consciousness within bisexuality as well: it's not just that you desire both men and women, it's the way you live that out, the way you think about it and how you see it fitting into the rest of society. A lot of people want to get married and have same-sex relationships on the side: I'm not saying, 'Don't do that, but be aware that you are buying into institutionalised slavery of women. There's no getting away from the fact that marriage is an oppressive institution that should be done away with, and when I hear bisexual women talking about getting married, I feel angry, I can't understand it. It's a great challenge to all of us to break out of this destiny which is forced on us the moment we open our eyes in this world. Yet there are bisexual people who would say we're giving them a bad name and bringing bisexuality into disrepute, dragging them out of the closet. I want to be clear what I'm coming out into before I do it, because there are lots of bisexual people who I feel are like a class enemy to me and I want to be able to say so constructively.

As more people identify as bisexual it will be more productive. A lot of lesbians and gay men are going to identify as bisexual; I'm not the only one. So you're talking about a movement with lots of people used to organising on a broad level, used to arguing, bringing a history with them. What I would like to see is a reframing of the whole debate so that lesbian, gay and bisexual are either all used or all dropped and another word adopted.

I don't think there is a bisexual politics yet. At the moment, it's a network of people bound together by a definition, 'bisexual', rather than a political allegiance. For instance, I've learned from black bisexuals that they need to be able to get together separately in order to form their own approaches to things. But it's a Catch 22 situation: you're not going to get autonomous black groups until there are enough black people involved, but only when you have a black agenda will you attract more black people.

There are all types of lesbians and gay men: greens, socialists, conservatives. But bisexuals are so marginalised they have to blur the differences in order to have some sort of cohesion. To me, the bisexual networks are too apolitical. They're trying to see bisexuality as a single issue, whereas the great challenge of bisexuality is the way it connects with everything else.

Jane

Jane is a twenty-two-year-old working-class black woman of mixed race, living alone in London.

Since I was about fourteen or fifteen, I've always known I was bisexual, that I was attracted to women. At that time I didn't have girlfriends – it wasn't something I had to do to find out I was bisexual. And I knew definitely that I was bisexual as opposed to being a lesbian.

I'm twenty-two now, and I haven't had many solid relationships with women. That's because I have been bisexual. Bisexual women have a bad name, and from my experience I can understand why, although I'm not like that. The women I used to meet when I was about seventeen tended to be women who weren't sure themselves whether or not they were bisexual, but it was a fantasy for their boyfriends or husbands. They didn't want to be with you, they just wanted sex – a threesome for their male partner. It's something I didn't want at all: if I wanted to have a relationship with a man, I'd choose my own. Most of these women I met through *Time Out* and *City Limits*; I didn't know any other bisexual women or lesbians at that point.

So I became completely disillusioned with women and decided not to seek out a relationship with a woman because I thought I'd be constantly disappointed. With men I was open to being disappointed, so I wasn't really; with women I didn't want to be disappointed, so it was a double blow when I was. For a while I was going out with a guy in his late thirties and having threesomes was one of his fantasies, so I didn't want to do it for that reason as well.

I haven't sought out relationships with men, but they have happened. I'm having one at the moment with someone I've known for a few years and he knows the situation, he knows how I feel. We have a very equal relationship, no sex roles. At the beginning, as I've found with quite a lot of men, he found the idea that I am bisexual exciting. But as he's got to know me, as he's realised it is something I really want, it has became more threatening to him, because if I do find a woman, what's going to happen to what he's got? But he won't try to stop me.

I'm seeing a woman at the moment and he knows all about it. I don't know whether I'll have a relationship with her; I think I probably won't for lots of reasons. I'm not meeting the sort of women now that I used to – I'm meeting women I'm physically attracted to, but I don't like their personalities. I know that if I get involved with them physically there's not going to be anything mentally, and that's not what I want. I don't know how it would go if I found a woman I really did like; I don't know which way it would go.

When I was younger I thought it would be ideal to be somebody who could appreciate both sexes, to be in the middle. I still feel that way, and if I had a child, I would like him or her to be like that. I also wish I could be lesbian and not have relationships with men, but I'm physically attracted to them and I won't deny that because it would be denying a part of myself; it would be dishonest. Still, it's difficult if you are bisexual and having a relationship with a man, because you're always going to want to be having a relationship with a woman. I don't know if bisexual women or men can ever be really happy, whereas if you are lesbian or gay, maybe it's easier.

In the past, I wanted to be more lesbian because of the difference in my feelings for men and women. My feelings for men are largely physical. If I find a man physically attractive, I'll make compromises that I wouldn't with a woman; if I find a man physically attractive but I don't like his personality, I'll still go ahead. But with a woman, like this woman I'm seeing at the moment, it's different. She's very physically attractive but she is a very selfish person. Yet if she'd been a man, I probably would have gone ahead with it.

It's not that I think I *should* be a lesbian, I really *want* to be. If I could choose (and you do get people who say lesbians have chosen, though I think that's silly), then I'd choose to be a lesbian. It's like feeling something but not being able to do anything about it. I can't make myself change and I wouldn't put myself through that unhappiness. I know I will always be bisexual; I'm quite willing to recognise that.

I was very interested in feminism when I was a teenager, but not actively. I used to read the books and practise it in my life, but I didn't go to the groups. When I was seventeen I worked in a refuge, and I found the women there too much, all their politics. I feel that women who are in the feminist movement aren't feminists at all and I find that disappointing. The women in the refuge would say they were feminists and didn't like men: most of them hadn't been lesbian all their lives – they'd had children and been with men, but they'd been particularly violent or verbally aggressive, so these women didn't only dislike men, they hated them. That's not what feminism is about: feminism is about equality for everyone.

When I go out I tend to go to mixed clubs, mixed gay men and women, because in women-only clubs there are all those roles being played, like butch and femme, just like heterosexual roles. A lot of the women look very macho; I don't like macho-ness in men, so I certainly don't like it in women. The reason I'm attracted to women is because they look like women, and a lot of these women don't. These are all debates within the lesbian community, and I wouldn't say you can't behave like that, but I feel I might as well go to a straight club; there'd be less dominance there.

I've never enjoyed going to clubs to pick people up, so I thought telephone dating might be a good way to meet people. I decided the best thing to do would be to put my own message on, because then I could say what type of person I'd like to meet. But the people I met obviously hadn't listened to the message; they all wanted an answer on the first night as to whether I was going to go out with them or not, when I'd only met them for an hour. I didn't meet any crazy people, just people who were already involved in terrible triangular relationships. If I do it again I won't have the expectation of making a relationship, though I have made some friends out of it.

The whole lesbian issue isn't addressed at all in the black community. There are people there who are very religious, for instance. I don't know whether black lesbians have an easier time dealing with bisexuals than white lesbians; my experience would say they don't. The black lesbians I've met don't like bisexuals because they've had bad experiences with them; I've had arguments with black lesbian friends who say all bisexual women are like this or that. A lot of black lesbians are very political, first about being black and second about being lesbian. They think if you're bisexual you're just flirting. They feel they are suffering so much oppression, and you're getting away with it. It's ridiculous: they feel themselves oppressed and they are oppressed, yet there they are going around doing the same thing. The white women I've known haven't been like that at all – maybe they feel they don't have any right to tell me what to do. A lot of black lesbians won't have relationships with bisexual women, whereas I think white lesbians do mix over. I know, and have known, more white bisexual women than black, and I don't think I would actively seek out black bisexual women.

I don't go to groups much, though I do go to a group that's just started for black lesbians. I feel quite comfortable there, whereas I don't feel I would be comfortable in a group for bisexuals. They don't even ask about your sexuality: they just accept that you're there and you want to be there. I don't know what their views are on bisexuals; it hasn't been an issue. I find with most groups it's going along and talking about yourself and your sexuality. I can understand the importance of that for some people, but I've never needed to do it as I've never had a problem with my sexual identity. I'm also a very private person and I wouldn't want to share that with people I'm probably not going to see next week.

Politically, I think the bisexual community should be part of gay liberation, but I don't know how, because they're not welcome in the gay movement. Maybe it's different for bisexual men: the gay men I know don't seem to mind the idea of bisexuality, whereas a lot of gay women see bisexual women as traitors. The gay movement is completely split, men and women on opposite sides. Then there's the whole bisexual debate, and we're told to go off somewhere else. I know bisexual people who try to make friends with gay people and some of them just don't want to know. I think some of them have had bad experiences and they seem to lump you all together.

I don't want to have lots of different relationships at one time, it's too complicated. I would like to be with one person, a regular thing. But whether that would be a man or a woman, I don't know. With the situation I'm in at the moment, I don't know how I would handle it if I met a woman. I wouldn't want to have two relationships going at once; I would want to make a commitment somewhere. So my bloke is very threatened, very scared. He's a sensitive type of person; he won't tell me not to do anything – he knows it wouldn't wash anyway. We don't have great discussions about it, but he does feel threatened by my women friends.

I used to think my ideal partner would be a bisexual man, and I still think this might be the case, though it frightens me from the HIV point of view that he might have had lots of relationships with other men. It frightens me and I do the best I can to protect myself. Maybe that's why I'm very selective now about who I sleep with. When I was younger, I wanted to experiment; now I think that even if AIDS wasn't the huge problem it is, I still wouldn't. I know that I'm looking after myself, but I could meet somebody who wasn't what I thought, and you don't have to sleep around to get AIDS, as we all know.

I will probably end up having a single relationship with a woman, because that's where my emotions lie, not with men. If I was in a relationship with a woman I would be honest about my feelings for men; I don't think it does you any good to be dishonest. Although I can't say that my relationships with men have been deep, they are long, so obviously they mean something. But I don't love them, and that probably says more about me than about them.

However long I have to wait for a relationship with a woman, it will be worth it. You can have so many relationships that last two or three years, but the feelings just aren't there. I think what will probably happen is that I'll have a relationship with a woman and it will sum all that up. But I will never deny my feelings for men.

Diane

Diane is a white working-class woman in her early forties, living alone in the Midlands.

My bisexuality was a physical thing at first: I fancied women and I thought I ought to explore things a little. I suppose the feeling started ten years or more before I began to think about doing something about it. For a long time it was at the back of my mind. It's a certain type of woman I'm attracted to: someone who's strong and independent, a bit like myself. I've always admired strong women who've got on with their lives in whatever way they wanted to.

I've never wanted to be married. I did go through the motions of courting and almost getting married, but I backed out at the last minute. To me, getting married and having a nice little home and two children is boring. I know some women now who are career women and manage a successful home life too, but ten or twenty years ago, there weren't many married women with a career. When I left school in 1964 they only wanted to get married and have kids and that's it.

I hated my looks when I was at school, and my teenage years weren't particularly happy. I never had any confidence, but I did normal girls' things. I chased boys; I still chase them now! I don't like to wait around to be picked up, I like to do the chatting up. The first time I went to bed with a boy I was nineteen, a bit of a late starter. I was frightened, because my mother had told me you shouldn't 'let' boys. But I found that men were attracted to me after that, and I think I used sex to attract them. I wouldn't say I was free and easy but I felt that if you acted a bit sexy somebody would fancy you more. At that time I didn't think of fancying women. I had boyfriends, and a couple of very intense relationships with men.

Later, I thought, 'Well, you can go on and on confused about women, and not understand, and I want to understand about myself'. I thought, 'I've got to do something about it, because I might end up on my death bed and wonder if it would have worked'. My idea of life is that you should live it to the full, you're only here once.

So then I thought about how I could go about meeting someone similar. You can't chat someone up in a pub, and I would have been too nervous to go to a gay club, although I don't think there are any around here, anyway. So I thought the next best thing would be to try an advert in *Forum*. I'd been reading it on and off for a few years, so I put in an advert and it brought quite a lot of replies.

I whittled the replies down to four. I wanted someone close by, but the first woman I picked out was from London. She had been in a long-term relationship with another female for quite a long time, which had recently broken up. We spoke on the 'phone, and we met when I happened to be down there for my job, but I wasn't interested. The next one I met wasn't too far away, slightly older than me, and I met her in a pub car park. We went for a drink and I thought she could be nice, but I wasn't sure about going to bed with her. She was married, but not happily, and she said she'd like to see me again. I can't remember what happened, but I decided she wouldn't be the one. Because I was looking for 'the one', you see. There was another lady; she was older than me, a widow with a couple of children, and we met midway. She seemed to like me a lot and I said I'd be in touch, but I knew it was 'no'.

The other one I did start a relationship with. It wasn't a particularly long letter, and she said she didn't like writing letters much, but it was neat and friendly. We arranged to meet at a lay-by off a motorway, by the colours of the cars. A van pulled up and she got out and I got out and when I saw her I thought, 'yes', definitely. So I suppose it was a physical thing. When you think about it, you're not supposed to judge people by their appearance, but when you meet anybody of either sex, the first thing you see is what they look like, and afterwards you find out their personality. She was divorced with a little girl. She said she was always a lesbian, but she went through the motions of marriage, and her husband was quite awful to her.

We met a few times, and then she came to my house with her daughter. The daughter was outgoing and friendly; they came in the afternoon, I made evening dinner and the daughter was happy to go to bed in the spare room. So we played records and sat on the floor and I remember exactly what happened, she just turned to me and kissed me. At that moment, I thought, 'My God, this woman's kissing me', and I thought, 'Well it's nice, I like it!' And we kept on from there, and it seemed the most natural thing in the world, and I wondered what I was getting worked up about. Once I had kissed her it was easy; I should have done it ages ago. It went on to be a relationship for several months, but she got very serious with me. I got warning bells, because I'd never been able to have a serious one-to-one relationship with a man that lasted more than eighteen months.

So I told her I didn't want to get too serious. There were two sides to it. Emotionally and practically it would be too difficult, because I like my freedom to come and go. She was a bit jealous and possessive, which I didn't like, and I thought it would be even more so if we lived together. It would have been nice to have someone in the house, since she didn't go to work because of the little girl. But I also worried about what other people would think. Generally I am an 'anything goes' type of person, but deep down I do care what people think. I do things to get people going and I behave in a particular way to shock people, but I think it's a bit more serious if you have a live-in lover.

I had told my sister about this. I thought she'd be quite modern in her thinking, but she wasn't. She was horrified and disgusted. So if she reacted like that, there are going to be a lot more who react like that as well. And I don't think I could really cope with people pointing at me as though I was a wierdo. I know I am different, not just because I fancy women, but in other ways as well. I'm just not a traditional woman.

After that relationship I did feel more at peace with myself, because I felt I could understand myself more. I was glad I did it, and that it was successful, and I thought that if I met somebody else, I would understand it more. I didn't go out and look for somebody else straight away; I thought it might happen, and if it did I would know why, and just accept it as part of me. I didn't think I should just try it and then forget about it.

I did tell a few people that I fancy women. I don't know if they all believed me, but some of them did. A lot of men think I'm winding them up, but some do believe me and their ears prick up and they say, 'Oh that's always been an ambition of mine'. I think almost every male wants to have two women in bed, but they don't realise that the two women probably wouldn't be interested in them.

I tend to have a number of different relationships at once because it's my job that dictates my social life and my first love has always been my job. I know people, but I don't socialise much here as I travel so much. I'm having a relationship at the moment with a married man and sometimes we don't see each other for a month. I don't want to be flitting about a lot, and I like this relationship because I don't want to be lumbered with him all the time. I don't seem to be able to have ongoing relationships because I move about too much. But it's my lifestyle and I choose to do it. I chose to be single, and part of the choice I made with the job is not being able to form permanent relationships. But it's hard at times when you want to see someone.

I haven't had a proper boyfriend for a long time, but I do have one or two lovers. I like to stick to the same ones – I've known them a long time – because I'm always aware I might catch something. I think you change with age as well. As I'm getting older, I have more tolerance about people's funny little ways. So it's possible in the future I might live permanently with someone, but I don't think it would be a female. I still like men. It's a funny situation, and I wonder whether I should be one or another. But then I think, I'm sure you can be in the middle. I think that's how I am.

I put another ad in *Forum* which brought hardly any replies, and I didn't follow any of them up. That was after the big AIDS scare, which has done a lot to cut people's promiscuity. Another reply to one of my ads was from a man who wanted his wife to have a relationship with another woman. I thought that was a bit strange. I think I might be happy having a relationship with a married woman, because she would have a separate life and wouldn't be totally dependent on me. But I talked to this woman and she wasn't sure, although she said she had considered it for herself. Then I had a telephone call from him. He sounded a real wierdo, and said I sounded very interesting, and wanted to meet me. I said definitely not. So he said, could he give my number to a female friend? I got warning bells about the second woman, he seemed to be in control of the two women, and I thought, 'No man's going to control me!' More recently, I replied to an advert from *Forum* and she wrote to me. She lives a fair way away. I'm not sure what to do about it yet.

Anyway, there was a woman at work who I thought might be gay and I wanted to know. We were quite good friends and we used to go out, but I couldn't ask her directly. Then one night we were having a drink and it came out. I told her about this other relationship and said, 'I hope I can talk to you, because it's been worrying me a bit'. She gave me the reaction I expected, and confessed that she was. I found it very easy to talk to her; I hadn't had much experience, but she'd had none at all, not daring to do much about it. She was in quite a high position at work and was frightened to death someone would find out. So then it went further. And she could see the men rallying around me at work but couldn't do anything about it. It was absolutely secret. We got on very well, we'd go out together, but it sort of fizzled out eventually.

We were at a works retiring party in the upstairs room of a pub and I took the leftover sandwiches downstairs. There was a table of about ten lesbians, I knew they were straight away, so I said to her, 'You'll never guess who's downstairs'. So we took down more sandwiches and stayed there for the rest of the evening. One particular girl caught her attention, youngish, obviously upset about something. She went into the toilet in tears, and my friend went into the toilet to comfort her, which was the start of a long relationship!

My relationships with men haven't been that different from my relationships with women. In my mind, there's no such thing as male or female and you can have the same feelings for either sex. Myself, I feel slightly masculine. I think of sex in the way men think of sex; I like to do the chasing. I'm happy to take the lead and if I feel randy, why should I wait around?

I'm worried about other people not understanding. I don't like the word 'lesbian', I prefer 'gay', although 'lesbian' is the proper word. But I don't think I am anyway. I don't want to be totally anything. I think I will probably end up in a permanent relationship with a man because it's easier. I suppose I could probably not have another gay relationship. But only recently I've met females I'd like to have relationships with; it's hard. I go through agonies with women: when I'm with a woman I'm really attracted to and want to touch and can't, I physically ache. I think that's what men feel and I feel it too with women.

I think lots of other people would be bisexual, but they are too scared. If only people would be more honest with themselves, they would be a lot happier.

Liz

Liz is a white middle-class woman aged thirty and living in southern England. She is married with a daughter.

The first inklings of my sexuality came when I was at secondary school. I was very close to a girl there and I knew it was more than just a friendship. Although I didn't verbalise it to anybody, not even to her, I was sure that there was more there than society accepted. But even from that early point it didn't worry me: I knew it wasn't going to be a problem as I was happy to be in the mainline heterosexual mould for most of the time.

Just before I went to college, I stayed with a friend whom I'd known for quite a few years – we'd met every so often in the course of group meetings. She was very responsive to my friendship and

I realised that this could be a physical thing, not just an emotional attachment. Although it was very brief, I realised this was a new direction that was open to me, and that was lovely.

By the time I'd got to college, and met my boyfriend D as well, I was beginning to wonder how being bisexual would fit into my life. For example, how would a male partner react to it? I also didn't know how I would find female lovers, apart from the friend I'd been to stay with. She was living in London, so I didn't see her very often, and as she was involved in a heterosexual relationship as well, it was difficult to fit in more than the odd cuddle.

As I got to know D, I was able to talk frankly about my feelings and he accepted the way I was and has supported me throughout. Once we were at a party together, and D met somebody he was interested in (we were quite liberal in our relationship at that time). He asked her if she'd like to go for a drink, and she said, 'No, I'm sorry, I can't, I'm gay'. He rushed downstairs and told me, because he knew that I liked her as well, and so I rushed upstairs and said, 'Will I do?' It was lovely – we went out for a walk arm-in-arm and it was an amazing realisation that there might be somebody out there who would accept my bisexuality.

She was lesbian; at that time she was completely lesbian. As a threesome we were very close and friendly. Often she and I would go off upstairs together and D would go for a drink with his mates. It was ideal. Her relationship with D was quite hesitant, because she'd made the decision not to be with men, but emotionally we were all very close. It didn't really last so long – I think she found it difficult to come to terms with the way we were in relation to her lesbianism. She began to pull away from D and only contact me or talk to me. I found it very hard that she should snub D; I felt my main loyalty was to him, and so we grew apart. But while it lasted it was idyllic. I look back on it fondly, and I hope she does too.

So that was my main love during college, apart from D. Other experiences during that time were with female friends I'd known for several years. I'm a very physical person, I like hugging and so on, and through comments and the way I acted they realised I was bisexual. I would just flirt with them and would manage to end up in bed with them if I was pushy enough. We would have one or two physical times, and then maybe nothing for a while, because they were off with their male partners or whatever. I'm still in contact with most of these women, but it has become more difficult for all of us since we've got our own relationships. There hasn't ever been a time to equal the freedom we had at college.

It takes quite an effort for me to go and meet people I'm not already friendly with, for example at a bar or disco. One of the worries is whether they are going to be lesbian or bisexual, and how to get across that barrier of saying, 'Are you lesbian or are you bisexual, because I've actually got someone at home?' I'd want to find someone quite unusual, who would accept a part-time relationship and would accept me going back into this very steady straight one, well straight-ish. I've never been in a situation where I risked all and asked someone I didn't know whether she was lesbian or straight or bi.

I answered an advert in *Time Out* for a lesbian wanting someone for friendship. It was when D was away for five months – it was a time when we'd both decided to have freedom to sort ourselves out. I wanted to try to discover what direction I was going in, whether I was going to become completely lesbian, or stay bisexual, or miss D so much that I'd remain straight and abandon everyone else.

G was very young. She wasn't the person who'd put the advert in; she'd answered the advert too and the person who put it in put her in touch with me. G was about seventeen and I was in my early twenties. She was really just starting out, trying to find her sexuality, although she said she was definitely lesbian and had been all her life. She really fell in love with me and that was before I had been able to state my position: that I had somebody who might come back to me and I couldn't guarantee that I'd be just for her and nobody else. I got far too involved with her and I'd hurt her before I knew where I was. Once I'd been with her, I realised it wasn't right for me at that time. I don't know whether it was just her, or the whole lesbian thing. I didn't want to get totally involved with her at the expense of everyone else, and I was taken aback to see how intense she was.

Nowadays, I know a few lesbians, through friends or college, but I feel very much that I can't really be part of the lesbian scene, that I have to keep away to a certain extent, because my situation is so different from theirs. I'm sorry that it has to be so separate, but it seems unfair for me to expect a lesbian to have a relationship with me when I've got a heterosexual relationship backing me up all the time. Maybe a part-time relationship would be enough for someone, and she'd be happy to go off and do her own thing, but it's presumptuous of me to expect anyone to accept my set-up. I think it's only another bisexual woman who would cope with it, because she may have her own family and we would be on a more equal footing.

I realise I'm in a privileged position: if you are purely lesbian, it must be very hard to try to make a relationship in a straight and intolerant world. I can see I have safety nets that lesbians don't have: for example, they have to cope with prejudice at work and keeping quiet about their lovers, whereas I can just talk about D and no one need be any the wiser about the other side of me.

I dislike the heterosexual couple scene, though I'm part of it. Most couples seem to exist within very rigid boundaries, which worries and saddens me, though I have no right to say how other people should live their lives. But it means there's little scope for other sorts of relationships that are more fluid and flexible. As we get older, most of the people we mix with are other heterosexual couples. It's especially true when you have a young child, because you tend to mix with other parents and that tightens up the family unit even more. So much energy is put into being with a child, there's little time to look around outside. There's also the question of whether you should have a looser partnership when there's a child who needs the security and the base. I love D and my daughter and get a large proportion of what I need from being with them. I wouldn't want to forsake what I have, but I do sometimes feel a sense of conflict between my personal needs and the time I want to devote to my family.

If you're talking about fancying, looking at people at parties, I look at women first. My whole thinking is geared towards making contact with women, but my situation is geared against it. I do feel a bit lost at the moment: where do I go, whom can I meet, how can I meet people? But then I think, 'I haven't got a lot of time to meet anybody and I'm quite happy so what am I worrying about?' But there's still something inside me which would love to be with a woman again.

It's hard to say what the difference is, because my image of being with a woman is comprised of the women I've been with. The relationships I've had have been very caring and tender, with a lot of emotion from very simple things. I don't think you get that feeling with a man, especially when you first meet, because there's so much weighing up with men – the power relationship – and you're always a little suspicious. When you meet a woman, you know that isn't going to happen – or rather it might, but I know I haven't ever felt that there was a power struggle.

With women the sexual side is... well, you just go on for hours and hours! You have to be more inventive, and women's bodies are so beautiful and soft. It seems to make common sense to me to be with someone of your own sex. Having said that, I need D too! But then our relationship was something that grew up over a period of knowing each other, so by the time we got to a physical situation we knew each other very well as companions.

I like the effect that being bisexual has had on my relationships with men as friends. I find I can be on a more equal level, because I know that I don't see men in a particularly sexual way. If they get to know about me and know that I'm possibly more interested in women, apart from D, then they don't see me sexually either. I find that very freeing, though as I'm not a single person, they probably wouldn't see me like that anyway.

If I didn't have my relationship with D, I don't know where I'd be, as I know my interest is so much towards women. Maybe it's just that D was the right sort of person for me and would have been whether he was a man or a woman. I like the upfront type of person in general – and quiet, soft men, gentle men. So I wouldn't say that I could never fall in love with a man. It would be ridiculous to cast men aside in that way, and say that because they are men they are no good. It's just that generally most of the men I've met are not the type of person I find attractive.

I feel happy and content as a person. I really believe that if your life isn't right, you can get out and alter it, you can change your circumstances. So I suppose, because I'm not doing a lot about changing it, I must be happy with what I've got. It's been easy for me to be bisexual. The biggest problem is not going out and trying to make more opportunities. If I feel that side of my life is at a bit of a standstill, then it's up to me to do something about it: I've got good support, I live in a good town, I won't be chastised and I don't have to do it undercover. My only problem is the conflict between enjoying being with my family and wanting to go out and meet people and be more involved with women again. But in general, I've found being bisexual hasn't been a problem.

6 Towards a definition of bisexuality

For the majority of people whose only desire is and has been for the opposite sex, sexual identity is not an issue: they automatically consider themselves 'normal', without even having to wonder what 'normal' means. Lesbians and gay men, by contrast, have needed to find their own identities to challenge heterosexist assumptions of normality – and to decide for themselves what it means to be a lesbian or gay man, which usually differs from what dominant ideology thinks it means.

The creation of the label 'bisexual' is a fairly recent phenomenon, in operation only over the past twenty years. There was always a recognition that some people (men) were 'really' homosexual, and that some acted that way only part of the time, a recognition which appeared in the Wolfenden Report on homosexuality in the 1950s. However, it was only within the contexts of sexual liberation and then gay liberation that bisexuality was recognised as a specific form of sexual behaviour. Like lesbian or homosexual, it was regarded as negative, with connotations of vacillation, indecision, 'sitting on the fence', 'having the best of both worlds', transition, hedonism. Nevertheless, it existed, and people could relate to it if they could overcome its negative associations.

So is the creation and solidification of the category 'bisexual' a positive or negative phenomenon? Once forms of sexuality are named, then people find that their longings, which had previously been lonely, unspeakable, perhaps unformed, have a home. Therefore it could be argued that once a particular sexuality is defined and named publicly, it attracts more active adherents. (This, of course, is one of the supposed justifications of Section 28.) The advantages of taking on an identity (as opposed to being labelled by others) are clear: an individual can work out for herself what it means to be bisexual (or lesbian); can regard it as positive rather than negative; can work to create a culture in which her sexuality is validated. Lesbians and gay men, and more recently bisexuals, have also used sexual identity as a rallying point for political action.

On the other hand, creating categories fixes sexuality, which for many individuals is a fluid concept. Some people are attracted to a certain type of person when they are teenagers, and remain attracted to that type, and only that type, for the rest of their lives. Other people like different genders, types of people, ages and activities at various stages. To box people into a fixed category, from which they can emerge only at great personal cost, is surely not a progressive aim. Another danger of identity politics is that the immense differences between various groups within the broad sexual categories can be glossed over and the most powerful group-within-a-group (white upper- and middle-class men, for instance, or white middle-class women within the feminist movement) be the only voices to be heard.

However, the creation of a common agenda which includes the acceptance of difference can be an important position of power from which to challenge dominant ideologies, and the validation of sexual identities other than heterosexual is a necessary strategy in the fight against heterosexism. But such identities should not be an end in themselves: we need them only so we can get to the stage where sexualities other than heterosexual are fully acknowledged and we can all be as sexually fluid (or not) as we like.

People who want to take on a bisexual identity, or do not consider they fit straightforwardly within any of the existing categories, have to decide what it means to identify as such. This chapter looks at how self-defined bisexual women see their sexual identity and its various components.

Identifying as bisexual

To describe a person as 'a homosexual', 'a lesbian' or 'a heterosexual' is fairly straightforward: they are 'oriented' towards same- or opposite-sex relationships. But one of the problems of defining oneself as bisexual is the lack of agreed meaning of the word. According to the *Oxford Concise English Dictionary*, bisexual means 'sexually attracted by members of both sexes'. However, within this broad definition, there are many different situations which may lead a woman to wonder if 'bisexual' is really the term to describe her feelings. If she has had many relationships with men, for instance, and then falls for a woman, was she really always a lesbian? If she is much more interested in one sex than the other (although she likes both), is she still bisexual? If she has only had relationships with people of one sex, but has strong desires for, sexual fantasies about, or deep and exciting emotional attachments to people of the other, can she say she is bisexual? As question-naire respondents' experiences show, the answer will vary from person to person.

How and why do women come to identify as bisexual, and what is the relationship between sexual activity, emotional involvement, political commitment and sexual identity? The call for ques-tionnaire respondents was directed specifically at women who considered themselves bisexual, so most respondents identified as such. Of the 142 women who filled in questionnaires, 108 identified as bisexual and 34 did not. 13 of the 34 identified as 'other' – most explained this choice by saying they would prefer not to label themselves at all. 10 women gave a variety of other responses ('confused', 'not sure', 'my sexuality is fluid', and so on). 8 women chose dual sexualities: 4 identified as heterosexual/bisexual; 2 as heterosexual and lesbian; 2 as bisexual/lesbian. 2 women said they were lesbian, and 1 that she was heterosexual. The women who identified as lesbian had formerly identified as bisexual; the woman identifying as heterosexual thought she was coming to identify as bisexual. The double identities given by the others will be discussed later.

In response to the question of why they identified as bisexual, the vast majority (97 of the 108 who so identified) said it was because they were sexually and emotionally interested in both men and women, whether or not this had been acted upon. 3 respondents said they were primarily interested in women, but retained some desire for men; 1 respondent said she preferred men, but liked women too.

I am bisexual because I am sexually attracted to both sexes. (98)

I recognise my capacity to be sexually attracted to women and men. (130)

Sexually attracted to men and women but mostly women. (33)

I feel myself as bisexual and not heterosexual with lesbian tendencies or vice versa. (105)

3 women said they needed a label for their sexual identity:

I'd rather not define myself at all – but it's necessary to stop people making wrong assumptions and to tell gay/bisexual people I'm on their side. My feelings for women and men sometimes include sexual feelings – so I suppose I'm bisexual. (14)

5 women gave more theoretical responses:

I believe that everyone is born bisexual and society forces us to be heterosexual. (128)

I know that I have many possible feelings and I can't see any sensible reason for deciding on 'one side'. (129)

It's natural to be bisexual. (15)

The question of how women came to identify as bisexual produced a wide range of responses. For 28 women, identifying as bisexual was the result of a significant attraction to/relationship with/falling in love with another woman within an otherwise heterosexual history. 21 women had moved from heterosexuality to lesbianism, and then realised that they were still also attracted to men. 6 women gave no details of their sexual history, but said that to identify as bisexual was a process that had taken many years.

I had relationships with men for most of my life and then fell in love with a woman. (138)

I first fell in love with a woman when I was seventeen or eighteen, and thought at first I might be lesbian, but came to the conclusion I was bisexual. It would be a lot easier at present for me to define myself as lesbian, but I do also love men, even though this takes second place at the moment. (126)

I suppose I've always felt this way – attracted to women before anything happened, and been afraid. Then something happened with a friend when I was drunk, and I just ignored it. Two years later I was confronted with it again by getting to know a lesbian closely and then sleeping with a woman. (127)

After thinking I was a lesbian I realised that I fancy men too and that I could not make the political choice to reject them completely. (118)

I defined myself as bisexual after developing a painfully intense crush on a woman when I was sixteen, and realising this didn't alter my sexual feelings for men. (28)

It was a long slow process of realisation. (142)

24 women had always been attracted to both women and men; 11 women identified as bisexual because it was the only label they felt they could apply to themselves; 4 women said they could not choose between men and women; 3 were told by others that they were bisexual. 5 women gave a variety of other reasons for identifying as bisexual.

I have had relationships with both sexes since I was ten. (129)

I always had a semi-awareness of my capacity to respond to both sexes, although this wasn't fully realised until twelve years ago. (17)

I have always been too aware of both heterosexual and lesbian feelings to define myself as anything other than bisexual. (57)

Several years ago one of my women friends was recounting a conversation she had had with someone else where she described me as bisexual. Listening, I realised she was right: I had always had relationships with women and men, but never labelled myself before. (115)

I saw the word 'bisexual' in a dictionary and realised It was a fairly accurate description of myself. (112)

A common myth about bisexual identity is that it is always a short-term measure – usually a stage on the way to becoming lesbian. While some respondents had identified as bisexual in the past and now identified as lesbian, many others had identified as bisexual over a long period of time. Of the 108 respondents who identified in this way, 11 had always identified as bisexual; 15 had identified as bisexual for over ten years; 24 for between five and ten years; 28 for between three and five years; 21 for between one and two years and only 9 for less than a year.

Of course, people who have identified in one way in the past (for however long) do change, as is shown by the respondents who changed from heterosexual or lesbian to bisexual. And for some bisexuals, bisexuality is necessarily a transitional state: a small-scale study conducted in California in 1976 indicated that 11 out of 15 people who currently identified as bisexual saw it in this way – though this may be less likely in the 1990s.[1] However, this can be true of other sexual identities too: 23 per cent of young lesbians in Shere Hite's *Women in Love*[2] felt that they would not necessarily always be lesbian, while according to Klein et al,[3] in a study where 384 people completed the Klein Sexual Orientation Grid, 25 per cent of heterosexual respondents indicated that they would ideally like to be more bisexual.

Uncertainty about sexual identity is something which no section of society allows; the pressure to decide which identity one is going to assume and to stick to it is enormous. For many people, this is achieved only at immense personal cost: surely it would be more useful to see *all* sexualities as states of transition and sexuality as fluid, within or outside a given identity?

Lesbians first

At present I only have relationships with women, but I would not be prepared to rule out the possibility of having another relationship with a man. It is very limiting and narrow-minded to believe you can only ever have sexual/social relations with one sex, although you may socialise predominantly with either one or the other. (33)

44 women (about 30 per cent of the sample) had identified as lesbian at some point in their sexual history and a further 15 had considered the possibility they might be lesbian. For 12 of the 44, their lesbian identity was shattered when they had a relationship with a man. For almost everyone, the change from lesbian to bisexual was a hard one.

It was difficult. Being a lesbian is a very strong identification and I would not have changed without a powerful motive. When I met B, I slept with him without sex for several months because I still felt that I was a lesbian. It took a lot of doing for me to accept that I *was* attracted to him and therefore was bisexual. When I had slept with men before I had always thought of it as a straightforward, purely physical process. (1)

I became extremely involved with a man and realised that I wanted sexual relations with men as well as women. (25)

The other 32 gave a variety of reasons for their change from a lesbian to a bisexual identity. 4 respondents felt that their lesbian identity had been politically motivated, 1 that she had identified as a lesbian for the sake of her lover, 2 women that they had consciously repressed their sexual feelings for men and 3 that their feelings had changed.

My first lesbian relationship made me so euphoric: I thought, 'Oh wow! I'm a lesbian, how wonderful'. But subseqently I realised that I was attracted to some men still, whether I liked it or not, so I thought I'd better come out as bisexual, as that was obviously what I was and I couldn't pretend that both sides weren't there. (16)

At around sixteen I felt guilty somehow for being bisexual and I tried to convince myself that I was lesbian. Eventually, I realised that I was deluding myself. (84)

My politics developed in such a way that I no longer saw men as the enemy or oppressor class. I started sleeping with men friends out of affection, and then I 'fell in love' with a man, and it didn't seem honest or fair to deny the relationship. (7)

I used to be attracted just to women, but I always kept open the option that a prince in shining armour would arrive. This happened when I was twenty-five. (15)

After my first love relationship with a woman I defined myself publicly as lesbian, although deep down I always felt bisexual but 'guilty'. It has taken me a long and painful time to accept my bisexuality and even now I am only out to close friends. (17)

Although I defined myself as a lesbian, I continued to have ambivalent sexual feelings towards men. There were also aspects of what I perceived as the 'lesbian lifestyle' which did not attract me. (40)

2 women said that they remained mainly lesbian, rather than bisexual; 1 felt she was still coming to terms with her bisexuality; another that she was becoming more aware of her bisexual feelings and another that she identified according to the sex of her current partner.

I am not sure I *became* bisexual: I have always been aware of my attraction to men and women, but I choose to identify with whatever connection is the most prominent at the time. (110)

There are many reasons why women have been led to deny their bisexuality – in some cases to themselves as well as to others – in favour of lesbianism. Pressure from friends or lovers; the desire to make a political statement for women; a distaste for the stereo-typical image of bisexual women as oversexed, available to men, trendy and decadent have all played a part. As the responses showed, some bisexual women had or did identify as lesbian politically and publicly, despite their bisexual feelings. This may be particularly true of women currently in primary relationships with other women. As these respondents said:

I am bisexual, because I am able to have sexual and emotional relationships with women or men and have done so. However, I now describe myself as lesbian as I have ceased to have sexual relationships with men and now consider only women as potential sexual partners. (115)

I am a bisexual lesbian feminist. (134)

Sexually I am bisexual with a strong lesbian identity; politically I identify as gay/lesbian. (109)

That women identify as both bisexual and lesbian can advance the cause of both movements. And it appears that the flow is not necessarily one way, as some women who identify predominantly as lesbian are now wanting to ally themselves with the bisexual community:

While I would be fairly happy with the word lesbian, and often use it to define myself, I think it's important to describe my potential to love men and women by the word 'bisexual'. Rather than jumping from one closet to the other, I want to keep the door open and identify with all bisexual people, whatever their sex or exact orientation. (81)

Within bisexual communities, particularly in the US, some women are now calling themselves 'lesbian-identified bisexual', to show where their political allegiance lies and where they choose to place their energy and have relationships. (2 questionnaire respondents identified in precisely this way.) Others call themselves 'heterosexual-identified' – to indicate their sexual preference, rather than their politics, as their presence within the bisexual community signals a political allegiance. Is this sexuality-within-a-sexuality a useful breakdown, or just an even narrower definition that limits sexual fluidity? And what about bisexually-identified bisexuals, who choose individuals as individuals, with no preference for one sex over the other? Though some bisexual activists have argued that it is a myth that bisexuals can be equally attracted to women and men,[4] a substantial number of respondents did not claim any preference. My own view is that bisexuality itself should encompass as broad a definition as possible, and that to produce even narrower categories is counter-productive.

Other respondents used multiple labels to describe themselves: 'heterosexual and lesbian', 'heterosexual/bisexual', 'lesbian and bisexual'. Of the 4 women who described themselves as 'heterosexual and bisexual', 3 were in long-term relationships with men and the other said she preferred men to women for sexual relationships.

I call myself bisexual now as shorthand – I prefer 100 per cent heterosexual and 100 per cent lesbian. 'Bisexual' is a convenience, but it doesn't adequately describe me in my entirety. (110)

I'm a lesbian who sleeps with men. (67)

I am a heterosexual, with bisexual tendencies. I am married and could not give that up, yet I need the freedom of the company of women. (52)

I define myself as bisexual/heterosexual. I use the terms to apply to my sexual preferences and behaviour. (41)

Lesbian and heterosexual, but more lesbian. (138)

For other women, being bisexual signalled a way of relating to people which looked beyond gender and opened the possibility of forming relationships whose patterns fell outside the sanctioned norms of heterosexual or lesbian culture.

I love having no limits on who I can get close to, and having several people who are 'special'. I love the richness of my experience and life. (123)

The fact of being bisexual has made me dislike conformity (or perhaps it was the other way round) and I find conventional sexual relationships unappealing, lesbian conventions included. (99)

Bisexual behaviour/other identities

12 respondents circled 'other' when asked how they identified. These women saw themselves as attracted to people of both sexes, but felt no need to label themselves. 2 women said that the

negative connotations of the word 'bisexual' were an additional reason not to use it.

I believe that we are all just 'sexual' and that the form this takes is determined by predisposing characteristics, our environment and circumstances. (38)

Although objectively people would define me as bisexual, I personally find the term too loaded to be happy about using it. (69)

I don't define myself as bisexual, because it implies a separation from those who don't consider themselves bisexual. (31)

I don't exactly define myself as bisexual because of what it has come to mean politically, but it most accurately describes my sexual behaviour. (32)

I have always had sexual relationships with people regardless of gender, but I don't really 'define' myself as anything. (111)

I am a woman and a feminist – these are the only two labels I am happy with or prepared to own. None of the sexual labels fits in with my view of myself. However, I do have sexual relationships with men and women. (63)

Many of the respondents who identified as bisexual also expressed a dislike for the limitations of fixed sexual identities. 56 women said they considered the use of sexual labels to be a negative thing, and only 11 women thought they were positive or helpful. 35 respondents had mixed feelings, while 16 thought of labels as a necessary political strategy, whatever their personal feelings about using them.

I dislike labels as such. I agree with the continuum theory that has gays and heterosexuals at opposite ends of a continuum of sexuality, with bisexuality in the middle. People move around so much that to label them is essentially false. (5)

I feel uneasy with the use of sexual labelling, because it seems to be restrictive. (78)

I think that as things are now, with a heterosexual and homophobic society which is hostile to any same-sex behaviour, labels such as 'lesbian', 'gay' and 'bisexual' are necessary and useful. They are necessary for us to be able to find others to identify with for strength and support and to create a community and politics. Similarly in lesbian and gay society, the label 'bisexual' has become an important one because it identifies a group who differ from that society in certain ways and are often rejected or ignored for their differences. (1)

Labels are helpful if used with thought and caution. It's a matter for individual choice. (10)

For 12 women, bisexual was a negative label.

The heterosexual and lesbian/gay labels seem fine because they are so specific, whereas bisexual seems a sort of wishy-washy melting-pot, implying one is ready to jump into bed with each and everyone. This doesn't have very much to do with my sexuality! (28)

At present, sexual labels are almost inescapable. Gay and heterosexual people are perceived and treated very differently, and people of all sexualities are anxious to 'place' the sexuality of others so as to know how to relate to them. The fact that bisexual people may not be so easily classifiable is often a cause for anxiety.

Although terms such as 'lesbian', 'gay', 'dyke' or 'queer' have negative connotations in mainstream society, the lesbian and gay communities are constantly challenging those definitions and forming and re-forming their own. Positive connotations for the word 'bisexual' are being formulated within the bisexual movement, but such changes in language take time and require the visible support of substantial numbers of people. This is perhaps why many people who by 'objective' criteria would be considered bisexual do not identify as such, and why 48 respondents said they knew people whose behaviour seemed to be bisexual, but who did not claim bisexual identity.

I do know others who appear bisexual, but it seems superficial, like a kind of act or game. I try not to get mixed up in that. (96)

I have several women friends who have had relationships with women and who are now involved with men. How important those relationships with women were and whether my friends would identify as bisexual I don't know. I've never asked them. (113)

There are many straight women who won't admit what lies behind their flirtation/warmth with women friends. Also I know people who admit to bisexual feelings but prefer not to define themselves that way. (81)

To claim a reviled sexual identity can be a radical act, and for many people there are other issues involved. Few respondents to the questionnaire came from traditionally marginalised groups: for instance, women of colour and women with disabilities were under-represented, as they are under-represented in the bisexual community. It seems likely that women who already suffer oppression for other reasons may be reluctant to take on a sexual identity which will result in further oppression. Many people of colour prioritise racial and cultural identity,[5] although the number of black people loosely connected with the bisexual community is growing and there is a more representative proportion of 'out' black bisexuals in the US. Women with disabilities are often thought of as asexual, Asian women as submissive, and working-class women, Jewish women and black women as hyper-sexual.[6] These pre-existing stereotypes can make the claiming of bisexual identity more difficult for women from these groups.

What bisexuality *is* remains unclear, and its definition varies from person to person. For instance, are married lesbians (women whose sexual and emotional inclinations are towards other women, but who are married) bisexual? Or what about women who consider themselves lesbians, but who nevertheless are sexually attracted to men? The issue was hotly debated at the 1991 National Bisexual Conference in London, in the light of a growing number of lesbians and gay men who are talking about having sex with each other, or recognising their attraction to the opposite sex. Similarly, heterosexual women may have had sex or intimate friendships with other women, but may nevertheless still see themselves as heterosexual. As a friend whom I consider to be bisexual said when I asked her to complete the questionnaire, 'Sex with women is much better, but I call myself heterosexual for emotional reasons'.

Fantasy (whether imagining sexual scenarios or 'daydreaming' about potential partners) is an important part of sexuality, and many respondents' identification of their bisexuality came from the fact that they fantasised about both women and men (only 10 respondents' fantasies were limited to one sex). Psychologists have claimed that the gender fantasised about is the key to determining a person's 'true' sexuality,[7] implying that fantasy is what people would like to do, but don't. But of course the connection between fantasy and action is more complex than this. Surveys ranging from the *Hite Report* to those in women's magazines such as *Elle*[8] indicate that some 6 per cent of heterosexually-identified women would like to have sex with women, that is would like to act on their fantasies, while for others, fantasy plays a different role: for example, imagined scenarios may be arousing precisely because they are forbidden (this is certainly the case for some lesbians, who enjoy sexual fantasies about men precisely because they feel sex with men is taboo).[9] The answer perhaps is that having sexual fantasies about women may lead an outwardly heterosexual woman to identify as bisexual (and having fantasies about men make a lesbian identify in this way, too) if they see them as important enough.

It is, in any case, possible to argue that sexual identities are a white western construct that does not apply through the rest of the world. In many cultures, bisexual behaviour – although not spoken about or labelled as such – is common. Men and women are expected to marry and have children, and locate themselves primarily in a family context, yet their strongest emotional, physical and often sexual relationships are with people of the same gender. This applies in places as diverse as parts of North Africa, where men will have sex with other men before and after marriage;[10] Kenya, where all women are or have been married, but form sexual friendship networks;[11] Nigeria, where it is common for women to be semi-sexual with each other, but to stop short of genital contact;[12] and Mexico, where men having sex with each other are not stigmatised as long as they play the 'masculine' role.[13] This is not to say that legitimised sexuality, as in the west, does not centre on the penis/vagina. But the prevalence of other scenarios clearly makes a mockery of definitions of sexuality which posit an absolute either/or for hetero/homosexuals.

Different ways of being bisexual

Women who identify as bisexual have a wide range of modes of behaviour, lifestyles, feelings and attitudes. Here are just some examples drawn from questionnaire respondents:

- A is largely celibate, because although she prefers sex with men, she doesn't like them emotionally
- B has only had one heterosexual relationship – with her husband. But she has had many women lovers
- C is an out lesbian and has a strong political analysis of lesbianism. But she is secretly bisexual

- D likes feminine men and boyish women. In general she finds men 'low quality', and now that she is in her thirties, finds it increasingly difficult to meet them
- E is a married woman and practising Catholic whose only sexual relationship has been with her husband. Yet she feels that her dreams, emotions and friendships make her bisexual
- F identifies publicly as heterosexual and her boyfriend does not know of her bisexual feelings, which have arisen since the relationship began
- G is active in the bisexual community, and has a ten-year history of committed multiple relationships with men and women
- H is a schoolgirl who has not yet had a 'full' sexual relationship, but feels she would like to explore intimate relationships with both sexes. She has felt this way since she was about ten
- J has had a number of relationships with men, and some (but a smaller number) with women. She would love the balance to be different, but can't see how she would be able to achieve this

Some women wanted different things from men and women: for example, they might fall in love with women and want sex with men; or find men exciting and women nurturing; or women passionate and men protective. Or vice versa. Others were attracted to individuals regardless of gender, and felt that the sex of the person they were involved with was irrelevant. For others, relationships with one sex (usually women) remained on a fantasy level, although the fantasies were strong and important. Some women had 'always known' they were bisexual, some came to realise it in the context of a heterosexual relationship, and some within a lesbian one.

Bisexuality is somehow seen as a soft option – the fact that I can only manage to define myself as a bisexual without being able to turn that into a real, material life, says that it isn't. (86)

In this section I shall discuss the different components of respondents' sexuality through an analysis of their responses to the Klein Sexual Orientation Grid. Fritz Klein, an American psychiatrist, drew up a grid in the 1980s as an elaboration of the scale developed by Kinsey, who places people's sexuality along a heterosexual to homosexual continuum from 0 to 6. The Klein grid recognises that people's sexuality may change over time and that their behaviour and what they would like to do is often significantly different. The grid also records variations in individuals' feelings and identity across different areas of their lives.

The grid sets out seven areas: sexual attraction, sexual behaviour, sexual fantasies, emotional preference, social preference, self-identification, and heterosexual/lesbian lifestyle. The respondent is asked to identify (on a scale of 1 to 7) the degree of heterosexuality/lesbianism she has or has had in these areas in the past, in the present and as an ideal. The degrees are: 1 heterosexual only; 2 heterosexual mostly; 3 heterosexual somewhat; 4 heterosexual/lesbian equally; 5 lesbian somewhat; 6 lesbian mostly; 7 lesbian only. The figures relate only to gender preference, and not to any other aspect of partner preference such as age or behaviour.

	Past	Present	Ideal
A. Sexual attraction			
B. Sexual behaviour			
C. Sexual fantasies			
D. Emotional preference			
E. Social preference			
F. Self-identification			
G. Heterosexual/lesbian lifestyle			

Questionnaire respondents' completed grids (figures are calculated on the 97 respondents who gave unequivocal responses to each category) displayed a wide range of variation. Some women's figures indicated that overall they identified as mostly lesbian; others as mostly heterosexual. Some women had similar figures for emotional and social preference, yet totally different figures for the three sexual categories; some had substantial variations between past, present and ideal figures.

The most 1s (heterosexual only) were in past lifestyle, which was the case for more than one-third of the sample (34 women), followed by past sexual behaviour, which 30 women marked as heterosexual only. No respondents marked heterosexual only for present self-identification, or for emotional preference. In general, there were few 1s in either the present or ideal figures.

4s (heterosexual/lesbian equally) were strongly represented across all categories in the present figures, and even more so in the ideal figures. For instance, 64 women (about two-thirds of the sample), were equally sexually attracted to men and women as an ideal, whereas the corresponding present figure was only 39.

The highest number of 7s (lesbian only) occurred in the grids of the 11 women whose current emotional preference was entirely lesbian; no women marked lesbian only for past sexual behaviour. For most categories, fewer than 5 women gave lesbian only, while 6 women seemed to be almost entirely lesbian in their present and ideal categories.

What follows is a category-by-category analysis of the figures:

A. *Sexual attraction*

	Past	Present	Ideal
1	12	1	1
2	30	3	2
3	15	13	2
4	25	39	54
5	6	20	14
6	8	17	16
7	1	4	8

(1 heterosexual only; 2 heterosexual mostly; 3 heterosexual somewhat; 4 heterosexual/lesbian equally; 5 lesbian somewhat; 6 lesbian mostly; 7 lesbian only)

Respondents' figures for sexual attraction indicate that the majority had been more sexually attracted to men than to women in the past, although most had been sexually attracted to women to some degree. Present figures indicate that almost 40 per cent of the sample were equally attracted to men and women, with a similar number being somewhat or mostly attracted to women, indicating a bias towards sexual attraction to women. Ideal figures were heavily weighted to equal attraction to men and women (over half the sample), with most of the rest indicating that they would rather be sexually attracted to women than to men.

B. *Sexual behaviour*

	Past	Present	Ideal
1	30	15	2
2	36	26	3
3	9	12	4
4	11	14	53
5	5	7	11
6	6	16	16
7	0	7	8

Respondents' past sexual behaviour was also mainly heterosexual, with about two-thirds having little or no past sexual experience with women. Present figures were more evenly distributed, though the number of respondents who had more sex with men than with women was about twice those who had more sex with women than with men. Over half the sample indicated that ideally they would like equal amounts of sex with women and men, while just over one-quarter wanted more sex with women than with men. 15 women were currently sexual only with men; 7 only with women. 2 women would ideally be sexual only with men (currently these 2 women were both happily monogamous); 8 women ideally only with women. These 8 comprised 3 women in monogamous lesbian relationships, and 5 who were not (it therefore did not include all the 7 women currently having sex only with women).

C. Sexual fantasies

	Past	Present	Ideal
1	8	3	1
2	25	8	3
3	20	9	2
4	17	38	54
5	9	12	15
6	17	20	16
7	1	7	6

Though figures for women's pasts were again weighted towards heterosexual experiences, only 8 respondents had no lesbian sexual fantasies in their pasts and about one-quarter of the sample had had more sexual fantasies about women than about men. In the present, most women considered men and women equally important in their sexual fantasies, though a third of the sample had more fantasies about women than about men, and only half that number more fantasies about men than about women. Only 10 respondents were monosexual in their fantasies. It is interesting to compare the figures for sexual fantasy with those for sexual behaviour: in both past and present categories, respondents who had fantasies about women significantly outnumbered those who were sexually active with women. Ideal figures again showed that more than half the sample would like to fantasise equally about women and men. Significantly more women (31) preferred to fantasise more about women than men than vice versa (5).

6 women who completed the rest of the grid did not complete the ideal part of the fantasy section, indicating that they would prefer not to have sexual fantasies at all. The reasons given were that they had been damaged by them, or that the fantasies evoked feelings they did not like. One of these women was a sexual masochist; 3 others were incest survivors. The remaining 2 felt that sexual fantasies were detrimental to forming genuine relationships.

D. Emotional preference

	Past	Present	Ideal
1	9	1	0
2	16	3	1
3	14	7	3
4	18	38	49
5	18	18	21
6	19	19	14
7	3	11	9

Respondents' past experience of emotional preference was more evenly distributed than for any other category, with significantly more women indicating a preference for women than in any other area of their lives. Present and ideal figures both showed the highest number of women as having no preference, with the vast majority of the rest falling on the lesbian side of the grid.

E. Social preference

	Past	Present	Ideal
1	15	2	2
2	28	10	2
3	17	7	3
4	19	52	60
5	10	15	16
6	6	7	12
7	2	5	4

Respondents' past social preference was fairly evenly distributed between heterosexual only and somewhat lesbian. In the present and ideal categories, over half the respondents indicated that they liked the company of women and men equally, with the next largest number indicating a slight preference for the company of women.

F. Self-identification

	Past	Present	Ideal
1	23	0	1
2	26	4	2
3	12	15	5
4	18	47	55
5	11	14	15
6	5	13	14
7	2	4	5

Respondents' past sexual identities were fairly evenly distributed between heterosexual only and somewhat lesbian, with about half the sample in the heterosexual mostly or only groups. Present and ideal figures showed a clear majority of 4s, indicating that most women identify as 50/50 bisexual, with more respondents identifying or wanting to identify as somewhat or mostly lesbian than as somewhat or mostly heterosexual.

G. Lifestyle

	Past	Present	Ideal
1	34	6	1
2	27	25	3
3	13	22	8
4	13	22	52
5	6	10	11
6	3	9	17
7	1	3	5

Respondents' past figures were significantly biased towards the heterosexual side of the grid, with the figure of 34 as the highest heterosexual only total for any category. In the present, a significant number of respondents had moved towards the centre of the grid, though more than half remained mostly or somewhat heterosexual. Just under one-quarter of respondents gave 4 as a response (the smallest number of any category), with a further quarter on the lesbian side of the grid. This implies that even women with significant amounts of lesbian sexual contact had somewhat heterosexual lifestyles. The ideal figures were again predominantly 4s, with about half the sample wanting to live a bisexual lifestyle. As an ideal, more women were on the lesbian side of the grid, with about one-third of the sample wanting somewhat or mostly lesbian lifestyles.

Overall, past figures in every category were weighted towards heterosexuality – and the numbers given seemed to indicate that even women who had identified as lesbian at some point had still had predominantly heterosexual pasts (3 women indicated that they had had two pasts and therefore could not complete the grid as it stood). Present figures indicated that women had moved towards the centre of the grid, with high numbers of 4s in most categories. Only 1 respondent gave 4s for all present categories. The lowest 4 figure in the present was for sexual activity (14 respondents), indicating that having equal numbers of male and female partners is not easy. It was, however, seen as the ideal for 53 women. There was very little consistency in figures given for pasts, presents and ideals whatever the category, as the sample grids below show.

Many women's ideal figures differed from their present ones. Below is a selection of responses to my question of why this was so (these are not quantified into types, as the answers are too specific and varied).

I think bisexuality is the only valid political choice, but I find men very difficult to relate to. There is one man that I am attracted to at the moment, but apart from him my desires are all directed towards women. (76)

(This respondent gave figures for the present which were biased more towards the lesbian side of the grid than her ideal figures.)

I have two children, and I respect the promises I made to their father. We have just moved and I hardly know anyone, and because the children are very young I cannot go out for long. I am consciously living in a self-imposed limbo, and will break out when I'm ready. (91)

(This respondent had present figures which ranged from 1 to 6, whereas her ideal figures were all 7s – i.e., her ideal life would be completely lesbian.)

There is a lack of availability of women, with fewer lesbians available than straight men, and the lesbian lifestyle is a little hard to get into. (87)

(This respondent's present figures were mainly 4s apart from current sexual behaviour and lifestyle, which were both 2s. Her ideal figures were all 4s.)

The differences between the figures are from the problems of managing to live openly as bisexual due to lovers' feelings, friends' feelings, family's feelings and society generally. (34)

(This respondent's ideals were all 4s. Within her present figures, sexual attraction, fantasies and self-identification were 4s whereas the rest, including sexual behaviour and lifestyle, were 6s and 7s.)

The difference in figures is due to lack of opportunity, perhaps a secret fear of changing my lifestyle; social conditioning; a need for sex, and heterosexual sex is much more available; having a deeper respect for women and therefore not pressurising a woman into having sex, which I might do with a man. I have a social dependency about men which I detest, but cannot deny. (18)

(This respondent's present figures ranged from 2 to 5, with most responses being 4. Her ideal figures were all 5s and 6s, indicating that she would rather be a little more lesbian.)

24 women gave all 4s for their ideal figures, and the majority of respondents' ideal figures ranged from 3 to 5. Few women's ideal figures were biased towards the heterosexual side of the grid: the highest number in any category was 8 women who indicated 3 (slightly heterosexual) for the lifestyle category. Several women consistently gave 6s and 7s as ideal figures and at least 5 women gave 7 (wholly lesbian) as their ideal in every category (although some women only gave one or two 7s in this section of the grid). At least 12 women gave 6 in every ideal category, and on the whole more women gave 6s than 5s. It would seem from these responses that a significant proportion of bisexual women would like to be mostly lesbian.

12 women rejected the idea of there being any ideal (and therefore do not appear in the 97 answers detailed above). The women who expanded on this said either that they did not know what their ideal would be, or rejected the idea of there being any ideal option.

I can't say I want to be this way or that. I just want to be happy, and will go the way I feel will give me the most happiness. (114)

I couldn't really say that ideally I want to be attracted more to one sex than to another. It seems to be an unreal limitation on the future – I just take things as they come. (48)

What cannot be seen from the previous analysis is the variations within individual's grids. The following complete charts give some idea of the range of responses:

Sonia

	Past	Present	Ideal
A. Sexual attraction	4	6	6
B. Sexual behaviour	2	6	7
C. Sexual fantasies	1	3	6
D. Emotional preference	5	7	7
E. Social preference	2	6	6
F. Self-identification	2	6	6
G. Heterosexual/lesbian lifestyle	1	3	6

Sonia's past was more heterosexual than not, although she had always somewhat preferred women to men emotionally. Her present figures were mainly lesbian, except in the areas of fantasy and lifestyle, which fell into the somewhat heterosexual band. At the time of answering the questionnaire, she had no significant sexual relationship. Her ideal figures were mainly lesbian, and she said that the differences in her chart occurred because: 'My sexuality has been and still is evolving'.

Denise

	Past	Present	Ideal
A. Sexual attraction	5	6	6
B. Sexual behaviour	2	2	2
C. Sexual fantasies	6	7	7
D. Emotional preference	4	6	7
E. Social preference	6	6	6
F. Self-identification	6	6	6
G. Heterosexual/lesbian lifestyle	2	4	6

Denise's past figures indicated that she considered herself mainly lesbian, except in the areas of lifestyle and sexual behaviour, which were predominantly heterosexual, and emotional preference, where she gave equal importance to men and women. Her present figures had moved towards the lesbian side of the grid, except for sexual behaviour, which had remained the same. Her ideal figures are different because she feels her sexuality is 90 per cent lesbian, yet she is in a long-term relationship with a man with whom she is, she says, 'definitely in love'. She has identified as bisexual for eight years.

Lorna

	Past	Present	Ideal
A. Sexual attraction	2	3	4
B. Sexual behaviour	2	6	4
C. Sexual fantasies	2	3	4
D. Emotional preference	5	5	5
E. Social preference	5	5	5
F. Self-identification	2	4	4
G. Heterosexual/lesbian lifestyle	2	6	4

Lorna's past figures showed that she was mainly heterosexual in all areas except emotional and social preference, where she somewhat preferred women. Her present figures indicated that while she was somewhat more sexually attracted to men and likely to fantasise about them sexually, her sexual behaviour and lifestyle were mainly lesbian. Ideally, she would give equal weight to men and women, except in the emotional and social preference categories, where she somewhat preferred women (these two categories were consistent through each of the chart's timescales). Lorna is in a long-term relationship with a woman, although her past relationships have been with men. She 'probably' prefers sex with men, but is emotionally closer to women.

Annette

	Past	Present	Ideal
A. Sexual attraction	4	1	4
B. Sexual behaviour	3	1	1
C. Sexual fantasies	3	2	4
D. Emotional preference	6	1	4
E. Social preference	5	4	4
F. Self-identification	4	4	4
G. Heterosexual/lesbian lifestyle	4	2	2

Annette's past included significant involvement with both men and women. Her present figures indicated that she had moved towards the heterosexual side of the grid, though her ideal figures moved back towards the centre, except in the areas of sexual behaviour and lifestyle. Her social preference and self-identification remained fairly consistent. Annette added: 'Looking at the figures, you have to take into account my current position as a woman in love and about to marry, with no intention of ever taking another sexual partner'.

Sheila

	Past	Present	Ideal
A. Sexual attraction	4	5	
B. Sexual behaviour	1	5	
C. Sexual fantasies	4	4	
D. Emotional preference	5	5	
E. Social preference	4	4	
F. Self-identification	2	4/5	
G. Heterosexual/lesbian lifestyle	2	4	

Although Sheila had no sexual contact with women in the past section of the chart, and her identity and lifestyle were mainly heterosexual, she gave figures for sexual attraction, fantasies and emotional and social preference that placed equal importance on men and women. Her present figures were fairly consistent, indicating that she preferred women somewhat. Sheila put 'N/A' in the ideal column: 'At present I am very confident about my bisexuality and happy in my relationship with my female lover. What more could I ask for – life is wonderful!'

Brenda

	Past	Present	Ideal
A. Sexual attraction	6	6	4
B. Sexual behaviour	6	4	4
C. Sexual fantasies	6	6	4
D. Emotional preference	6	4	4
E. Social preference	6	4	4
F. Self-identification	6	5	4
G. Heterosexual/lesbian lifestyle	6	3	4

Brenda's past was consistently mainly lesbian. Her present figures showed mainly lesbian sexual attraction and fantasies; sexual behaviour and emotional and social preferences directed equally towards men and women; a somewhat lesbian self-identity and a somewhat heterosexual lifestyle. Her ideal figures showed that she would like to have no preference between men and women in any area of the grid. Brenda is married and in a 'traditional family' set-up with the only man with whom she has been sexually involved. Her past was almost entirely lesbian, and she still has women lovers as she does not believe in monogamy.

Rosa

	Past	Present	Ideal
A. Sexual attraction	3	3	4
B. Sexual behaviour	2	1/2	3/4
C. Sexual fantasies	3	4	4
D. Emotional preference	3	4	4
E. Social preference	3	3	4
F. Self-identification	3	2	4
G. Heterosexual/lesbian lifestyle	1	1	3

Rosa's past figures were slightly heterosexual overall, with an exclusively heterosexual lifestyle, which was unchanged in her present figures. In all other areas, she had moved towards a more equal balance between women and men. Her ideal figures indicated that she would like this move to continue. Rosa is in a relationship with a man, but most of her other intimate relationships are with women. She has identified as bisexual for five years – following 'an enormous crush' on a woman, which was unrequited.

A future bisexuality

How do we define bisexual? It is apparent from the analyses in the previous section that a bisexual identity encompasses many different elements, and as bisexuality as an identity gains strength and visibility, more people will probably come to identify in this way. Could it be that everyone is bisexual, as 15 respondents specifically stated?

Everyone is bisexual – but they don't admit it, they repress it. (21)

I think everyone is born bisexual. I was: and I rediscovered it when I was seventeen. (121)

Yet even if everyone has the potential to be bisexual, and in an ideal world in which gender would not matter, the majority of people would behave bisexually, it does not mean that everyone is bisexual here and now.

Perhaps the easiest option is to claim as bisexual anyone who defines themselves in this way. Unlike 'lesbian' or 'heterosexual', 'bisexual' does not describe a specific sexual activity, and to link bisexual identity to behaviour, whereby people could only claim to be bisexual if they have currently or recently had sex or a relationship with people of both sexes, would limit the number of people who could use bisexual as a consistent identity. In my view, one is bisexual through feelings, fantasies, attractions, identifications, friendships, community and political activity – whether one is celibate, in a monogamous relationship with a person of either sex, or having multiple relationships. It is an identity which cannot be altered by a partner – whoever they are, whatever the type or length of the relationship. The only person who can decide on your sexual identity is you – and no matter how hard other people might try, they cannot dictate your feelings.

As Colin Spencer writes:

> As far as I can detect, I have always felt bisexual, strongly and equally attracted to men and women. At certain stages in my life, for psychological reasons, I have felt impelled to love and be loved by a man instead of a woman, or vice versa.[14]

Bisexuals, like people of other sexualities, often see their own orientation as superior. And although bisexuality may not be the best of both worlds, it can be a bridge between the two, pulling together two sides of sexuality which are usually distant. It can be a way of expressing a sexuality which sees the person rather than the gender; it can be a way of having relationships which do not rely on stereotypes; it can be a way of relating more closely to people of both sexes; it can encompass many types of sexuality and many different people. Ideally, bisexuality is a way of forming relationships without putting boundaries on them because of gender.

Defining and labelling sexuality is not an end in itself. Ideally, labels will become irrelevant, and everyone will be able to have sexual/emotional relationships with whomsoever they choose. But that day is a long way off: at present, bisexuality has negative connotations for the vast majority of people and the only way to change that is for people who consider themselves to be bisexual to say so, loudly. To define oneself in any way is, perhaps, restrictive, presupposing a fixed identity which for many people is not possible; however, bisexuality does allow for a multiplicity of behaviours and is a more open label than most.

Notes

1. Jack Leroy Harwell, *Bisexuality: Persistent Lifestyle or Transitional State?*, Dissertation to Graduate Faculty School of Human Behavior, United States International University, San Diego, 1976
2. Shere Hite, *Women in Love,* Penguin, 1989
3. Fritz Klein, Barry Sepekoff & Timothy J. Wolf, 'Sexual Orientation: A Multi-Variable Dynamic Process' in Klein & Wolf (eds), *Two Lives to Lead (Bisexuality in Men and Women)*, Harrington Park Press, 1985
4. For example, Sharon Forman Sumpter, 'Myths and Realities of Bisexuality' in Hutchins and Kaahumanu (eds), *Bi Any Other Name*, Alyson Publications, 1991
5. Pratibha Parmar in Cherry Smyth's *Lesbians Talk Queer Notions*, Scarlet Press, 1992 and Carmen, Gail, Neena, Tamara in 'Becoming Visible: Black Lesbian Discussions' in Feminist Review (ed), *Sexuality: A Reader*, Virago, 1989, make this point
6. See, for instance, Charles H. Stember, *Sexual Racism*, Elsevier, 1976 and D. Bullard & S. Knight (eds), *Sexuality and Physical Disability*, Mosby, 1981
7. Anna Freud, *Before the Best Interests of the Child*, New York, 1979, p121
8. *Elle*, April 1992
9. See, for example, Pat Califia, *Macho Sluts*, Alyson Publications, 1988
10. Interview with Mohammed from forthcoming Off Pink Collective book
11. Gill Shepherd 'Rank, gender and homosexuality: (Mombasa as a key to understanding sexual options)' in Pat Caplan (ed), *The Cultural Construction of Sexuality*, Tavistock, 1987
12. Buchi Emecheta, *New Internationalist*, November 1989
13. J.M. Carrier, 'Mexican Male Bisexuality' in Fritz Klein & Timothy Wolf (eds), *Two Lives to Lead*, Harrington Park Press, 1985
14. Colin Spencer, *Which of Us Two?*, Viking, 1990, p259

7 The politics of bisexuality

In its broadest sense, politics affects every aspect of our lives. What we can and cannot do, even what we are able to think, are all constructed by 'society' and our place within it. And in order for there to be a true acceptance within society at large that gender is immaterial in the choice of sexual partner, enormous changes will have to be made.

The degree of choice and control each individual has over his or her life depends on a number of factors, including gender, race, class, poverty/affluence, age, physical attributes, personality and so on, the relative importance of which varies from person to person. Certain groups in society have power at the expense of other groups, and our relationship to that power is an important aspect in determining our freedom of sexual expression. But though our options may be curtailed by circumstance, everyone does have some degree of choice over how to live their lives, however difficult their choices may be.

Several respondents saw their sexual identity as connected with other political struggles. One respondent wrote (after Adrienne Rich) that bisexuals have an 'outsider's vision' – that because we are not accepted by society and do not find images of ourselves in society's norms, bisexuals easily identify with other oppressed groups. While it is true that many of the advertisements seeking questionnaire respondents were placed in left-ish or 'alternative' publications, the number of respondents who identified with other political struggles was surprisingly high: 90 described themselves as some form of socialist (from Labour voters to revolutionary socialists); 30 described their politics as green; 10 were anarchist; 10 were 'liberal' or middle-of-the-road; 5 said they had no political opinions; 2 were right wing and 2 were not sure. (Some respondents gave more than one answer.) From reading respondents' comments and from personal observation, it seems that a substantial number of bisexuals seek what could broadly be called

184

'alternative' lifestyles, including anarchist/hippy/punk, or have a commitment to non-monogamy, ecology, communal living and so on.[1]

So much that is wrong with the world relates to these screwed-up hierarchies of gender. I see my sexuality as a way to combat sexism – and in turn racism, militarism, imperialism – and the ways human beings defined as 'other' are dehumanised and oppressed. (56)

By refusing to limit my sexuality to the accepted heterosexual mould, I am challenging the 'status quo' e.g. nuclear family; male/female roles. (48)

Bisexual women are an oppressed group and must fight back to re-educate themselves and others. (83)

In answer to the question, 'Do you see your sexuality in any sense as political?', 86 women said 'yes', 31 'no', and 22 were not sure. However, individuals who answered 'yes' had very different views of where the political dimension of their sexuality lay.

Is my sexuality political? I can't see what else it could be! (110)

It is political in that it is essentially self-defined, which in itself is political – the power of groups to name themselves rather than have definitions imposed upon them is crucial. (57)

For some women, it was having relationships with other women, and thus breaking the dominant mould of sexuality, that upturned the status quo. For others, the political challenge lay in being outside the heterosexual/homosexual opposition. Some women believed that their bisexuality enabled them to form different types of relationships with men or that it was their rejection of traditionally feminine behaviour that was political.

My lesbianism is definitely political. It is choosing to act only on part of my sexuality. I still (occasionally) see/meet men I find attractive but I don't act on it – as I don't act on every instance of finding a woman sexually attractive. (115)

I'm very aware of men as oppressors (whether they individually mean to be or not) and find it hard to separate relationships with men from that oppression. (100)

I do think that bisexuality or lesbianism is a political standpoint in that it rejects society's norm and accepted morality. Coming out is

also a political statement – but politics did not cause my bisexuality. **(97)**

Bisexuality is definitely political: it's a resistance to being pushed into a gay or straight category and thus challenges such categories and categorisation generally. **(76)**

I can't behave as most men want women to be: dinky, pretty, sweet housewifely. I'm big, tall, clever and decisive: I'm not as tolerant of men as when I was younger. **(59)**

At present it is impossible within society at large for relationships that are not based on the model of the heterosexual nuclear family to exist without comment. Many lesbian and gay groups are fighting for tolerance and/or for equal rights; however, tolerance and uncritical acceptance are not the same thing. Same-sex couples may eventually be allowed to marry, for instance, and homosexuals may be publicly acknowledged within certain spheres (for example, the arts), but there is a vast gap between this recognition of difference (or deviancy) and the acceptance of homosexuality as natural, normal and unremarkable.

The realisation that equal rights on paper will not necessarily lead to profound social change is one of the impulses behind the new queer politics, spearheaded in the UK by the groups ACT-UP and OutRage. Proponents of queer believe that gay liberation has not achieved enough, and that rather than seeking acceptance, people who do not identify with the mainstream heterosexual world should fight back with anger. Adherents of queer are turning their backs on straight society and seek – at least in theory – to bring together people of both sexes and of all races whose sexuality is proscribed, actively including bisexuals, to participate in the struggle. Queer activists set out to challenge all proscriptions on sexual behaviour and can be as critical of feminist sexual norms as of any others. And they believe in having fun with their politics, with demonstrations that include wink-ins, kiss-ins and the outing of army generals.

Queer is fighting a society in which homophobia is endemic and is actively promoted by legislation and most of the media. All legislation and representations that assume that people who are not heterosexual are inferior, sick, wicked or sad, is homophobic and preys on the fears of those who are looking for scapegoats for society's (or their own) problems. Obviously homophobia is suffered directly by bisexuals in same-sex relationships, but those in opposite-sex relationships feel it too, in more subtle ways. Bisexuals may find that their heterosexual side is accepted and encouraged, and their homosexual side ignored or derided. The construction of homosexuality as a deviation from the norm means that people are assumed to be heterosexual until proved otherwise, so bisexuals may find themselves silenced and unable to talk about half their feelings. This may be a less threatening form of oppression than queer-bashing, but it is oppression nonetheless.

The word 'biphobia' – irrational prejudice against bisexuals – has recently been coined to describe discrimination that results not from bisexuals' desire for same-sex relationships, but from their capacity for relationships with people of both sexes. It is biphobia that has created the myths that bisexuals are oversexed, can't choose, want the best of both worlds and, in the age of AIDS, are responsible for the spread of HIV to the heterosexual and/or lesbian communities. Biphobia is exhibited by lesbians and gay men as well as by heterosexuals: bisexuals are believed to break lesbians' hearts, to take from lesbians and give nothing in return, and to have the 'disgusting' desire to relate to men. (This is not the same as lesbians who believe bisexuals should choose to be same-sex-identified for political reasons, which is a more complex issue; biphobia is *unreasonable* prejudice similar to that propagated against lesbians by heterosexuals.) As with homophobia, biphobia is kept in place by fear – of the unknown; of the freedom to choose lovers regardless of gender; of the weakening effect this could have on the norms on which the heterosexual and/or lesbian and gay communities are based.

All oppressed peoples recognise the need to work twice as hard to prove themselves, and biphobia has created a pressure on bisexuals to prove that we are better than other people – less liable to break hearts, more committed and monogamous, less confused. But always trying to avoid making mistakes in order to combat unfair stereotypes and constantly having to defend one's own and other bisexuals' behaviour and world view can create unrealistic expectations. Many feminists in the 1970s entered lesbian relationships fully believing that their sexual/emotional problems would be over and that relationships with other women would automatically be rewarding and egalitarian; the gap between expectation and reality was for many women a great disappointment. It is important to be realistic about bisexuality too: of course some bisexuals are confused; some are in transition; some break hearts;

some use people. It also may be true that some stereotypes can become self-fulfilling prophecies: if you are constantly told you are confused, you will begin to feel and act that way; if your partner constantly tells you that because you are bisexual you will leave her/him, then the chances are this is what will happen.

The oppression facing bisexuals means that many come to believe the myths themselves. People with bisexual desires have often thought that they were bad, confused and greedy, or have repressed their feelings. They begin to wonder why they cannot choose one sex over another – what is wrong with them. To swallow the idea that to have sexual/emotional feelings towards people of both sexes is wrong is a powerful form of self-oppression.

Respondents' feelings about their own sexuality varied, though in general they were positive rather than negative. 59 felt good about their sexuality, 7 simply felt that it was normal for them.

I like my sexuality. I used to wish for something simpler – one or the other – but I don't any more. (1)

I am happy about my sexuality most of the time and increasingly becoming positive about it as I meet other bisexuals. (2)

My sexuality seems natural and obvious to me. (98)

I now have the confidence to define myself as I feel, not as I think I ought to feel. (131)

41 respondents said they had mixed feelings, 18 felt confused, and 5 felt bad about their sexuality.

I feel strong in my definition but still feel guilty about the heterosexual side. I feel defiant, lonely. I feel I'm never going to be fulfilled, whatever choice I make. (85)

Confused! And happy (not necessarily in that order). (21)

I feel mostly good. It's not being bisexual that mixes me up but feelings about being non-monogamous. (25)

Most respondents had been helped in their positive feelings towards their sexuality by role models, both male and female. 48 respondents said that they had had positive role models for their sexuality, many of whom were not necessarily bisexual, though respondents may have perceived them as being so. The majority were famous people or characters in books; some women mentioned archetypes, such as 'the earth mother'. As most women said they had known no other bisexuals before identifying as such (and some still knew very few) such models were very important.

The bisexual community

Meeting other people who identify as you do, for whom a basic level of explanation is not necessary, and with whom a certain amount of acceptance goes without saying, has been a lifeline for all sorts of oppressed people. The knowledge that other bisexuals exist – whether from personal contacts, books such as this, television programmes or articles in the press – helps to forge a sense of community as well as promoting a social climate in which bisexuality is recognised. While the eventual goal must be for there to be no further need for communities based on sexuality, in the short term, they play a vital role in giving members of oppressed groups strength in the face of a generally hostile society.

Bisexual groups at present represent most clearly the public face of the bisexual community, though not everyone wants to attend a group where people meet solely on the basis of sexuality – and, for practical reasons, not everybody can. Unfortunately, there is as yet no bisexual club scene, such as lesbians and gay men enjoy in most metropolitan areas in the UK: the nearest to it is probably some mixed gay clubs and 'queer' clubs, such as the mainly SM Saidie Maisie club in London, where gender seems almost irrelevant.

At the time of writing there are thirteen mixed bisexual groups and five bisexual women's groups in the UK – and more are starting up. The most enduring is the London Bisexual Group, started from an anti-sexist men's group in 1981, which now has approximately equal numbers of male and female members. The group has weekly discussion-based meetings, with business dealt with by an elected committee. It also runs a helpline two evenings a week, does referrals to other bisexual groups or contacts around the country, and provides speakers for events. Also very active is the Edinburgh Bisexual Group, started in the mid-1980s. It also meets weekly, offering support and discussions. Other groups have been set up more recently in Norwich (which also runs a national newsletter, *Bi-Frost*), Nottingham and Leeds, and two groups organised specifically for bisexual political activism are starting. The London Bisexual Women's Group, which began in 1984, was the second to arise from the feminist movement (the first, which began in 1983, fizzled out as the second was formed). Initially, there was little contact between the London women's and mixed groups, though over the years more links have been forged. The women's group has operated mainly as an emotional and social support group, but is now considering more political activity. The other women's groups are based in Birmingham, Manchester, Nottingham and Sheffield.

44 questionnaire respondents had attended a bisexual group: 23 a mixed group, 15 a women's group, and 5 both. 34 women found attending the groups useful and/or important; 6 found it somewhat important; 4 felt the experience had been negative. Some women said they would not want to go to a mixed group on the grounds that talking about sexuality is political, and they did not trust men to share their political perspective.

Most men I have met at bisexual events have been OK to great, but there always seem to be one or two who are really predatory, or who take over the group completely, or who come out with unthinking sexism they won't even consider. (99)

A primary reason for joining a group is to meet other bisexuals. 103 respondents knew other self-identified bisexuals, though 26 said they knew very few. A further 26 knew none at all. Some women had found attending a bisexual group useful and important, but now wanted more.

When I was 'coming to terms with my sexuality', going to a bisexual group – in my case a women-only group – was essential. Now I feel comfortable with my sexuality, I'm not sure what I would get out of it. (99)

Yes! Going to the group is both important and useful, but I would like to be in a group that did things in a wider political sense, in order to change people's perceptions of bisexuality. (11)

Bisexual groups to date have offered social networking, discussion and emotional support. This kind of support is vital, but in order to bring about any kind of political change, more is needed, hence the newly formed bisexual activist networks. Some bisexuals do not want the movement to engage in political activity, believing that people whose sexuality does not fit the norm should keep quiet and 'act respectable'. But as years of quiet behaviour have got bisexuals nowhere, simply perpetuating bisexuality as invisible, some bisexuals, along with lesbians and gay men, are now considering queer activism as the way forward. Bisexual men have also become involved in campaigns around AIDS and have worked with official bodies to set up projects to educate men who have sex with men – regardless of self-definition – and to target bisexual men in particular.

The increasing popularity of the bisexual conferences which have been held at various locations since 1984 is also indicative of the changing climate of opinion towards bisexuality and the growing sense of community. Initially, the events were fairly low-key, but now ever larger numbers gather for increasingly sophisticated debate. The 1991 conference included sessions on: Outing; The Suppression of Freud's Theory of Bisexuality; Monogamy and Multiple Relationships; Transsexuality; Quakerism; Feminism; Queer; Bisexuality and Astrology; Black and Bisexual; the Bisexual Erotic Imagination and many more. The conferences tend to be more politically oriented than the group meetings and attract people who for various reasons do not attend groups. These gatherings of people from diverse areas, lifestyles and backgrounds for a weekend of intense discussion have helped many isolated people get by from year to year.

It has been argued by some that it is difficult for bisexuals to form a sustained community because of the shifting population of those who identify in this way,[2] and certainly in the past, particularly in the US, groups have come and gone, seemingly leaving little behind. People who define their sexuality on the basis of the gender of their current partner, rather than on their own continuing feelings, will, of course, move between heterosexual and homosexual identification, and many bisexuals are also part (for some at different times, for others always) of both heterosexual and homosexual communities. Bisexuals locate their identities and live their lives in very different ways, and at present there is no bisexual culture or 'look' (for example, bisexual clothes or hair cuts!). Bisexuals are too obviously diverse for that.

At the time of writing, bisexual groups are known to exist in Germany, the Netherlands, Japan and New Zealand, but it is in the US that they have most obviously flourished. The one or two groups which stopped and started in the 1970s and early 1980s have now given way to a strong nationwide network: according to the North American Multi-Cultural Bisexual Network, there are over 100 bisexual organisations in the US and Canada, some general, others highly specialised (e.g. Bisexual Adult Children of

Alcoholics). Three books on bisexuality have been published in the US in the past three years, and others are in preparation.[3]

The US bisexual community at the time of writing is more active and overtly political than that in the UK. Women are in more prominent positions, there are more visible bisexuals of colour, and issues of racism, anti-semitism, sexism and disability are firmly on the agenda. In addition, bisexuals seem to be more involved in US queer groups, including LABIA (an acronym for 'Lesbians and Bisexuals in Action'). There is also a group called 'UBIQUITOUS': 'Uppity Bi Queers United in their Overtly Unconventional Sexuality'.

Close links have been established in recent years between bisexual groups in the US and UK, as well as between individual activists, with people crossing the Atlantic in both directions to address meetings, attend conferences and help to develop ideas. The 1990 US National Bisexual Conference in San Francisco was attended by a UK contingent and 1991 saw the first International Bisexual Conference in Amsterdam, which attracted delegates from the UK, US, Austria, France, Germany, Belgium, Canada, and of course, the Netherlands. Clearly this conference was not truly international, but it did allow valuable connections to be made between individual struggles in different countries. A second international conference was held in London in 1992.

Bisexuality and the lesbian/gay communities

One of the reasons that a bisexual movement in the UK has become established now, rather than fifteen years ago, is the current strength of the lesbian and gay communities. Section 28 has been followed by other threatening legislation such as Clause 25 of the Criminal Justice Bill, which could recriminalise some forms of sexual behaviour between consenting adult men; the Operation Spanner case, where men were imprisoned for consensual sado-masochistic sex; and the guidelines to the 1990 Children's Act, which seek to prevent lesbians and gay men from fostering children. Together with the homophobia stirred up by the AIDS epidemic, such precedents have led many previously apolitical lesbians and gay men to rethink their position. Greater numbers of gay people are now unapologetic about their sexuality, are speaking out about it in public, and are developing stronger networks and an autonomous culture with its own novels, poetry, music, academic and political theory, newspapers and television programmes.

Bisexuals have always worked within lesbian or gay groups – but usually without being open about their sexuality. As the first bisexual groups were formed, and bisexuality was more publicly acknowledged, it gradually became easer to identify as bisexual, though this could still be problematic within lesbian or gay organisations. It is essential for bisexuals to be open about their sexuality whenever possible in these groups: ensuring that bisexual issues are heard is the responsibility of politically active bisexuals to those people who are not yet out or active. But that is not the same as pushing bisexuality down gay people's throats when you are working for the same things – or insisting that everyone is really bisexual.

The threats to freedom of sexual expression that face us all in the 1990s are extensive, and we need to fight an oppressive, heterosexist society on all fronts. Bisexual women and lesbians need to work with bisexual and gay men – at this point in our history, we simply cannot afford to be divided. Our sexual lives are a direct challenge to the status quo and we are all punished, in various ways and to various extents, for not living within the mythical norm. No bisexual, lesbian or gay man can possibly accept the narrow definition of condoned sexual relationships, and we need to oppose that definition in an atmosphere of mutual respect.

The climate of opinion towards bisexuality within the lesbian and gay communities has changed considerably in the last couple of years. The existence of bisexuals is more often taken for granted, we are no longer automatically presumed to be in transition or cowards, neither are bisexuals necessarily thought to be devious heartbreakers until proved otherwise. The reasons for this change are complex. In part, studies of lesbian and gay history and discussions of various issues of sexuality worldwide, together with first-hand experience of twenty years of gay liberation, have shown that many people do not and cannot fit on one or other side of a neat heterosexual/homosexual divide. Research on HIV transmission has revealed that many people have sex with the 'wrong' gender – for instance, Project Sigma at South Bank University in London, whose research sample was 930 'men who had sex with men', discovered that 12 per cent of participants also had female partners in the course of a year. And when even government health campaigns admit the existence of married men who have affairs with other men (and ask the advice of bisexual

men about how best to portray this), the lesbian and gay communities too have to take notice. Lesbians, who have taken the
lead in discussing safer sex for women, have had to acknowledge
that lesbians have had and do have sex with men – and still
consider themselves lesbian. With such knowledge, it is not so
simple to condemn bisexual women out of hand.

Within the climate of increased homophobia of the past ten years,
more and more bisexuals are doing what we were always assumed
not to do: stand up and be counted even when the going is tough.
Far from retreating into a heterosexual closet, many bisexual
women have publicly allied themselves with lesbian causes. The
increasingly visible presence of bisexuals in gay groups bears this
out. Many mixed gay groups now include bisexual in their titles
– and the campaign literature for actions against Clause 25 in the
UK specifically includes bisexual men. The London Lesbian and
Gay Centre now allows bisexual groups to meet there, and the
National Union of Students has a Lesbian, Gay and Bisexual
campaign. The word 'bisexual' is often mentioned in gay/lesbian
contexts, and queer groups welcome people of all sexualities.

A lesbian and gay community which is increasingly strong and
thought-out *within itself* can accept diversity more readily, and
not rely on a false image of homogeneity. In the US, the 1993
Equal Rights march on Washington D.C. will be for bi (but not
bisexual), as well as lesbian and gay rights, and the annual Gay
Pride marches in London look set to follow suit. Though the fact
that groups have added bisexual to their titles might not immediately signal any profound changes in their politics, increased
visibility and at least paper acceptance of bisexuals as part of the
gay struggle will, it is to be hoped, lead to a genuine mutual
respect in the long term.

The rise of queer culture in the 1990s, with its radical, often
disturbing challenges to fixed notions of gender, has also helped
to create a climate in which sexual desire can go beyond a simple
opposition between masculinity and femininity. Some lesbians
and gay men have started to look at how they can use each
other's culture and images, and to acknowledge that in some cases
they may even desire each other sexually on some level. This is
important for bisexuality because it is a further challenge to the
monolithic view of sexuality which says that people are only ever
attracted to maleness or femaleness.

Although the queer movement is dominated by white gay
men, and it is men who have tended to exploit most fully the

gender-bending possibilities of drag, it is women who have pushed back the boundaries of gender and sexuality in the most interesting ways, both personally and artistically. Far from moving towards androgyny, they are deliberately subverting gender in ways which are transgressive of any and every sexual norm. Della Grace, for instance, is a photographer whose work on lesbian boys (i.e. lesbians who look like young gay men) caused flurries of desire among gay men unsure of who or what it was they were desiring.[4] These images developed from Grace's previous work on butch-femme and lesbian sado-masochism and was carried to an extreme in the 'Daddy Boy Dykes' series, which featured female couples wearing highly realistic, penis-like strap-ons.[5]

Grace's work comes out of the sex-radical lesbian community, but Carol Queen, whose reputation in the UK came from a couple of readings of one short story, is a bisexual activist. Queen writes explicit erotic stories about women who desire wild sex, particularly the sort of sex men have with each other. In her most quoted story, the female character dresses as a man to have sex with gay men, and then changes back and forth to play different gender roles.[6] As with Grace, Queen's work appeals to both women and men, and to people whose stated sexual identity could be anything as long as it's queer.

Feminism and lesbian feminism

There are now several cross-overs between the lesbian and gay male communities, particularly since the campaigns around Clause 28 and AIDS have created a climate in which lesbians and gay men are organising together more frequently than in the early 1980s. But there is also still a strong and separate lesbian feminist movement and lesbian culture (for those who know where to find it) including clubs, pubs, publishing houses, hotels, therapists and workplaces, some of which are almost apolitical. Lesbian feminism covers a wide range of political perspectives, from those who believe that all women can and should reject men totally and choose to be lesbians, to those who think that the fixing of people into pre-set categories (whether of sexuality or gender) is not possible or desirable. So how and where do bisexual women fit into both lesbian feminism and feminism in general?

As discussed in Chapter 3, bisexual women have in the past often felt unwelcome in the feminist movement. This movement, now less organised and more fragmented than during the past twenty years, is still vital for women. Despite the watered-down versions of feminism readily available in women's magazines, women are still oppressed – and this is not going to change on its own. A feminist theory which excludes large numbers of women, for whatever reason, is inadequate. Theory must work from the actual, not the ideal, and if bisexual women exist, then feminist theory must acknowledge them. Workshops on feminism at bisexual conferences until about 1990 were often guilt-ridden, with women feeling that they ought to make the choice to be lesbian. Many bisexual and heterosexual feminists have berated themselves for having relationships with men; if these relationships were rewarding, they have felt guilty and confused, as though they were letting the side down. But there needs to be some recognition within feminist theory that although men oppress women and heterosexual couple relationships are a paradigm for this, it does not necessarily follow that all such relationships are oppressive.

Lesbianism is a strong identity and political force. And while it is true that bisexual women, who may have considerable contact with men, could lessen the political impact of women 'doing it for themselves', in certain circumstances their co-operation could be valuable. For example, bisexual women often have more contact with heterosexual women than do lesbians, and could be valuable bridge-builders between the two communities. It is important that bisexual women and lesbians organise politically, both together and separately. While there are political and personal issues that affect only lesbian or only bisexual women which need to be discussed separately, there are also a vast range of issues that affect us both, where working together can only strengthen our movement.

As yet, there has been little open lesbian-feminist debate on bisexuality in the UK, unlike in the US, where lesbians have become polarised on the issue. Many have been supportive of political bisexual organising, as have most gay men, but there is nevertheless a substantial and vocal group that does not consider bisexuals to be oppressed, and thinks that to include them in lesbian and gay groups or marches, to allow them to meet in lesbian and gay centres, and to deal with bisexual issues in lesbian and gay publications dissipates the energy of the gay movement. Lesbians (like bisexual women, and, to a great extent, women in general) have very little power or visibility and want to keep what they have. However, this kind of separatism is not the way to succeed, and may lead to increasing factionalism.

Where to now?

The 1990s is an exciting time for bisexuals and the bisexual community. 1991/92 alone in the UK saw a dramatic upsurge in the number of bisexual groups, the introduction of a bisexual political network, the launching of a bisexual newsletter, and the opening of a 'bisexual night' in a London bar – as well as the usual group meetings and the national conference. Over the past few years, indeed over the period in which I have been writing this book, bisexuality has moved in progressive circles from an undiscussed, invisible identity to one whose radical potential is increasingly being realised.

The comedienne Sandra Bernhard, for instance, whose show 'Giving Till It Hurts' played two packed-out seasons in London during 1992, gets her audience to out themselves as gay, bisexual or ('that least interesting group'), heterosexual. Her shows contain sketches about relationships with both men and women. Bernhard talks in interviews about her past relationships with both sexes: whether or not she still has any sexual interest in men depends which one you read. Susie Bright, aka Susie Sexpert, long-time editor of the lesbian sex magazine *On Our Backs*, reveals in *Susie Bright's Sexual Reality* that she is and always has been bisexual.[7] There is even a bisexual woman character on the primetime television programme, *LA Law*. C.J. Lamb is pleasant, amusing, attractive, a good lawyer and has rewarding sexual relationships with both women and men.

The existence of prominent role models is obviously positive, but where should bisexual activists or the bisexual movement be directed in the future? I would like to suggest some areas which could be explored.

First, bisexual feminists need to enter into an active dialogue with lesbians, with the aim of becoming involved in joint political activity. We have an enormous amount in common, but before we can work together, we need to work out precisely what the overlaps are. Mixed bisexual/lesbian groups have been formed in the US, following a positive debate between bisexual women and lesbians at the 1990 San Francisco bisexual conference. The development of a feminist bisexual politics is under way, and the first-ever national UK conference for bisexual feminists was held in June 1992. (A one-off conference, unconnected to any wider movement, was held in 1978). The recent conference, which attracted sixty women, was of the opinion that bisexual women have a great deal to offer feminism (and the political will and energy to do so).

I hope that soon a feminism that has learned from bisexuality – not least about the importance of acknowledging and respecting difference – will emerge and will acknowledge that bisexual women can and do choose to have relationships with men, while remaining allied with and attracted to women. It would be a feminism that would put women first, but without moralising, and would deal with reality rather than an ideal. It would also embrace rather than marginalise women who do not fit the stereotype of bisexual, or feminist, or any other stereotype: in terms of race and class, but also of behaviour and lifestyle.

One of the reasons a conference for bisexual feminists was organised was because many women feel that the bisexual community as it is currently constituted does not address issues important to them. Certainly, the community appears to be mainly white, male and middle class – although it purports not to be. (This is also true of the queer community.) One of the great strengths of the bisexual community has been its ability to accept diversity: this is one of the reasons why transvestites and trans-sexuals have found a place within it. However, for there to be actual diversity, the bisexual community at large (rather than a small part of it) needs to engage with wider political struggles. It needs to look at how all kinds of oppressions work and where bisexuality fits into this framework. This may mean that the bisexual community will have to form a greater number of sub-groups, but it is to be hoped that these will also be able to come together for more general action.

On a more lighthearted note, there should be more clubs and social situations in which bisexuals can meet. Ideally, a bisexual club would be a place where women could meet men or women without pressure, but could take the initiative; where there would be no assumptions made about a person's sexuality. Bisexuals should also make greater incursions into the lesbian and gay communities – both the queer sectors, and those which operate in more conventional ways. This should include involvement in the many intellectual debates by lesbian and gay academics, in which at present there is scant bisexual involvement.

I believe the analogy [to bisexuality] is interracial or multiracial identity... a multi-cultural, multi-ethnic, multi-racial world view. Bisexuality follows from such a perspective, and leads to it as well... If you are free, you are not predictable and not controllable. To my mind, that is the keenly positive, politicizing significance of bisexual affirmation.[8]

As June Jordan says here, bisexuality has a great potential for crossing many barriers, for creating a truly different society. Society at present in the UK, much of the rest of Europe, and the US is increasingly right wing and repressive: it is essential now, more than ever, to fight for what we want and need. A society in which true freedom of sexual expression is possible would require the transformation not just of attitudes to sexuality, but of all areas in which oppression operates. Bisexuality is, will be and has to be part of the struggle to build that society.

Notes

1. See Loraine Hutchins & Lani Kaahumanu (eds), *Bi Any Other Name*, Alyson Publications, 1991, where contributors talk about involvement in all of these
2. Chuck Misham, 'The Bisexual Scene in New York City', in Klein & Wolf (eds), *Two Lives to Lead*, Harrington Park Press, 1985
3. In *Bi Any Other Name*, op cit, bisexual men and women cover a wide range of themes, including AIDS, gender, politics, marriage and community; *Bisexuality: A Reader and Sourcebook* (edited by Thomas Geller) is a collection of illustrations, writings, songs and a filmography; *Closer to Home* (edited by Elizabeth Reba Weise) is discussed on pages 58–9
4. Paul Burston, 'Falling From Grace' in *Capital Gay*, 21 June 1991, and letters in subsequent issues
5. *Quim*, issue 2, Summer 1991
6. Carol Queen's work is not published in the UK, and is only available in the US in 'zines such as *A Taste of Latex* (see 'When the Lights Changed' in *A Taste of Latex*, vol 1, No 4, Winter 1990–91)
7. 'Blindsexual' in *Susie Bright's Sexual Reality: A Virtual Sex World Reader*, Cleis Press, 1992
8. June Jordan, 'A New Politics of Sexuality' in *The Progressive*, July 1991

Resources list

Bisexual groups

Listed below are the most established bisexual groups in the UK. Information on other groups in the UK and mainland Europe can be obtained through *Bi-Frost* or the phonelines (see below).

Women's groups

London
c/o BM Box LBWG
London WC1N 3XX

Manchester
c/o Vi
WBG
PO Box 153
Manchester M60 1LP

Sheffield
SBWG
LBG Room
Octagon Centre
Sheffield University
Western Bank
Sheffield S10

Mixed groups

Edinburgh
58a Broughton Street
Edinburgh EH1 3SA

Liverpool Freedom of Sexuality Group
c/o Friend Merseyside
36 Bolton Street
Liverpool

London
Box BM/BI
London WC1N 3XX

Norwich
EABN
PO Box 117
Norwich NR1 2SU

Nottingham
Box B
Hiziki
15 Goosegate
Hockley
Nottingham NG1 FE

Worldwide
International Directory of Bisexual Groups
Robyn Ochs (ed)
East Coast Bisexual Network
PO Box 639
Cambridge
MA 02140
US
Published twice a year, $5

Phonelines

Bisexual Helpline (run by London group)
081 569 7500 (Tuesdays and Wednesdays) 7.30 – 9.30pm

Bisexual Phoneline (run by Edinburgh group)
031 557 3620 (Thursdays) 7.30 – 9.30pm

Publications

BiFrost
PO Box 117
Norwich NR1 2SU

Monthly bisexual newsletter – for sample issue send SAE.

There are also several good bisexual women's newsletters in the US. Subscription details may be obtained from:

North Bi Northwest
c/o SBWN
PO Box 30645
Greenwood Station
Seattle WA 98103-0645
US

Bi Women
338 Newbury Street, 202C
Boston
MA 02115
US

Anything That Moves
c/o BABN
2404 California Street #24
San Francisco
CA 94115
US

Bibliography

Bisexuality: further reading

Mentioned below are the few books which deal specifically and positively with bisexuality; others which I have used to develop my arguments and which are particularly valuable or interesting are starred (**) in the main bibliography. Most books on bisexuality are either out of print and/or were never widely available in the UK. Exceptions are marked (*).

Blumstein, Philip & Schwartz, Pepper, 'Bisexual Women', in Wiseman, J.P. (ed), *The Social Psychology of Sex*, New York: Harper Row, 1976 (short but positive article about bisexual women)

Bode, Janet, *A View from Another Closet: Exploring Bisexuality in Women*, New York: Hawthorn, 1976 (until the recent publication of *Closer to Home*, this was the only sensible book published on women and bisexuality)

Boston Lesbian Psychology Collective (eds), *Lesbian Psychologies*, Urbana, Chicago: University of Illinois Press, 1987 (excellent book dealing with various aspects of lesbian psychology; consideration of bisexuality runs throughout the book, and several essays deal with it specifically)

(*) Bright, Susie, *Susie Bright's Sexual Reality: A Virtual Sex World Reader*, Pittsburgh, San Francisco: Cleis Press, 1992 (includes 'Blindsexual', essay on Bright's bisexuality)

(*) Cartledge, Sue & Ryan, Joanna (eds), *Sex and Love: New Thoughts on Old Contradictions*, London: The Women's Press, 1983 (essays on aspects of feminist sexuality, including chapter on bisexuality)

Fast, Julius & Wells, Hal, *Bisexual Living*, New York: Pocket Books, 1975 (interviews with ten bisexuals, followed by a benign 'analysis' of their behaviour)

Geller, Thomas (ed), *Bisexuality: A Reader and Sourcebook*, Ojai, California: Times Change Press, 1990 (anthology of essays and articles about bisexuality including information on plays, films, etc which deal with bisexuality)

(*) Hutchins, Loraine & Kaahumanu, Lani (eds), *Bi Any Other Name: Bisexual People Speak Out*, Boston: Alyson Publications, 1991, imported to UK by Gay Men's Press (anthology of bisexual people's stories, ranging from personal histories to political theory)

Jay, Karla & Young, Allen (eds), *After You're Out*, New York: Link, 1975 (contains several positive articles on bisexuality)

Klein, Fred, *The Bisexual Option*, New York: Priam Books, 1978 (a discussion – by a psychiatrist – of healthy and neurotic bisexuality from the standpoint that bisexuality is potentially the most healthy way of relating)

Klein, Fritz & Wolf, Timothy (eds), *Two Lives to Lead: Bisexuality in Men and Women*, New York: Harrington Park Press, 1985 (sociological/psychologically biased academic book looking at a variety of issues pertaining to bisexuality; excellent bibliography)

Kohn, Barry & Matusow, Alice, *Barry and Alice: Portrait of a Bisexual Marriage*, New York: Prentice Hall, 1980 (Alice and Barry talk about how they came to realise their bisexuality and how it affects their lives)

(*) Off Pink Collective, *Bisexual Lives*, London: Off Pink Publishing, 1988 (women and men talk about being bisexual, together with articles on AIDS and a resource guide)

(*) Spencer, Colin, *Which of Us Two?*, London: Viking, 1990 (largely autobiographical book which also has a section on Spencer's theories of bisexuality)

Valverde, Mariana, *Sex, Power and Pleasure*, Toronto: The Women's Press, 1985 (feminist analysis of the subject, includes a good chapter on bisexuality)

(*) Weise, Elizabeth Reba (ed), *Closer to Home: Bisexuality and Feminism*, Seattle: Seal Press, 1992, imported to UK by Airlift (essays on many aspects of bisexuality and feminism, including personal stories, critiques of feminist theory and political analysis)

Wolff, Charlotte, *Bisexuality – A Study*, London: Quartet, 1977 (the only serious analysis of the subject ever published in the UK)

Psychology/sexology

Anon, *Everywoman's Book of Love, Marriage and Family Life*, Amalgamated Press, c1930s

Berg, Charles & Krich, A.M. (eds), *Homosexuality: A Subjective and Objective Analysis*, London: Allen & Unwin, 1958

Bergler, Edmund, *Homosexuality: Disease or Way of Life?*, New York: Collier, 1956

Bergler, Edmund & Kroger, William, *Kinsey's Myth of Female Sexuality*, New York: Grove and Stratton, 1954

Brecher, Edward, *The Sex Researchers*, London: Deutsch, 1970

Brown, James A.C., *Freud and the Post-Freudians*, London: Pelican, 1961

Browne, Stella, *Sex Variety and Variability Among Women*, London: The British Society for the Study of Sexual Psychology, 1915

Bryan, Douglas, 'Bisexuality', *International Journal of Psychoanalysis*, vol 11, 1930

Cory, Donald W. & LeRoy, John P., *The Homosexual and His Society*, New York: Citadel, 1963

Day, Beth, *Sexual Life Between Blacks and Whites*, London: Collins, 1974

Deutsch, Helene, 'Homosexuality in Women', in *International Journal of Psychoanalysis*, vol 14, 1933

——, *The Psychology of Women*, New York: Grove and Stratton, 1945

Douglas, Jason, *Bisexuality*, London: Canova, 1970

Ellis, Albert (ed), *Sex Life of the American Woman and the Kinsey Report*, New York: Greenberg, 1954

Ellis, Havelock, *Sexual Inversion, Studies in the Psychology of Sex*, vol 2, Philadelphia: F.A. Davis, 1924

Ernst, Morris & Loth, David, *Sexual Behaviour and the Kinsey Report*, London: Regular Publications, 1949

Ford, Clellan S. & Beach, Frank, *Patterns of Sexual Behaviour*, London: Eyre and Spottiswoode, 1965

Fordham, Frieda, *An Introduction to Jung's Psychology*, London: Pelican, 1953

Freud, Anna, *Before the Best Interests of the Child*, New York: The Free Press, 1979

Freud, Sigmund, 'Femininity', in *New Introductory Lectures on Psychoanalysis*, London: Pelican, 1979

——, 'The Psychogenesis of a case of Homosexuality in a Woman', in *Standard Edition*, vol 18, London: Hogarth Press, 1955

——, *On Psychopathology*, London: Pelican, 1979

——, *On Sexuality*, London: Pelican, 1979

Gorer, Geoffrey, *Sex and Marriage in England Today: A Study of the Views and Experiences of the Under-45s*, London: Panther, 1973

Henry, George, *Sex Variants*, New York: Paul B. Hoeber Inc, 1948

Hill, Ivan, *The Bisexual Spouse*, New York: Harper and Row, 1987

Hirschfeld, Magnus, *Sexual Anomalies & Perversions*, London: Torch, 1946

'J', *The Sensuous Woman*, London: Mayflower, 1970

Jung, Carl Gustav, 'The Love Problem of a Student', in *Civilisation in Transition, Collected Works*, vol 10, London: Routledge & Kegan Paul, 1970

——, *Memories, Dreams, Reflections*, London: Flamingo, 1963

Kinsey, Alfred, Pomeroy, Wardell B. et al, *Sexual Behaviour of the Human Female*, Bloomington, Indiana: Sanders, 1953

Krafft-Ebing, Richard von, *Psychopathia Sexualis*, London: Mayflower Dell, 1967

Lacan, Jacques (and the Ecole Freudienne), Mitchell, Juliet & Rose, Jacqueline (eds), *Feminine Sexuality*, London: Macmillan, 1982

Lynne, David, *The Bisexual Woman*, New York: Midweek, 1967

Magee, Bryan, *One in Twenty*, London: Corgi, 1968

Masters, William & Johnson, Virginia, *Human Sexual Response*, Toronto, London: Bantam, 1980

——, *Homosexuality in Perspective*, Toronto, London: Bantam, 1982

Poland, Jefferson F. & Alison, Valerie, *Records of the San Francisco Sexual Freedom League*, London: The Olympia Press, 1971

Rado, Sandor, *Psychoanalysis of Behaviour*, New York: Grove and Stratton, 1956

Stekel, Wilhelm, *Bisexual Love*, New York: Physicians and Surgeons Book Co, 1934

Stopes, Marie, *Married Love*, London: G.P. Putnam's Sons, 1923

Velde, Theodore van de, *Ideal Marriage*, London: Heinemann, 1965

Welldon, Estela, *Mother, Madonna, Whore*, London: Free Association Books, 1988

Wright, Helena, *The Sex Factor in Marriage*, London: Noel Douglas, 1930

——, *More About the Sex Factor in Marriage*, London: Williams and Norgate, 1947

Feminist/progressive sexual theory

Abbott, Sidney & Love, Barbara, *Sappho Was a Right-On Woman*, New York: Stein and Day, 1972

Allen, Susana, 'Bisexuality: the best of both worlds', in *Spare Rib*, April 1973

Ardill, Susan & O'Sullivan Sue, 'Sex in the Summer of '88', in *Feminist Review*, issue 31, Spring 1989

Benn, Melissa, 'The Passion of Decency: Thoughts on Feminism & Bisexuality', in *Spare Rib*, February 1989

Bright, Susie, *Susie Sexpert's Lesbian Sex World*, San Francisco, Pittsburgh: Cleis Press, 1990

Bullard, David & Knight, Susan (eds), *Sexuality and Physical Disability: Personal Perspectives*, St Louis, London: Mosby, 1981

(**) Caplan, Pat (ed), *The Cultural Construction of Sexuality*, London: Tavistock, 1987

Carlin, Norah, 'The Roots of Gay Oppression', in *International Socialism*, 2:42, 1989

Chodorow, Nancy, *The Reproduction of Mothering: The Psychoanalysis and Sociology of Gender*, Berkeley, London: University of California Press, 1978

Connexions, 'Global Lesbianism', Winter 1982

Coveney, Lal et al (eds), *The Sexuality Papers*, London: Hutchinson, 1984

Coward, Rosalind, 'Sexual Liberation and the Family', in *M/F*, issue 1, 1978

Dinnerstein, Dorothy, *The Rocking of the Cradle and the Ruling of the World*, London: The Women's Press, 1987

Dollimore, Jonathan, *Sexual Dissidence*, Oxford: Oxford University Press, 1991

Dworkin, Andrea, *Intercourse*, London: Secker and Warburg, 1987

Ehrenreich, Barbara, Hess, Elizabeth & Jacobs, Gloria, *Re-making Love: The Feminization of Sex*, London: Fontana 1987

Faderman, Lillian, *Odd Girls and Twilight Lovers: A History of Lesbian Life in Twentieth Century America*, London: Penguin, 1992

——, *Surpassing the Love of Men*, New York: Morrow and Co, 1981

Feminist Review (ed), *Sexuality: A Reader*, London: Virago, 1987

Feminist Review, Spring 1986

(**) Foucault, Michel, *The History of Sexuality, Vol 1: An Introduction*, London: Allen Lane, 1979

Friday, Nancy, *My Secret Garden (Women's Sexual Fantasies)*, London: Quartet, 1976

Galland, Victoria, *Bisexual Women*, unpublished PhD thesis, California School of Professional Psychology, Berkeley, 1975

Gochros, Harvey & Jean (eds), *The Sexually Oppressed*, New York: Associated Press, 1977

Harwell, Jack Leroy, *Bisexuality: Persistent Lifestyle or Transitional State?*, unpublished dissertation, Graduate Faculty of the School of Human Behavior, US International University, San Diego, 1976

Heath, Stephen, *The Sexual Fix*, London: Macmillan, 1982

Heresies, 'Sex Issue', 1981

Hite, Shere, *The Hite Report*, New York: Summit Books, 1977

——, *Women in Love*, London: Penguin, 1989

Hocquenghem, Guy, *Homosexual Desire*, London: Allison & Busby, 1978

Hooper, Anne, *The Thinking Woman's Guide to Love and Sex*, London: Futura, 1983

Humphries, Steve, *A Secret World of Sex*, London: Sidgwick & Jackson, 1988

Jackson, Stevi, *On the Social Construction of Female Sexuality*, London: WRRC Pamphlet, 1978

Jeffreys, Sheila, *Anti-Climax*, London: Virago, 1987

—— (ed), *The Sexuality Debates*, London: Routledge & Kegan Paul, 1987

Kirkpatrick, Martha (ed), *Women's Sexual Experience*, New York: Plenum, 1982

(**) Kitzinger, Celia, *The Social Construction of Lesbianism*, London: Sage, 1987

Kitzinger, Sheila & Celia, *Women's Experience of Sex*, London: Penguin, 1984

Koedt, Anne, 'The Myth of the Vaginal Orgasm', in Wiseman, J.P. (ed), *The Social Psychology of Sex*, New York: Harper Row, 1976

Lazarre, Jane, *On Loving Men*, London: Virago, 1981

Loulan, JoAnn, *Lesbian Sex*, San Francisco: Spinsters Ink, 1984

Meulenbelt, Anja, *For Ourselves*, London: Sheba, 1981

(**) Mieli, Mario, *Homosexuality and Liberation*, London: Gay Men's Press, 1980

Nestle, Joan, *A Restricted Country*, Ithaca, New York: Firebrand, 1987

Norris, Stephanie & Read, Emma, *Out in the Open: People talking about being Gay or Bisexual*, London: Pan, 1985

O'Sullivan, Sue & Parmar, Pratibha, *Lesbians Talk (Safer) Sex*, London: Scarlet Press, 1992

Phillips, Eileen (ed), *The Left and the Erotic*, London: Lawrence & Wishart, 1983

(**) Plummer, Kenneth (ed), *The Making of the Modern Homosexual*, London: Hutchinson, 1980

Ponse, Barbara, *Identities in the Lesbian World*, Westport, Connecticut, London: Greenwood Press, 1978

Richards, Dell, *Lesbian Lists*, Boston: Alyson Publications, 1990

Roelofs, Sarah, 'A Reply', in *Spare Rib*, March 1989

Rule, Jane, *Lesbian Images*, London: Peter Davies, 1976

Scarlet Women, issue 13, May 1981

Sherfey, Mary Jane, *The Nature and Evolution of Female Sexuality*, New York: Random House, 1972

Sisley, Emily & Harris, Bertha, *The Joy of Lesbian Sex*, New York: Simon & Schuster, 1977

(**) Smyth, Cherry, *Lesbians Talk Queer Notions*, London: Scarlet Press, 1992

Snitow, Ann, Stansell, Christine, & Thompson, Sharon (eds), *Desire: The Politics of Sexuality*, London: Virago, 1984

(**) Vance, Carole (ed), *Pleasure and Danger*, Boston: Routledge & Kegan Paul, 1984

Walkowitz, Judith, *Prostitution and Victorian Society*, Cambridge: Cambridge University Press, 1982

(**) Weeks, Jeffrey, *Coming Out*, London: Quartet, 1977

(**) ——, *Sex, Politics and Society: The Regulation of Sexuality Since 1800*, London: Longmans, 1981

(**) ——, *Sexuality and its Discontents*, London: Routledge & Kegan Paul, 1985

Wittig, Monique & Zeig, Sande, *Lesbian Peoples*, London: Virago, 1980

Wolff, Charlotte, *Love Between Women*, London: Duckworth, 1971

Feminism

Barrett, Michèle, et al (eds), *Ideology and Cultural Production*, London: Croom Helm, 1979

Beauvoir, Simone de, *The Second Sex*, London: Jonathan Cape, 1953

Bryan, Beverley, Dadzie, Stella & Scafe, Suzanne, *Heart of the Race: Black Women's Lives in Britain*, London: Virago, 1985

Coote, Anna & Campbell, Beatrix, *Sweet Freedom*, London: Picador, 1982

Coward, Rosalind, *Patriarchal Precedents*, London: Routledge & Kegan Paul, 1983

Ernst, Sheila & Maguire, Marie (eds), *Living with the Sphinx*, London: The Women's Press, 1987

Firestone, Shulamith, *The Dialectic of Sex*, London: The Women's Press, 1979

Foreman, Ann, *Femininity as Alienation*, London: Pluto, 1977

Gallop, Jane, *Feminism and Psychoanalysis: The Daughter's Seduction*, London: Macmillan, 1982

German, Lindsey, 'Theories of Patriarchy' in *International Socialist*, 2:12, 1981

Greer, Germaine, *The Female Eunuch*, London: MacGibbon & Kee, 1970

Griffin, Susan, *Pornography and Silence*, London: The Women's Press, 1981

Holdsworth, Angela, *Out of the Dolls House*, London: BBC Enterprises, 1988

hooks, bell, *Feminist Theory: From Margin to Center*, Boston: South End Press, 1984

——, *Talking Back: Thinking Feminist Thinking Black*, London: Sheba, 1989

Jordan, June, *Moving Towards Home*, London: Virago, 1989

Lederer, Laura (ed), *Take Back the Night: Women on Pornography*, Toronto, London: Bantam, 1980

Millett, Kate, *Sexual Politics*, London: Virago, 1977

Mitchell, Juliet, *Psychoanalysis and Feminism*, London: Penguin, 1975

——, *Women – the Longest Revolution*, London: Virago, 1984

Onlywomen Collective (ed), *Love your Enemy?*, London: Onlywomen Press, 1981

Segal, Lynne, *Is the Future Female? Troubled Thoughts on Contemporary Feminism*, London: Virago, 1987

——, (ed) *What is to be Done about the Family?* London: Penguin, 1983

Spare Rib, vol 1, 1972 onwards

Wandor, Micheline, *The Body Politic: Writing from the Women's Liberation Movement in Britain*, London: Stage 1 Publications, 1972

Wilson, Elizabeth, *Only Halfway to Paradise: Women in Postwar Britain 1945-68*, London: Tavistock, 1980

——, & Weir, Angela, *Hidden Agendas: Theory, Politics and Experience in the Women's Movement*, London: Tavistock, 1986

Political theory

Goldman, Emma, *Anarchism and Other Essays*, London: Mother Earth, 1971

Kollontai, Alexandra, *Sexual Relations and the Class Struggle*, London: SWP, 1984

Mount, Ferdinand, *The Subversive Family*, London: Jonathan Cape, 1982

Reich, Wilhelm, *The Function of the Orgasm*, London: Panther, 1968

——, *The Mass Psychology of Fascism*, London: Penguin, 1977

——, *The Sexual Revolution*, London: Peter Nevill, Vision Press, 1952

Miscellaneous

Alexander, Jane, 'Sex Survey', in *Elle*, April 1992

'Anastasia', 'Gender Benders', in *Bi-Monthly*, February/March 1989

Bradley, Ann, 'Love-All', in *Company*, September 1990

Children Come First, London: HMSO, 1989

Delcourt, Marie, *Hermaphrodite*, London: Studio Books, 1961

Formaini, Heather, 'The Scary Truth about Male Sexuality', in *Cosmopolitan*, December 1990

Heilbrun, Carolyn, *Towards Androgyny*, London: Gollancz, 1973

Herrera, Hayden, *Frida: A Biography of Frida Kahlo*, New York: Perennial, 1983

Horner, Tom, *Sex in the Bible*, Rutland, Vermont: Charles E. Tuttle, 1974

Hyam, Ronald, *Empire and Sexuality*, Manchester: Manchester University Press, 1991

Jordan, June, 'A New Politics of Sexuality', in *The Progressive*, July 1991

Kabbani, Rana, *Europe's Myths of Orient*, London: Pandora, 1988

Marcuse, Herbert, *Eros and Civilization*, New York: Vintage, 1955

Millett, Kate, *Flying*, St Albans: Paladin, 1976

Moss, Rachel (ed), *God's Yes to Sexuality: Towards a Christian Understanding of Sex, Sexism and Sexuality*, London: Collins, Fount, 1981

Office of Population Censuses and Surveys, Social Services Division, *General Household Survey 1989*, London: HMSO, 1989

Owens, Tuppy, *The (Safer) Sex Maniac's Bible*, London: Tuppy Owens, 1990

Report of the Committee on Homosexual Offences and Prostitution, London: HMSO, September 1957

Richardson, Diane, *Women and the Aids Crisis*, London: Pandora, 1988

Singer, June, *Androgyny: Towards a New Theory of Sexuality*, London: Routledge & Kegan Paul, 1977

Social Community and Planning Research (Jowell, Roger & Airey, Colin, eds), *British Social Attitudes 1984*, Aldershot: Gower Publishing Company, 1984

Social Community and Planning Research (Jowell, Roger, Witherspoon, Sharon & Brook, Lindsey, eds), *British Social Attitudes 1988/89*, Aldershot: Gower Publishing Company, 1989

Social Trends, no 6, London: HMSO, 1975

——, no 19, London: HMSO, 1989

Spencer, Colin, 'How it feels to be Bisexual', in *Cosmopolitan*, June 1990

Stember, Charles, *Sexual Racism*, New York: Elsevier, 1976

Thompson, Tierl, *Dear Girl*, London: The Women's Press, 1987

Whitehouse, Mary, *Whatever Happened to Sex?*, Hove: Wayland, 1977

Appendix 1: the questionnaire

Below is the questionnaire from which statistics and information have been compiled, reprinted in full.

This is a long questionnaire. Please feel free to answer as much or as little as you wish, or is relevant to you. All information will be treated in confidence, and you need only give your name and address if you wish to take part in a further interview. It is for any woman who feels she is bisexual, regardless of behaviour or lifestyle.

Age:

Are you:
Black	White
African	N. European
Afro/Caribbean	S. European
Asian	Other
Other	

How would you describe your class background?

Are you employed / unemployed / student / looking after children / other?

Is your income level high / medium / low?

What educational qualifications do you have?

What is your living situation (e.g. alone, with partner, collective house etc)?

Do you live in a city, town, small town, rural area?

In which area do you live?

Do you consider yourself a feminist?

What are your other political convictions?

Have you ever sought professional counselling about your sexuality?

Identity

Do you define yourself as heterosexual / lesbian / bisexual / other?

Why?

If you do, how did you come to define yourself as bisexual?

How long ago was this?

Have you ever defined yourself as lesbian?

If yes, how did you then become bisexual?

Do you feel part of the lesbian community?

If you do, are you there as bisexual or lesbian?

How do you feel about it?

How do you feel about your sexuality?

Do you consider that your sexuality is a choice, or that you were born / made bisexual?

Are you 'out' as bisexual to:
a) friends: all / some / none
b) family: all / some / none
c) at work
d) in general

What kind of reaction have you had?

Do you know other self-defined bisexuals?

Do you know other people who appear to you to be bisexual?

What do you feel about sexual labels like bisexual, etc?

Have you ever been part of a bisexual group? Was it mixed or women-only?

Was it useful / important to you?

Do you see your sexuality in any sense as political?

Background

As far as you know, are / were your parents heterosexual?

Do you consider your childhood to have been happy?

Your adolescence?

How did you perceive your sexuality as an adolescent?

Did you / do you get on well with your mother? Your father?

What influence do you feel your family background has had on your sexuality?

What about the influence of the wider society in terms of options which were open to you?

What effect does your family / community still have on you?

Was your upbringing religious? If yes, what effect did it have?

Do you practise a religion now? Which?

If you do, what effect does it have on your sexuality?

Did you know anyone as a child who was not heterosexual? What did you think about them?

Have you ever had any positive role models for your sexuality? If so, whom?

Have your parents pressurised you to marry?

How did you respond?

Do you have children? If they are old enough, what do they know about your sexuality?

Have you made compromises about your sexuality / living conditions because of them?

Relationships

Do you have a main sexual relationship?

If yes, what sex is your lover?

Does this person know of your bisexuality?

If yes, what is their reaction to it?

If no, why not?

Do you have other sexual relationships?

If yes, what role do they play in your life?

How do you meet other lovers?

What effect do they have on your main relationship?

If you don't have other lovers, why not?

Are you married? Why?

If you have been married, why did it end?

Do you have simultaneous 'open' relationships (i.e. have several lovers who theoretically have the same importance)?

How does this work in practice?

Is this an emotional / sexual / political decision?

What are your feelings about monogamy generally?

Do you prefer sex with women or men?

How many sexual partners have you had? Male? Female?

If you have had more sexual partners from the group you do not prefer, why do you think this is?

Are your most emotionally intimate relationships with women or men?

Are you at present celibate?

Have you had periods of prolonged celibacy, whether through choice or not?

Why do you think this was?

Have you ever had sex with more than one person at a time?

If yes, how often?

What was the context, e.g. all women, two men and you etc?

Was any one person the initiator, and if so who?

How did you feel about it?

Have you ever used a) contact magazines like *Forum* or b) lonely-hearts columns, and with what result?

If you have a physical disability, how has this affected your ability to become part of the lesbian / bisexual community, join groups, etc?

How has it affected your choice of lovers?

Lastly, please could you complete the following. The numbers 1 to 7 indicate various degrees of heterosexual / lesbian feelings or behaviour as follows:

1 heterosexual only; 2 heterosexual mostly; 3 heterosexual somewhat; 4 heterosexual/lesbian; 5 lesbian somewhat; 6 lesbian mostly; 7 lesbian only

Please would you fill in which figure applies to you for each of the following categories. It should be done three times: a) for your past (the most representative period of your past life); b) for the present; c) for how you would ideally like it to be.

	Past	**Present**	**Ideal**
A. Sexual attraction			
B. Sexual behaviour			
C. Sexual fantasies			
D. Emotional preference			
E. Social preference			
F. Self-identification			
G. Heterosexual/lesbian lifestyle			

If there is a large difference between the present / ideal sets of figures, why do you think this is?

Thank you very much for filling in this questionnaire. Please feel free to add anything else you feel is relevant.

Appendix 2: the answers

These figures are based on the replies given by 142 respondents. Where relevant, numbers of those who gave no reply are included.

Age

Under 20	11
21–30	64
31–40	27
41–50	14
51 and over	5
No reply	21

Are you

White, northern European	123
(includes 4 Irish and 3 Jewish women)	
Afro-Caribbean	6
Southern European	3
Other European	3
(includes 2 Jewish women)	
Japanese	2
Afro-Caribbean/Irish	1
Asian-southern European	1
Mexican-American	1
Pacific-American	1
Australian	1

How would you describe your class background?

Upper-middle class	8
Middle class	60
Lower-middle class	11
Working class	34
Mixed	16
No reply	13

Are you

Employed	77
Working part-time	15
Student	23
Unemployed	10
Looking after children	6
Retired	1
No reply	10

Is your income level

High	8
Medium	70
Low	59
No reply	5

What educational qualifications do you have?

O levels or less	13
A levels or less	15
Post-A level qualifications	21
Degree	40
Postgraduate qualifications	26
No reply	27

What is your living situation?

With male partner	59
Alone	46
With others	22
With family of origin	10
With female partner	5

Do you live in a

City	90
Town	19
Small town	18
Rural area	8
No reply	7

In which area do you live?

Greater London	51
North-east	15
Midlands	14
South-east	14
North-west	10
Scotland	8
South-west	7
East Anglia	5
Wales	4
Ireland	3
USA	2
Canada	2
Germany	2
Japan	1
No reply	4

Do you consider yourself a feminist?

Yes	121
Sometimes	18
No	3

What are your other political convictions?

Socialist	90
Green	30
Anarchist	10
Liberal	10
None	5
Not sure	2
Right wing	2

(Some respondents gave more than one answer)

Have you ever sought professional counselling about your sexuality?

Yes	11
No	100
Other counselling	17
Other	7
No reply	7

Identity

Do you define yourself as

Bisexual	108
'Other'	13
Other replies	10
Heterosexual/bisexual	4
Heterosexual/lesbian	2
Bisexual/lesbian	2
Lesbian	2
Heterosexual	1

Why (of 108)

Attraction to men and women	96
I needed a label	3
I like women mainly but some men	3
Men mainly but some women	1
Other	5

If you do, how did you come to define yourself as bisexual?

Heterosexual, and fell in love with a woman	28
Was always bisexual	24
Lesbian, fell in love with a man	21
Only label applicable to me	11
Couldn't choose between men and women	4
Others told me	3
Other	5
No reply	12

How long ago was this?

Always	11
Over 10 years	15
5–10 years	24
3–5 years	28
1–2 years	21
Less than a year	9

Have you ever defined yourself as lesbian?

Yes	44
Maybe	15
No	80
No reply	3

If yes, how did you then become bisexual?

Fell in love with a man	12
My politics changed	4
Lesbian identity, not feelings	4
Feelings changed	3
Had repressed feelings	2
Still mainly lesbian	2
Other	6

Do you feel part of the lesbian community?

Yes	18
Sometimes	21
No	79
No reply	24

If you do, are you there as bisexual or lesbian?

Bisexual	17
It depends	6
Lesbian	5
Not sure	5
As a woman	3
No reply	3

How do you feel about it?

Unhappy	16
Happy	12
OK	12
A fraud	9
Angry	9
Wish it was better	8
Resigned	3
Other	2
No reply	71

How do you feel about your sexuality?

Good	59
Mixed	41
Confused	18
Normal for me	7
Bad	5
No reply	12

Do you consider that your sexuality is a choice,
or that you were born/made bisexual?

Choice	43
Born	27
Difficult to say	24
Made	14
All three	12
Born/choose to act	12
Not a choice	3
Made/choose to act	2
Other	4
No reply	1

Are you 'out' as bisexual to

a) friends: all 30 / some 100 / none 6 / no reply 6
b) family: all 10 / some 65 / none 40 / no reply 27
c) at work: all 22 / some 26 / none 65 / no reply 29
d) in general: yes 24 / sometimes 22 / no 58 / no reply 38

What kind of reaction have you had?

Good	58
Mixed to good	27
Mixed	37
Mixed to bad	10
Bad	7
No reply	3

Do you know other self-defined bisexuals?

Yes	103 (26 knew very few)
No	26
No reply	13

Do you know other people who appear to you to be bisexual?

Yes	48
No	17
No reply	77

What do you feel about sexual labels like bisexual, etc?

They're negative	56
Mixed feelings	35
Necessary	16
'Bisexual' is a negative label	12
Positive	11
No reply	12

Have you ever been part of a bisexual group?
Was it mixed or women-only?

Mixed group	24
Women-only group	15
Both	5

Was it useful/important to you?

Yes	34
Somewhat	6
Negative	4

Do you see your sexuality in any sense as political?

Yes	86
No	31
Not sure	22

Background

As far as you know, are / were your parents heterosexual?

Yes	133
Not sure	7
Mother a lesbian	1
Mother had lesbian relationship	1

How did you perceive your sexuality as an adolescent?

Heterosexual	40
Confused	22
Bisexual	18
Asexual	17
Heterosexual with crush on girls	14
Unhappy about it	8
Lesbian	6
'Promiscuous'	5
No reply	12

What influence do you feel your family background has had on your sexuality?

Restrictive	28
Positive female role models	20
None	18
Liberal upbringing	15
Happy childhood	10
Sexual abuse	10
Don't know	10
Heterosexism	9
Other	22

What about the influence of the wider society in terms of options which were open to you?

Compulsory heterosexuality	41
Bisexuality not possible	21
Few influences	11
Sexual liberation	8
Lesbianism	8
Education	8
Feminism	8
Made to keep sexuality quiet	7
Peer pressure	3
Other	10
No reply	17

What effect does your family / community still have on you?

None	28
Restrictive	15
Positive	15
Induces conformity	11
Need to protect family	10
Have little contact	10
Need their approval	3
Live in two worlds	2
Rural life constricts	2
Other	23
No reply	23

Was your upbringing religious?

Yes	58
No	80
No reply	4

If yes, what effect did it have?

Negative	27
No lasting effect	23
Mixed to positive	8

Do you practise a religion now? Which?

'My own'	6
Church of England	5
Matriarchal/pagan	5
Catholic	3
Jewish	3
Quakers	3
Christian without church	3
Buddhist	2
Baptist	1
Transcendental meditation	1

If you do, what effect does it have on your sexuality?

Positive	12
None	7
Affects ethics	6
Negative	3
Mixed	2
No reply	2

Did you know anyone as a child who was not heterosexual?

No	100
Yes	36
Only on TV	6

Have you ever had any positive role models for your sexuality?

Yes	48
No	38
No reply	56

Have your parents pressurised you to marry?

Yes	24
Yes – covert	15
Pressure not to	11
No	92

How did you respond?

Married   14
Ignored   7
Laughed   5
Got angry 3
Disagreed 2
Other   9

Do you have children?

Yes   35
Trying to   6

If they are old enough, what do they know about your sexuality?

May know   9
Told something   7
Too young   7
Nothing   7
Other   2
No reply   3

*Have you made compromises about your sexuality /
living conditions because of them?*

Yes   15
No   15
Not sure   2
No reply   3

Relationships

Do you have a main sexual relationship?

Yes   97
No   40
No reply   5

If yes, what sex is your lover?

Male   68
Female   26
One of each 3

Does this person know of your bisexuality?

Yes   85
No   12

If yes, what is their reaction to it?
Positive   41
Mixed   29
Negative   9
No reply   6

If no, why not?
Not relevant to tell   4
Don't want to upset him   2
Husband narrow-minded   2
I may be a lesbian   1
Female lover is anti-bisexual   1
No reply   2

Do you have other sexual relationships?
No   53
Yes   39 (14 had no main partner)
Occasionally 19
No reply   31

If yes, what role do they play in your life?
Little   20
Friendship   12
Excitement   6
It varies   6
Emotional   5
Sex   5
Make me feel 'really bisexual'   5
Other   7
(Some respondents gave more than one answer)

How do you meet other lovers?
'Through living'   27
Various ways   27
Friends first   22
Work   10
Lonely-hearts columns   10
Don't but wish I did   7
Lesbian scene   3
Other   3

What effect do they have on your main relationship?
Little effect   21
Negative   6
Positive   5
Depends   4
Other   6

If you don't have other lovers, why not?
Don't want to   28
Partner wants monogamy   9
Don't want the complications   8
Looking for another lover   6
Choosy about lovers   4
Other   4

Are you married?
No   114
Yes   28
(Divorced 16)

Why? (women who are married)
Love   15
Parental pressure   6
I expected to   4
Not sure   4
Security   3
(Some respondents gave multiple reasons)

Why? (women who are not married)
Disagree with marriage 20
Not interested   18
Too young   10
Haven't met Mr Right   6
Other   8

If you have been married, why did it end?
We grew apart   11
Wanted to be with same sex 3
Violence   2

Do you have simultaneous 'open' relationships (i.e. have several lovers who theoretically have the same importance)?

No   72 (8 strongly disapproved)
Have done   21
Yes   14
No reply   35

How does / did this work in practice?

It works well   4
It's hard   4
They meet different needs   3
It doesn't work   3
They live in different places   2
Other   5

Is this an emotional / sexual / political decision?

Emotional   11
A mixture of all three   9
Sexual   7
Political   4
It just happened   4

What are your feelings about monogamy generally?

Mixed   52
In favour   51
Monogamy is destructive   23
It depends on situation   7
No reply   9

Do you prefer sex with women or men?

Women   37
Particular individual(s)   35
Not enough experience to say   25
No preference   21
Men   9
Other   9
No reply   6

How many sexual partners have you had? Male?

Over 50	7
21–50	18
11–20	23
6–10	30
1–5	46
0	4
No exact figure	14

Female?

11–20	10
6–10	20
1–5	86
0	17
No exact figure	9

If you have had more sexual partners from the group you do not prefer, why do you think this is?

Heterosexist society	32
Interest in women recent	23
No available women	13
Fear of rejection by women	8
Heterosexual sex easier to get	8
Lesbian scene intimidating	3
Other	11

Are your most emotionally intimate relationships with women or men?

Women	92
Certain individuals	28
Men	11
Not sure	5
Other	6

Are you at present celibate?

No	104
Yes	35
Maybe	3

Have you had periods of prolonged celibacy,
whether through choice or not?

Yes   62
No   32
No reply 48

Why do you think this was?

Lack of opportunity   21
Shy   9
No desire   9
Sex is special   8
End of relationship   8
Energy on other things   8
Confused about sexuality   7
Went off men   4
Other   9

Have you ever had sex with more than one person at a time?

No   77
(No but want to   8)
Yes   60
Other   2
No reply   3

If yes, how often?

Once   23
1–4 times   24
Over 4 times   7
'Many' times   5

What was the context, e.g. all women, two men and you etc?

Various contexts   19
Another woman, one man   18
Mixed groups over three people   4
All women   2

Was any one person the initiator, and if so who?

It just happened   17
Respondent   15
The man   11
It varied   10
Another woman   6

How did you feel about it?

Good	25
Bad	14
OK	11
Mixed (over different experiences)	8

Have you ever used a) contact magazines like Forum *or b) lonely-hearts columns and with what result?*

Contact magazines	9
Bad experience	5
OK experience	2
Led to sexual relationship	2
Lonely-hearts columns	42
Bad experience	23
Good experience	11
OK	8

If you have a physical disability, how has this affected your ability to become part of the lesbian / bisexual community, join groups etc?

4 women said they had a disability. All felt it had not affected their behaviour or choice of lovers.

Respondents first read or heard about the questionnaire in:

Guardian	45
Through bisexual groups or conferences	20
Spare Rib	15
Shocking Pink	10
Personal contacts	10
Time Out	8
Forum	6
Bi-Monthly	5
Lesbian and Gay Socialist	4
City Limits	4
Gay Scotland	4
Bookshops (various)	4
Women's News (Belfast)	1
Women's groups	1
Unidentified	5

Index

Abbott, Sidney 45
abortion 8, 40, 43
ACT-UP 186
activism; bisexual 105, 116, 118, 164, 189, 190, 192, 195, 197; gay 118; queer 186, 191
adolescence 30, 96, 97–8
advertising, and commoditisation of sex 8
Africa, and AIDS 117
Afro-Caribbean community 67, 99
AIDS 76, 115, 116–19; and bisexual men 19, 116–18, 147, 191; campaigns around 195; exploitation of the epidemic 10; as a heterosexual disease 117; and HIV infection 118; and homophobia 117, 192; and homosexuality 117; and non-monogamy 85–6; and promiscuity 16, 151
AIDS-activist community 118
'alternative' lifestyles 15, 185
'amphigenic inverts' 29
androgyny 21, 25–8, 52, 195
anti-gay attitudes, marked increase in 20
anti-semitism 192
anti-vice campaigns 39
Any Woman Can (play) 47
Arena 3 (magazine) 18
arts, the; and commoditisation of sex 8; and homosexuals 186
Asian women 168
Augustine, St 11
Austria, bisexual conference delegates 192

Barnard conference (1982) 52
bars 78, 154, 197
Beauvoir, Simone de 40–1, 85
Belgium, bisexual conference delegates 192
Benkert, Dr Karoly Maria 16
Benn, Melissa 56–7
Bennett, Kathleen 59
Berg, Charles 31
Bergler, Edmund 31, 32
Bernhard, Sandra 197
Beveridge Report (1942) 13
Bi-Frost (national newsletter) 189
Bi-Lifestyles 115
Bible, interpretation of 11
biology 30, 34
biphobia 116, 118, 187
Birmingham 190
Bisexual Adult Children of Alcoholics 191–2
bisexual community 36, 105, 189–92; ability to accept diversity 198; and coming out 104; development of theory and practice within 5; and disabled women 168; feminist 3; and gay liberation 146; labelling in 164; nascent 19; rapidly growing 1; and safer sex 118; and women of colour 168
bisexual conferences 191, 192, 196, 197–8
bisexual groups 189–92, 193, 197; men's 124, 189; mixed 189, 190, 200–201; women's 124, 125, 189–90, 200

234